P9-BJI-354

Left, Right

Marching to the Beat
of Imperial Canada

By Yves Engler

Copyright © 2019 Yves Engler
All rights reserved. No part of this book may be reproduced or transmitted in any
form by any means without permission in writing from the publisher, except by a
reviewer, who may quote brief passages in a review.

Black Rose Books No. SS397

Cover by Frank Myrskog
Printed and bound in Canada by
Marquis Printing
A co-publication of
RED Publishing
203 32nd Street West
Saskatoon, Saskatchewan
S7L 0S3 and

Black Rose Books
C.P. 35788
Succ. Léo Pariseau
Montréal QC
H2X 0A4
CANADA
www.blackrosebooks.com

Library and Archives Canada Cataloguing in Publication

Engler, Yves, 1979-, author
    Left, right : marching to the beat of imperial Canada / Yves Engler.

Issued in print and electronic formats.
ISBN 978-1-55164-665-7 (hardcover).--ISBN 978-1-55164-663-3 (softcover).--
ISBN 978-1-55164-667-1 (ebook)

    1. New Democratic Party. 2. Labor unions--Political activity--Canada.
3. Right and left (Political science)--Canada. 4. Canada--Foreign relations.
I. Title.

JL197.N4E54 2018   324.27107   C2018-903596-X
                                                             C2018-903597-8

Ordering Information

USA/INTERNATIONAL
University of Chicago Press
Chicago Distribution
Center
11030 South Langley
Avenue
Chicago IL 60628
(800) 621-2736 (USA)
(773) 702-7000 (World))
orders@press.uchicago.edu

CANADA
University of Toronto Press
5201 Dufferin Street
Toronto, ON
M3H 5T8
1-800-565-9523
utpbooks@utpress.utoronto.ca

UK/EUROPE
Central Books
Freshwater Road
Dagenham
RM8 1RX
+44 (0) 20 852 8800
contactus@centralbooks.com

Table of Contents

Abbreviations

American Federation of Labour (AFL)
Canadian Congress of Labour (CCL)
Canadian Council for International Cooperation (CCIC)
Canadian Forces (CF)
Canadian Institute of International Affairs (CIIA)
Canadian International Development Agency (CIDA)
Canadian Labour Congress (CLC)
Canadian Union of Public Employees (CUPE)
Communications, Energy and Paperworkers Union (CEP)
Congress of Industrial Organizations (CIO)
Cooperative Commonwealth Federation (CCF)
Department of National Defence (DND)
Global Affairs Canada (GAC)
International Confederation of Free Trade Unions (ICFTU)
Labour International Development Program (LIDP)
North Atlantic Treaty Organization (NATO)
Organización Regional Interamericana de Trabajadores (ORIT)
Trades and Labour Congress (TLC)
World Federation of Trade Unions (WFTU)

Introduction

AS I HAVE DISCUSSED IN PREVIOUS BOOKS the Big Lie is that Canada has long been a force for good in the world. This book details the contribution of "the left" to confusing the public about Canada's international policies. It seeks to answer why Canadians overwhelmingly believe this country is a benevolent international actor despite a long history of supporting empire and advancing Canadian corporate interests abroad.

In *A Propaganda System: How Canada's Government, Corporations, Media and Academia Sell War and Exploitation* I outlined the main obstacles Canadians face in understanding their country's role in world affairs. Every year the Department of National Defence (DND), Veterans Affairs and Global Affairs Canada (GAC) spend hundreds of millions of dollars articulating a one-sided version of Canadian foreign policy. In addition to massive PR departments, DND and GAC also operate history departments, university initiatives and their own media. Alongside government communications initiatives, international and military focused corporations finance university programs, think tanks and PR efforts. Additionally, the corporate media (and CBC/Radio Canada) only permit a narrow spectrum of opinion regarding Canadian foreign policy.

The propaganda system outlined in my previous book is 90 percent of the answer to why Canadians think their country is a force for good in the world. But, the left has also played a part in justifying Canada's role within an unfair and unsustainable world economic system. This book is about the other 10 percent of the answer to the question: Why do Canadians think their country is a benevolent international force?

Initially conceived as part of *A Propaganda System*, this volume details NDP, labour unions and other left commentators' roles in confusing Canadians about their country's international policies. It also looks at how left nationalist ideology, as well as First Nations and Quebec sovereigntists, have warped the foreign policy discussion. While less influential than the institutions detailed in *A Propaganda System*, the left's promotion of imperial policies and nationalist myths contributes to popular confusion about Canada's place in the world. Instead of exposing the bad things our governments and corporations do abroad the left has remained silent, or worse, actively enabled the imperial behaviour.

In the years following World War II Canada's major left-wing party backed NATO and the Korean War. More recently, the NDP endorsed bombing Serbia and Libya. Over the years they've also supported military spending, Western policy in the Ukraine and the dispossession of Palestinians.

Closely tied to the NDP, labour unions often challenge the corporate perspective on domestic issues. But, that's rarely true with international affairs. In the two decades after World War II unions supported the Marshall Plan, NATO, the Korean War, assassination of Patrice Lumumba, Bay of Pigs invasion, etc. While no longer gripped by Cold War thinking, unions seldom devote energy to challenging foreign policy decisions.

Partially funded by the labour movement, left-wing think tanks mostly ignore international affairs or present highly circumscribed opposition. Sometimes they also promote foreign policy myths. A long-time employee of Foreign Affairs and NATO leads Canada's preeminent left-wing foreign policy think tank.

To survive in the mainstream, left commentators concede a great deal to the dominant ideology. Whether it's Linda McQuaig turning Lester Pearson into an anti-US peacenik, Stephen Lewis praising Canada's role in Africa, Michael Byers supporting military spending, or any number of individuals mindlessly demanding more "peacekeeping", leftist intellectuals regularly confuse our understanding of international relations.

Left Canadian nationalism is an important explanation for this confusion. Viewing Canada as a semi-colony struggling for its independence has blinded progressives to Canada's destructive international policies. In an extreme example, the left nationalist prism has contributed to distorting global understanding of an important historical event, which has paved the (ideological) path to enormous suffering in eastern Africa.

Even the Canadian state's primary victims have been ensnared by foreign policy nationalism. First Nations have fought in Canada's wars and upheld its international mythology.

While the Québécois led domestic opposition to a number of wars, the official sovereigntist movement largely acquiesced to Western imperialism before the first independence referendum in 1980. Progressive Québec nationalists generally backed a violent 2004 coup in Haiti and overwhelmingly ignore the deleterious effects of the province/nation's international policies.

By backing a number of morally unjust policies, the NDP, unions and left commentators have contributed to confusing the public about Canada's role globally. But, they've probably done as much damage by simply remaining silent about important aspects of foreign policy. Staying quiet about the vast diplomatic efforts employed to advance Canadian mining interests abroad doesn't make this country's corporate interests any less central to foreign policy decision making. Similarly, ignoring the geostrategic aims of naval exercises or international military training doesn't eliminate these aims from planners' thinking.

By failing to question every day pro-corporate/empire policies left institutions engender ignorance of Canadian policy. Systematic silence on important subjects is a form of complicity. As US historian Howard Zinn put it, "you can't be neutral on a moving train."

Though details in the story below are unique to Canada, its broad dynamics aren't. To some extent the mainstream left has been willing to criticize the dominant economic system and to offer alternatives to the "greed is good" narrative of the hardline supporters of capitalism. But, the mainstream left has mostly ignored international affairs, focusing on local and immediate problems facing voters and union members.

Around the world left parties and movements have had difficulty criticizing their own government/ruling class's imperialism. Socialist or social democratic parties and labour unions in Europe have largely failed to confront their countries' aggressiveness abroad. The Labour Party, for instance, administered British colonialism after World War II. While it adopted a variety of important social reforms at home, Labour initiated a brutal counter-insurgency war in Malaya, punished Iran for nationalizing its oil and pushed to develop nuclear weapons. In 2003 Tony Blair's Labour government invaded Iraq.

The mainstream left has often supported imperialist wars, colonialism and capitalist exploitation, so long as these destructive behaviours have profited their nations' companies. The pressure to be patriotic, especially during times of war, can be immense. In the best-known example of leftists succumbing to patriotic fever, most of the Second International abandoned their internationalist rhetoric and supported the slaughter at the start of World War I. The group of 20 socialist parties, which launched the working-class May Day celebration and International Women's Day, was unable to maintain even its "Eurocentric internationalism". (The Second International's operations and rhetoric barely extended to non-white colonies.)

After the Russian Revolution the left became divided between supporters and enemies of "Bolshevism". This introduced a new layer of obfuscation to the understanding of foreign affairs and led to widespread confusion on both sides of the divide about national interests and working-class internationalism. The Cold War deepened this confusion.

***

Since each circumstance is unique there is no simple formula for what constitutes "good" or "bad" international policy. But there are broad principles by which to judge foreign relations. One possibility is the Golden Rule, versions of which exist in every culture and religion. Do unto others as you would have them do unto you. In other words, we should attempt to examine policy from the standpoint of the "other side". Before we send troops to another country to fight a war, we should ask ourselves: Is this something we would wish for Canada? Before we support corporations abroad we should ask ourselves: Is their manner of operating something we would want to see here? Before we send aid to another country we should ask ourselves: Is what we are paying for, and the manner in which we are doing it, something we would want to see in Canada?

In the *Black Book of Canadian Foreign Policy* I offered a Golden Rule standard for judging international policy: "I believe Earth is our home and we are its stewards. While citizens of Canada, we are also neighbours to everyone who shares this planet. We must be good neighbours. That should be the underlying premise of Canada's foreign policy."

In this book I will borrow from healthcare to offer another simple prescription: First Do No Harm. As in healthcare the world of foreign policy is full of altruism, people seeking to help others and professionals dedicated to service. But, like healthcare, foreign policy is also shaped by individual and corporate greed and is rife with snake oil salesmen attempting to sell us military power or other harmful products as remedies to whatever ails us. As in the medical industry, responsible practitioners of foreign policy should be mindful that the "treatments" offered often include "side effects" that can cause serious harm or even kill.

That part of the Hippocratic oath stating, "First do no harm" includes a commitment to seek and tell the truth. Unfortunately, in foreign affairs, as in medicine, truth can often seem elusive amidst competing claims, vested interests, propaganda and outright lies. In both medical care and foreign affairs, many well-meaning people distort the truth. This is dangerous to our health and the world.

***

This book is not intended to cause offence or attack individuals, but rather to assess the responsibility of "the broad left" in misleading the public about Canada's role in world affairs. When individuals are named it is to offer concrete examples of the points made. In fact, those named are assumed to broadly represent "our side", which includes organizations associated with the working class, women, First Nations, oppressed minorities and various "progressive" causes. Along with being considered "on our side" comes greater expectations regarding an understanding of how capitalism, patriarchy, racism, colonialism, imperialism, etc. function. We can only make a better world if those we look to for leadership tell the truth about the actions of our government, military, corporations and other organizations. Just because something is called "aid" or "peacekeeping" or "responsibility to protect" or "war to end all wars" doesn't make it good for ordinary people. Just because Ottawa or Canadians pursue an international policy, doesn't mean it should be supported, either actively or through our silence. In fact, when something is done in our name, we have a particular responsibility to analyze and criticize it to ensure it does no harm.

Left intellectuals and representatives generally understand that when given unfettered power within Canada corporations do what most profits their shareholders regardless of the ill effects on workers, communities, the environment or democracy. Of course Canadian companies function the same way elsewhere. In fact, their actions are usually more damaging the weaker the country. Additionally, government support for Canadian corporations' operation is generally starker the greater the international power imbalance.

Yet somehow this reality is more difficult for many to see in Latin America, Africa, the Caribbean or Asia. Why? How come many progressives are fooled into thinking that exploitation, war and political subversion are okay over there? Does this blindness to imperialism reveal a shallowness of understanding about how capitalism works as an international system or a lack of commitment to defend all people everywhere on our planet? Is it as simple as not being able to see what lies beneath the Team Canada jersey?

The answers to these questions are important to constructing a more just foreign policy and to building more effective organizations of the left. Solidarity has always been the central organizing principle of the working class and excluded. Dividing to conquer has always been the way ruling classes maintain power for themselves. Today when one can communicate instantaneously across the planet, our solidarity must be worldwide. The only way to build a just and environmentally harmonious world is for common people to work together across the planet.

NDP/CCF

"[Canada has] a special place of trust among the developing nations. We emerged as an independent nation almost a century before them, but we also emerged out of colonial status. We have never [had] an imperial goal or imperialistic intentions"
— David Lewis, 1969

IN A PARLIAMENTARY DEMOCRACY opposition parties are supposed to question government policies. Official party status confers various privileges to hold the government accountable, including public funds for research and the ability to ask questions in the House of Commons.

Through parliamentary debates, party lists, public events, statements to the press, etc. the NDP is well positioned to inform the public about political developments. If they consistently challenged unjust foreign policy decisions the NDP would help counter the propaganda system outlined in my previous book. But instead of criticizing the geo-strategic and corporate interests driving foreign policy decisions, the NDP/CCF has often supported them and contributed to Canadians' confusion about this country's international relations.

While the party has played an important role in mitigating the worst effects of capitalism inside Canada when it has been in power provincially and through pressure from the left federally, it has regularly failed to defend the rights of ordinary people across the planet, particularly the victims of the British and American empires that Canada's ruling class has aligned with. A short history of NDP/CCF positions on foreign affairs follows.

The Cooperative Commonwealth Federation (CCF) was born a decade and a half after an inter-imperialist conflict that left 15 million dead. Considered the CCF's founding document, the 1933 Regina Manifesto expressed some of the pacifist, even anti-imperialist, sentiment of the post-World War I period. Point No. 10 on "External Relations" notes: "A Foreign Policy designed to obtain international economic cooperation and to promote disarmament and world peace. Canada has a vital interest in world peace. We propose, therefore, to do everything in our power to advance the idea of international cooperation as represented by the League of Nations and the International Labour Organization. We would extend our diplomatic machinery for keeping in touch with the main centres of world interest. But we believe that genuine international cooperation is incompatible with the capitalist regime which is in force in most countries, and that strenuous efforts are needed to rescue the League [of Nations] from its present condition of being mainly a League of capitalist Great Powers. We stand resolutely against all participation in imperialist wars. Within the British Commonwealth, Canada must maintain her autonomy as a completely self-governing nation. We must resist all attempts to build up a new economic British Empire in place of the old political one, since such attempts readily lend themselves to the purposes of capitalist exploitation and may easily lead to further world wars. Canada must refuse to be entangled in any more wars fought to make the world safe for capitalism."[1]

But, the Regina Manifesto and other early CCF documents downgraded foreign-policy questions. In an analysis of key early CCF manifestos (Calgary Program, League for Social Reconstruction, Regina Manifesto, etc.) Alan Whitehorn found the word "imperialism"/"imperialist" was only mentioned once while "capitalism" was used 18 times, "socialization" 21 times and "nation"/ "national" 25 times.[2]

WAR AND EMPIRE

Besides downgrading foreign policy, the Regina Manifesto ignored important ongoing injustices. It said nothing about Canadian banks' substantial influence over Caribbean finance or Canadian companies' international operations more generally.[3] Written when Europeans ruled most of Africa, the Caribbean and Asia, the Regina Manifesto ignores Canadian complicity in European colonialism, notably the universities that recruited students to join Britain's colonial service and the Canadians who governed African colonies.[4]

In response to a brutal, high profile instance of European subjugation of Africans, the CCF equivocated. In 1936 the National Executive "deferred a press statement and left the question of recognition of Italy's conquest of Ethiopia to the CCF caucus."[5]

That same year the CCF criticized London and Ottawa's refusal to support Spain's elected Republican government against Franco's fascists, who were backed militarily by Hitler and Mussolini. The Spanish Civil War made many distrust London and Ottawa's subsequent hostility towards Germany and Italy. Britain and Canada's position during the Spanish Civil War suggested that tension between Britain and Germany reflected an inter-imperialist conflict similar to WWI rather than an antifascist battle. Many in the CCF distrusted British/ Canadian motives and feared being "duped" into supporting another "European dogfight".[6] CCF defence critic Grant McNeil, reports military historian Roger Sarty, "attacked the [pre-WWII] rearmament program as ill-disguised preparation for the dispatch of expeditionary forces blindly to repeat the horrors of 1914 – 1918."[7] But, by the time of the outbreak of the conflict most of the party supported war.[8] Yet on the eve of WWII party leader J.S. Wordsworth personally stood against involvement.

As Hitler's barbarity and ambition grew, antiwar sentiment within the party largely disappeared. The CCF eventually backed total war, including conscription, which reversed Prime Minister Mackenzie King's promise at the outset of the conflict. In an article titled "Pacifism or anti-imperialism?: The CCF response to the outbreak of World War II" James Naylor claims the party's position was partly a matter of succumbing to the prevailing political winds. Alluding to what also happened during the First World War, he writes, "on one level, socialists once again had been drawn into the nationalist and ideological vortex of war."[9]

Confirming Naylor's analysis, the CCF's alignment with External Affairs continued after the war. Despite opposition from many party activists, the CCF mostly backed Ottawa's expansionist post-war policies.

In 1948 the B.C. CCF opposed arms sales to the Chinese Kuomintang, who were then fighting Mao's forces.[10] The provincial party convention also criticized the evolving North Atlantic treaty.[11] During this period 11 CCF members in Manitoba published an open letter opposing the North Atlantic pact and Marshall Plan, which the provincial party's convention condemned in 1948.[12] Notwithstanding these efforts, challenging foreign policy, notes John Warnock, "had little support in the CCF leadership and was easily silenced by M.J. Coldwell and the right wing of the party."[13] In an article titled "Confronting the Cold War: The 1950 Vancouver Convention of the Co-operative Commonwealth Federation" Benjamin Isitt echoes this assessment. By the time of the convention on the west coast there was no more "serious radical criticism of the [External Affairs leaders] St Laurent-Pearson-Wrong obeisance to Washington."[14]

The CCF backed the 1947 Marshall Plan. Long time CCF National Secretary David Lewis later wrote, "most of us in the CCF greeted the Marshall Plan as an imaginative and generous policy urgently needed to rebuild the economies of Europe."[15]

Named after US Secretary of State George Marshall, the postwar reconstruction financing of Western Europe sought to counter left-wing influence.[16] During WWII self-described communists opposed Mussolini in Italy, fought the fascists in Greece and resisted the Nazi occupation of France. As a result, they had a great deal of prestige after the war, unlike the wealth holders and church officials who mostly backed the fascists. If not for US/British interference, communists — without Moscow's support — would probably have taken power in Greece and won the 1948 election in Italy. In France the Communist Party won 30 percent of the first post-war vote, filling a number of ministries in a coalition government.

The aim of the Marshall Plan was also to protect "individual initiative and private enterprise."[17] According to Michael Hogan, the Marshall Plan was designed "to avert 'economic, social and political' chaos in Europe, contain Communism (meaning not Soviet intervention but the success of the Indigenous Communist parties), prevent the collapse of America's export trade, and achieve the goal of multilateralism."[18] It also "set the stage for large amounts of private U.S. direct investment in Europe," according to the US Commerce Department in 1984.[19]

The Marshall Plan laid the foundation for the North Atlantic Treaty Organization (NATO). In the words of then US President Harry S. Truman, the Marshall Plan and NATO were "two halves of the same walnut."[20]

The CCF also backed NATO. In early 1949 the National Council of the party announced, "the CCF believes that Canada should support and join a North Atlantic security pact."[21] At its 1950 convention the party passed a resolution supporting NATO and, in coded reference to his aggressive response to its opponents, David Lewis writes, "the NATO issue did not disappear. It had to be dealt with at every subsequent convention, and always produced one of the most heated debates."[22] Army Captain and party advisor Desmond Morton describes the battle over a compromise resolution on military alliances at the NDP's founding convention in 1961. The motion to abandon NORAD, but stay in NATO, was "subjected to a bitter, emotional attack from the floor. As they had done in so many CCF conventions, Coldwell, [Tommy] Douglas and Lewis came to the microphones to hammer back the unilateralists."[23]

Party leaders did not only employ the power of persuasion. In addition to benefiting from the dominant ideological winds, the leadership employed the levers of power within the party. On one occasion, Coldwell threatened to resign as party leader if members did not support the North Atlantic treaty.[24] When a group of Manitoba CCF members, including individuals elected to the provincial legislature, organized an anti-NATO group the provincial secretary blocked their access to the party's mailing list.[25] Federal MP and future party leader, Stanley Knowles also intervened to pressure the Manitoba CCF to punish prominent opponents of NATO and the provincial party expelled two former members of the Manitoba legislature for campaigning against the North Atlantic accord.[26]

Two decades after its creation the NDP finally called on Ottawa to withdraw from NATO. But, its 1969 position was partially reversed in the mid-1980s, culminating in a 1987 "security" policy paper that equivocated on the subject.[27] In a 2015 federal election debate party leader Tom Mulcair called the NDP "proud members of NATO" and said his government would make the alliance a "cornerstone" of its foreign policy.[28]

Officially a response to an aggressive Soviet Union, NATO was established to blunt the European left and extend North American/European power in light of the de-colonization taking place in Asia and the Middle East. NATO planners feared a weakening of self-confidence among Western Europe's elite and the widely held belief that communism was the wave of the future. During Italy's 1948 elections Deputy Under-Secretary for External Affairs Escott Reid explained: "the whole game of the Russians is obviously to conquer without armed attack."[29] George Kennan, the top US government policy planner at the time of NATO's formation, considered "the communist danger in its most threatening form as an internal problem that is of western society."[30]

The other major factor driving the creation of NATO was a desire to rule the world. For Canadian officials the north Atlantic pact enabled European/North American dominance across the globe. As part of the 1949 NATO parliamentary debate external minister Lester Pearson said, "there is no better way of ensuring the security of the Pacific Ocean at this particular moment than by working out, between the great democratic powers, a security arrangement the effects of which will be felt all over the world, including the Pacific area."[31]

(Exactly how little NATO had to do with the Cold War is demonstrated by how the alliance has become more aggressive since the demise of the Soviet Union. In 1999 Canadian fighter jets dropped 530 bombs in NATO's illegal 78-day bombing of Serbia while during the 2000s tens of thousands of Canadian troops fought in a NATO war in Afghanistan. In 2011 a Canadian general led NATO's attack on Libya and in a dangerous game of brinksmanship NATO amassed troops and fighter jets on Russia's border in 2016-18.)

For Pearson and some US leaders NATO's first test took place far from the north Atlantic in Korea.[32] After the Communists took control of China in 1949 the US tried to encircle the country. They supported Chiang Kai-shek in Taiwan, built military bases in Japan, backed a right-wing dictator in Thailand and tried to establish a pro-Western state in Vietnam. The success of China's nationalist revolution also spurred the 1950-1953 Korean War in which eight Canadian warships and 27,000 Canadian troops participated. The war left as many as four million dead.

The CCF approved the US-led (though UN sanctioned) war in Korea. Deputy leader and party spokesperson Stanley Knowles immediately endorsed the deployment of Canadian naval units to the Western Pacific, which the government sent in case they "might be of assistance to the United Nations and Korea."[33] On the eve of a party convention a month into the war the CCF Executive Council put forward a resolution calling on the government to deploy ground troops and Coldwell announced its position to the press. Lewis writes, "Coldwell had not only declared the Council position to be CCF policy but had done so vigorously and in tones which excluded the possibility that the convention might change it. The Vancouver press carried full reports of Coldwell's speech the next day and, since Korea was prominently in the news, gave his remarks on that subject a great deal of space."[34] Coldwell's move angered party members who wanted to debate the issue at the convention, but they were forced to either repudiate the party's leader or support the executive's resolution.[35] After the convention, author S. W. Bradford bemoaned the CCF "out-shooting the Tories in calling for greater participation in the Korean conflict."[36]

The CCF started to shift its position on the Korean War when Washington had the UN condemn Chinese "aggression" six months into the fighting. After pushing North Korean troops back to the 38th parallel, the artificial line that divided the North and South, the US-led force moved to conquer the entire country. UN troops continued north in a bid to undermine China's new government. US officials, particularly UN force commander Douglas MacArthur, repeatedly attacked Mao's government and before China entered the war American aircraft bombed that country while carrying out air missions in northern Korea.[37] Even more ominous, both MacArthur and (later) President Truman publicly discussed striking China with nuclear weapons.[38]

UN troops pushed north even after the Chinese made it clear they would intervene to block a hostile force from approaching their border. Beijing was particularly worried about northern China's dependence on energy from the Yalu

River power station in northern Korea. From the Chinese perspective the People's Liberation Army defended the country's territorial integrity, which was compromised by US bombings and the control of Formosa (Taiwan) by foreign-backed forces. The CCF opposed labeling China an aggressor out of fear it might lead to "a general war".[39]

During the Korean War the CCF deterred members from signing a Canadian Peace Congress petition that was part of the Stockholm Appeal to ban atomic bombs. Signed by tens of millions of people worldwide, the Stockholm Appeal called for "the outlawing of atomic weapons as instruments of intimidation and mass murder of peoples ... We believe that any government which first uses atomic weapons against any other country whatsoever will be committing a crime against humanity and should be dealt with as a war criminal."[40]

The CCF newsletter "Across Canada" claimed the petition was a front for "international communism" and the party's 1950 convention condemned the Stockholm Petition.[41] (But, some prominent members added their names to the appeal, including then Saskatchewan premier Tommy Douglas.)[42] Coldwell berated Canadian Peace Congress president James Endicott for "spreading communist propaganda".[43] In early 1952, reports J. T. Morley, the Ontario CCF decided it would have "no dealings with the Canadian Peace Congress because it was viewed as a communist front even though its sponsors included prominent churchmen and other public figures."[44]

In the decades after World War II the CCF's ties to the British Labour Party influenced its international policy. A history of the CCF explains, "by 1950 the position of the party caucus on foreign affairs was fairly orthodox, that is, it hewed closely to the line of the British Labour party, which was itself quite orthodox."[45] As the government between 1945 and 1951, Labour was responsible for initiating a brutal military campaign against an independence struggle in Malaysia, undermining Iran's effort to benefit from its oil and maintaining the British Empire in Africa and the Caribbean.

A few months after Labour took office in London the president of the Saskatchewan CCF privately called on the national executive to criticize their British brethren's "continuation of old imperialist policies."[46] In a sign of the executive's indifference to British colonialism, which Canada supported in a multitude of ways, the federal CCF leadership refused.[47]

John Price describes the "CCF subordinating its views to retain friendly ties with the British" Labour Party during a 1947 conference of Commonwealth labour parties held in Toronto. In "Canadian Labour, the Cold War and Asia, 1945-1955" Price points out that none of the non-white Commonwealth countries' labour parties made it to the conference and "neither did the issue of decolonization."[48]

In 1952 the CCF leadership rejected members' efforts to invite Aneurin Bevan to Canada. Bevan had resigned as the minister of health in the Labour government over the "introduction of prescription charges for dental care and spectacles — created to meet the financial demands imposed by the Korean War."[49] Instead, the CCF invited Labour leader Clement Attlee and Jimmy Griffiths who "appropriately, had been Secretary of State for the colonies in the Attlee government."[50]

In the early 1950s Iranians pushed to gain greater benefit from their huge oil reserves. But, British Labour and Conservative governments had different plans. As one of the earliest sources of Middle Eastern oil, the Anglo-Iranian Oil Company (BP's predecessor) had generated immense wealth for British investors since 1915. With Anglo-Iranian refusing to concede any of their immense profits, Iran moved to nationalize the country's oil industry.

Despite calling for the nationalization of numerous sectors of the Canadian economy, the leader of the CCF criticized Iran's move. In October 1951 Coldwell told the House of Commons: "What happened recently in Iran [the nationalization of oil] and is now taking place in Egypt [abrogation of a treaty that allowed British forces to occupy the Suez Canal region] is an attempt on the part of these reactionary interests to use the understandable desire of the great masses of the people for improvements in their condition as an excuse to obtain control of the resources of these countries and to continue to exploit the common people in these regions."[51] The CCF leader then called on the federal government to "give every possible aid to the United Kingdom in the present crisis."[52]

Mohammad Mossadegh's move to nationalize Iran's oil would lead the US and UK to orchestrate his overthrow in 1953. The CCF failed (or at least it's not recorded in Hansard) to criticize Ottawa for backing the overthrow of Iran's first popularly elected prime minister.

In 1960 the UN launched a peacekeeping force that delivered a major blow to Congolese independence aspirations by undermining elected Prime Minister Patrice Lumumba. As detailed in *Canada, the Congo Crisis, and UN Peacekeeping, 1960-64*, Canadian soldiers played a significant role in the Organisation des Nations Unies au Congo (ONUC) force that enabled Lumumba's assassination. Before Ottawa decided to deploy troops CCF MP Herbert Wilfred Herridge asked the House of Commons, "in view of news reports over the CBC this morning to the effect that Soviet personnel will be employed in the Congo under United Nations auspices, will the minister now state whether the government has made a firm offer to the United Nations to supply up to the equivalent of a battalion of French speaking or bilingual forces for service in the Congo?"[53]

Lumumba called for a UN force to protect the newly sovereign country's territorial integrity from a Belgian-backed secessionist movement in the eastern Katanga province. But Washington used the UN force to undermine the anti-colonial leader and pushed Ottawa to participate.[54] Lumumba didn't openly oppose Canadian military involvement in his country but made his preference for African and Asian troops clear.

Herridge seems to have understood that Lumumba was popular but the CCF MP was extremely naïve about Canada's actions. After Lumumba was captured by UN-US-Canada backed forces and beaten, Herridge told the House, "knowing of his concern with this problem ... I wonder whether the [external] minister has any further information to report to the House."[55] But, external minister Howard Green was antagonistic to the elected Congolese prime minister. In a private conversation with Green, Prime Minister John Diefenbaker called Lumumba a "major threat to Western interests" and said he was "coming around to the conclusion" that an independent Western-oriented Katanga offered "the best solution to the current crisis."[56]

Canadian troops dominated intelligence-gathering positions within the UN mission and they worked to undermine Lumumba. After the PM escaped house arrest and fled Leopoldville for his power base in the Eastern Orientale province, Canadian Colonel Jean Berthiaume assisted Lumumba's political enemies by helping recapture him.[57] Kept in place by Ottawa, the UN Chief of Staff tracked the deposed prime minister and Berthiaume informed the head of the military, Joseph Mobutu, of Lumumba's whereabouts.[58] Soon after the elected prime minister was killed.

Ignorant or indifferent to Canada's role in Lumumba's assassination, Herridge asked the House, "has the government given consideration to what contribution we will make to meet the situation that will flow from this unfortunate incident?"[59]

I was unable find any CCF criticism of Canada's role in Lumumba's assassination or ONUC. Yet, tens of thousands around the world demonstrated against the killing of the Congolese independence leader. A front-page *Montreal Gazette* story reported on African students living in the city protesting "the external forces that have contributed to this savagery and the attitude of foreign nations who made possible the assassination of a great African nationalist leader."[60] A number of countries also withdrew their troops from ONUC to protest the UN force's role in Lumumba's murder.[61]

Whether it flowed from ignorance, fear of being considered "Communist" or from white supremacy, CCF support for Belgian and western imperialism across Africa was wrong. The Congolese and other Africans continue to suffer its consequences and Canadians certainly would not want our elected prime minister overthrown and killed by foreign forces. While Lumumba's murder was a high-profile example of Canadian social democracy's failure to oppose colonialism and white supremacy, it was not an isolated incident. To this day the NDP has often been seduced into silence or even support for Canada's not insignificant role in supporting Western imperialism in Africa, Asia, Latin America and the Caribbean. As well the party generally seems to believe anything called "peacekeeping" is good, whatever its actual motive.

PALESTINE

During its first decade the CCF largely opposed the imperialism and nationalism associated with Zionism. Since that time, however, the party has often backed Canada's contribution to the dispossession of Palestinians.

In 1938 CCF leader J. S. Woodsworth said, "it was easy for Canadians, Americans and the British to agree to a Jewish colony, as long as it was somewhere else. Why 'pick on the Arabs' other than for 'strategic' and 'imperialistic' consideration."[62] At its 1942 convention the CCF condemned Nazi anti-Semitism but refused to endorse Zionism. "The Jewish problem can be solved only in a socialist and democratic society, which recognized no racial or class differences," explained a party resolution.[63]

But before Israel's creation the CCF officially endorsed the establishment of a Jewish state on Palestinian land. A 1944 CCF resolution called for "governments to implement fully the Balfour Declaration of 1917, solemnly made by the government of Great Britain and endorsed by the League of Nations, to facilitate the establishment of Palestine as a Jewish homeland which should lead to the development of a Jewish Commonwealth."[64] This statement in support of British Foreign Secretary Arthur Balfour's crass expression of colonial thought is considered the first time a Canadian political party formally supported a Jewish state.[65]

Subsequently Young Poale Zion would become affiliated with the CCF. At the behest of this Jewish labour Zionist group CCF MP Alistair addressed the Anglo-American Commission of Inquiry on Mandatory Palestine in 1946.[66]

CCF leaders M.J. Coldwell, Tommy Douglas, Ted Joliffe and Stanley Knowles were members of the Canadian Palestine Committee (CPC), a group of prominent non-Jewish Zionists formed in 1943 (future external minister Paul Martin Sr. and Alberta premier Ernest C. Manning were also members). In 1944 the CPC wrote Prime Minister Mackenzie King that it "looks forward to the day when Palestine shall ultimately become a Jewish commonwealth, and member of the British Commonwealth of Nations under the British Crown."[67]

Many CPC members' Zionism was motivated by religious belief. Both Knowles and Douglas were Protestant ministers and their Zionism was partly inspired by biblical teachings. As an indication of the extent to which religion shaped Douglas his main biography is titled *Tommy Douglas: The Road to Jerusalem.*

In 1945 CCF leader Coldwell attended the International Christian Conference on Palestine in Washington, DC.[68] The next year the Anglican politician traveled to Houston, Texas, for a Christian Zionist conference there.[69]

CCF officials promoted the 1947 UN Partition Plan, which gave the Zionist movement 55% of historic Palestine despite Jews making up a third of the population and owning less than 7% of the land.[70] In 1948 CCF MPs opposed arms restrictions to Zionist forces in Palestine and complained that the British foreign office was appeasing Arabs.[71] At the time of Israel's creation "the CCF called for an end to violence and terrorism and urged the Security Council 'to warn the Arab states that, as members of UN, they are obliged to accept UN decisions, and that if they persist in supporting acts of aggression, the

Security Council will be compelled to take appropriate action.'"[72] When Prime Minister McKenzie King delayed immediately recognizing Israel, which captured 22% more Palestinian territory than allotted under the already unjust UN Partition Plan, the CCF called on Ottawa to recognize the Zionist movement's declaration of independence.[73]

Not long after 750,000 Palestinians were ethnically cleansed from their homeland in 1947/48 CCF officials said the refugees should not be allowed to return.[74] Despite the UN adopting Resolution 194 in support of Palestinian refugees right to return to their homeland, CCF MP Alistair Stewart said that taking in anything more than a small proportion of the refugees might destroy Israel and would be "asking more than any modern state would be prepared to accede to."[75]

Notwithstanding the party's general misgivings towards arms sales, CCF leader M.J. Coldwell backed Canada selling 24 F-86 Sabre jets to Israel in the lead-up to its 1956 invasion of Egypt.[76] The party justified Israel's invasion alongside declining Middle East colonial powers Britain and France. Coldwell said, "Israel had ample provocation for her action in marching into Sinai ... Egypt's insistence that Israel be made to obey United Nations resolutions [while it had] hampered Israel's shipping without lawful excuse. Egypt's insistence that Israel be made to obey United Nations resolution sounds no less than cynical coming as it does from a government which for years ignored and flouted the Security Council and United Nations when they ordered free passage for Israel's ships through Suez."[77]

The NDP also took up Israel's justification for invading its neighbours in 1967. They criticized Egypt's blockade of Israeli shipping while ignoring that country's strategic objectives, which the CIA concluded were the: "Destruction of the center of power of the radical Arab Socialist movement, i.e. the Nasser regime." (2) "Destruction of the arms of the radical Arabs." (3) "Destruction of both Syria and Jordan as modern states."[78]

Despite Ottawa's strong pro-Israel alignment, NDP leader Tommy Douglas criticized Prime Minister Lester Pearson for not backing Israel more forthrightly in the 1967 war. Describing the NDP convention shortly after the Six-Day War *Toronto Star* reporter John Goddard wrote, "the delegates were solidly behind Israel. I remember David Lewis leading the discussion at the Royal York Hotel, the look of steely resolve on his face, and the sense of relief in the room over the defeat of the Arab armies."[79]

After Israel conquered East Jerusalem in 1967 the party came out in favour of a "united Jerusalem". "The division of Jerusalem," said David Lewis, "did not make economic or social sense. As a united city under Israel's aegis, Jerusalem would be a much more progressive and fruitful capital of the various religions."[80]

As Israel occupied the West Bank, Gaza, Golan Heights and Egypt's Sinai, Lewis made "impassioned warnings that Israel was in danger."[81] During his time as federal leader from 1971 to 1975 Lewis also spoke to at least one Israel Bonds fundraiser, which raised money for that state.

The NDP vociferously opposed the UN granting the Palestinian Liberation Organization observer status in 1974. Federal party leader Ed Broadbent called the PLO "terrorists and murderers whose aim is the destruction of the state of Israel."[82] In the late 1970s the NDP called on the federal government to intervene to block Canadian companies from adhering to Arab countries' boycott of Israel, which was designed to pressure that country to return land captured in the 1967 war.[83]

Ontario NDP leader from 1970 to 1978, Stephen Lewis was stridently anti-Palestinian. He demanded the federal government cancel a major UN conference scheduled for Toronto in 1975 because the PLO was granted observer status at the UN the previous year and their representatives might attend.[84] In a 1977 speech to pro-Israel fundraiser United Jewish Appeal, which the *Canadian Jewish News* titled "Lewis praises [Conservative premier Bill] Davis for Stand on Israel", Stephen Lewis denounced the UN's "wantonly anti-social attitude to Israel." He told the pro-Israel audience that "the anti-Semitism that lurks underneath the surface is diabolical. The only thing to rely on is Jew helping Jew."[85]

In the 1989 book *The Domestic Battleground: Canada and the Arab-Israeli Conflict* Irving Abella and John Sigler write, "historically, the New Democratic Party (NDP) has been the most supportive of the Israeli cause, largely because of its close relationship to Israel's Labour party, and to the Histadrut, the Israeli trade union movement."[86]

Excluding non-Jewish workers for much of its history, the Histadrut was a key part of the Zionist movement. Former Prime Minister Golda Meir remarked: "Then [1928] I was put on the Histadrut Executive Committee at a time when this big labor union wasn't just a trade union organization. It was a great colonizing agency."[87] For its part, Israel's Labor party (and predecessor Mapai) was largely responsible for the 1947/48 ethnic cleansing of Palestine, 1956 invasion of Egypt and post-1967 settlement construction in the West Bank. In 2017 its leader Avi Gabbay came out against removing the most isolated illegal settlements in the West Bank and told party activists that "the Arabs have to be afraid of us ... They fire one missile – you fire 20. That's all they understand in the Middle East."[88]

NDP relations with Israel's Labor party continue. At the party's 2018 convention Labor Knesset Member Michal Biran was photographed with NDP leader Jagmeet Singh.[89] In the lead-up to that event Biran wrote, "Western progressives must not buy into the simplistic notion that peace is Israel's gift to bestow upon the Palestinians."[90]

Extreme pro-Israel rhetoric also remains a feature of the party. In 2008 NDP MP and later party leader Tom Mulcair told a French-language Jewish publication "I am an ardent supporter of Israel in all situations and in all circumstances."[91]

In another example of extreme pro-Israel policy, NDP officials continue to associate with the openly racist Jewish National Fund. Five months after speaking at the 2016 American Israel Public Affairs Committee (AIPAC) conference in Washington D.C., Hélène Laverdière participated in a JNF tree planting ceremony in Jerusalem. During a visit to Israel with Canada's Governor General the NDP's foreign critic attended a ceremony with JNF World Chairman Danny Atar and a number of other top officials of the JNF (KKL in Israel).[92] During the Harper regime NDP MP Pat Martin spoke at a JNF event at the prime minister's residence in Ottawa to "recognize and thank the people that have helped to make JNF Canada what it is today."[93] A Centre for Israel and Jewish Affairs board member at the time of publication, Nova Scotia Premier Darrell Dexter planted a tree at a JNF garden in 2011.[94] Manitoba NDP Premier Gary Doer was honoured at a 2006 JNF Negev Dinner in

Winnipeg and cabinet minister Christine Melnick received the same honour in 2011.[95] During a 2010 trip to Israel subsequent Manitoba NDP Premier Greg Selinger signed an accord with the JNF to jointly develop two bird conservation sites while water stewardship minister Melnick spoke at the opening ceremony for a park built in Jaffa by the JNF, Tel Aviv Foundation and Manitoba-Israel Shared Values Roundtable.[96] (In 2017 Melnick won a B'nai Brith Zionist action figures prize for writing an article about a friend who helped conquer East Jerusalem and then later joined the JNF).[97]

The JNF owns 13 per cent of Israel's land, which was mostly taken from Palestinians forced from their homes by Zionist forces in 1947-1948.[98] It discriminates against Palestinian citizens of Israel (Arab Israelis) who make up a fifth of the population. According to a UN report, JNF lands are "chartered to benefit Jews exclusively," which has led to an "institutionalized form of discrimination."[99] Echoing the UN, a 2012 US State Department report detailing "institutional and societal discrimination" in Israel says JNF "statutes prohibit sale or lease of land to non-Jews."[100] Indicative of its discrimination against the 20% of Israelis who aren't Jewish, JNF Canada's Twitter tag says it "is the caretaker of the land of Israel, on behalf of its owners — Jewish people everywhere."[101] Its parent organization in Israel — the Keren Kayemet LeYisrael — is even more open about its racism. In 2018 its website noted that "a survey commissioned by KKL-JNF reveals that over 70% of the Jewish population in Israel opposes allocating KKL-JNF land to non-Jews, while over 80% prefer the definition of Israel as a Jewish state, rather than as the state of all its citizens."[102] The JNF is an openly Jewish supremacist organization operating in a Jewish/white supremacist state.

Again, the NDP has supported policies in Israel that party members would not accept in Canada. Racist land covenants were outlawed in this country in the 1950s and religious/ethnic states run counter to the secular tradition from which socialist and social democratic parties emerged. While some might argue that the Nazi Holocaust explains the support Canadian social democracy offered Israel, and that the country's early "socialism" made it popular with leftists, many on the left (including some Jews) have long warned of the dangers of building an ethno-religious settler state. Instead of listening to those voices the CCF/NDP chose to side with an outpost of Western imperialism in a strategically important part of the world. Is this a coincidence or part of a consistent pattern?

MILITARY INTERVENTIONS AND COUPS

For a party founded on anti-capitalist and anti-war principles, the NDP has often supported the use of military force to overthrow governments seen as challenging Western interests. While it's generally justified with humanitarian language, great harm has been inflicted on people living in countries Canada has bombed, invaded or simply interfered in.

The NDP backed Canada's significant contribution to NATO's 1999 bombing of the former Yugoslavia. In the House of Commons foreign critic Svend Robinson endorsed "military action against selected Serbian military targets to address the humanitarian crisis ... We in the New Democratic Party accept that the use of military force as a last resort is sometimes necessary in grave humanitarian crises, when all efforts at diplomatic settlement have failed, and we believe this meets that test."[103] (The party only turned critical over a month after the bombing began.) Contravening international law, the

78-day bombing campaign killed hundreds and spurred the ethnic cleansing of Albanian Kosovars — exactly what NATO officials claimed to be trying to stop.[104]

The NDP initially supported Canada's October 2001 invasion of Afghanistan. In 2006 they called for Canada to withdraw from Afghanistan, but the party never mobilized against a war that saw 40,000 Canadians deployed halfway across the globe.[105]

Two days after the George W. Bush administration declared war, NDP leader Alexa McDonough and defence critic Peter Stoffer issued a "joint statement", saying they "completely back the men and women in the Canadian military assigned to the U.S. coalition."[106] Despite an ongoing military presence, the issue remained on the back burner until Canada took responsibility for an intense counterinsurgency war in the southern Afghan province of Kandahar.

To prepare soldiers and the public for the deployment to Kandahar, Chief of the Defence Staff Rick Hillier said, "we are going to Afghanistan to actually take down the folks that are trying to blow up men and women." He added, "we're not the public service of Canada, we're not just another department. We are the Canadian Forces, and our job is to be able to kill people."[107]

The NDP leader labeled Hillier's bombastic comments an "appropriate response" to the circumstances. Jack Layton told the *Globe and Mail*, "we have a very committed, level-headed head of our armed forces, who isn't afraid to express the passion that underlies the mission that front-line personnel are going to be taking on."[108]

Eight months after the CF took charge in Kandahar, Layton called for peace talks with the Taliban and withdrawal of the

2,000 Canadian troops from southern Afghanistan within six months.[109] (He didn't call for the 50 troops in the north to be withdrawn.) But, Layton made the demand a week before the party's Québec City convention, reportedly, "to discourage the party from adopting a more controversial resolution."[110] The September 2006 NDP convention overwhelmingly supported a resolution calling for Canadian Forces to be withdrawn from Afghanistan. The resolution called for "the safe and immediate withdrawal of Canadian troops from Afghanistan", but also included wording pushed by the NDP leadership to soften the "troops out" demand. It called for "support[ing] the continuation of development assistance to Afghanistan and democratic peace building in that country so that reconstruction efforts and good governance are achieved."[111]

While government officials and right-wing commentators dubbed him "Taliban Jack" for supporting negotiations with the Taliban, Layton's criticism of the occupation never came across as sincere or principled. He complained the mission was "not clearly defined" and lacked an "exit strategy".[112] In calling for the removal of troops from Kandahar prior to the 2006 convention Layton declared: "Our efforts in the region are overwhelmingly focussed on military force — spending defence dollars on counter-insurgency. Prime Minister Harper need only look at the experience in Iraq to conclude that ill-conceived and unbalanced missions do not create the conditions for long-term peace. Why are we blindly following the defence policy prescriptions of the Bush administration? This is not the right mission for Canada. There is no balance — in particular it lacks a comprehensive rebuilding plan and commensurate development assistance."[113] Layton did not criticize Canada's role in propping up the Hamid Karzai regime. Nor did he question how linking feminism to foreign occupation would impact Afghan women over the long term or how the government could claim to 'fight for women's rights in Afghanistan' while its policies in Haiti at the time contributed to a massive increase in rape. (According to the *Lancet* medical journal, 35,000 women were raped in Port-au-Prince in the 22 months after the 2004 Canada-backed coup discussed below.[114])

The "Taliban Jack" backlash, election of the more popular Barrack Obama — who expanded the Afghan war — and a short-term alliance with the Liberal Party led the NDP to stop calling for withdrawal. Between October 2008 and August 2009 the party did not issue a single press release calling for Canadian troops to be withdrawn from Afghanistan.[115] In December 2008 the NDP formally announced it would stop opposing the war while it worked with the Liberals to defeat the minority Conservative government.[116]

In mid-2010 the Liberals called on the Conservatives to extend the Afghan mission after an announced withdrawal in 2011. With Liberal foreign critic Bob Rae calling on Ottawa to "see this thing through", notes Derrick O'Keefe, "the leadership of the New Democratic Party (NDP) remained utterly silent on the question of Afghanistan. For NDP leader Jack Layton this was true to his form over the past couple of years. As the war in Afghanistan expanded, the social democratic opposition became more muted. Save for the occasional de rigueur mention of the party's official policy calling for troop withdrawal, after late 2008 the since deceased Layton rarely criticized the war."[117]

The NDP was also wishy-washy on the February 29, 2004, US/France/Canada coup in Haiti. In the House of Commons ten days later Svend Robinson rightly called for an investigation into elected President Jean-Bertrand Aristide's removal. He also requested the tabling of documents concerning the January 2003 Ottawa Initiative on Haiti, where high level US, Canadian and French officials discussed overthrowing Aristide.[118] Robinson asked if "regime change in Haiti" was discussed at this meeting.[119]

On March 10 Layton described the situation in Haiti as "very grave." But instead of "holding Paul Martin's feet to the fire" regarding Haiti, as the NDP leader claimed he would do, the party largely dropped the issue. During the June 2004 federal election debate Liberal leader Paul Martin and Bloc Québecois leader Gilles Duceppe agreed that Canada's involvement in Haiti was a success. Layton didn't object, wasting an opportunity to provide an alternative view of Canada's disastrous role in the Caribbean nation.

Throughout this period the Canada Haiti Action Network was in contact with party officials. Staff in foreign critic Alexa McDonough's office intimated that their interventions would be shaped by media considerations. After a spate of press articles exposing the Canadian-backed government's violence in Haiti were printed in March 2005, the NDP released two press releases concerning human rights violations in Haiti.

In another example of using humanitarian language to mask western imperialism, in 2011 the party supported two House of Commons votes endorsing the bombing of Libya. "It's appropriate for Canada to be a part of this effort to try to stop Gadhafi from attacking his citizens as he has been threatening to do," said Layton. "It's "important that we get (this mission) right."[120] But, the NATO bombing campaign was justified based on exaggerations and outright lies about the Gaddafi regime's human rights violations (see *The Ugly Canadian* for details). Additionally, NATO forces explicitly contravened the UN resolutions sanctioning a no-fly zone by dispatching troops and expanding the bombing far beyond protecting civilians. Canada also defied UN resolutions 1970 and 1973 by selling drones to the rebels.[121]

After Gaddafi was savagely killed, NDP interim leader Nycole Turmel released a statement noting, "the future of Libya now belongs to all Libyans. Our troops have done a wonderful job in Libya over the past few months."[122] As this book went to print in 2018, Libya was still divided into various warring factions and hundreds of militias operated in the country of six million.[123] Clearly, ordinary people have been harmed.

The NDP also failed to oppose Canada's low-level war against Iran. During Stephen Harper's reign Canadian naval vessels ran provocative manoeuvres off Iran's coast, Canadian troops occupied a bordering state, Ottawa targeted Iran at the UN, listed that country as a state sponsor of terrorism and cut off diplomatic relations with Iran. The NDP largely ignored these developments and in September 2012 NDP foreign critic Paul Dewar was rebuffed by party leader Tom Mulcair after he meekly criticized the Conservatives' move to sever diplomatic ties. "For us to make a difference, we have to be there [in Iran]," Dewar told CTV News. "We have to show up, and now we're walking away."[124]

But that was too much for Mulcair. "I think one of the concerns that Paul [Dewar] was expressing there was with Canadians who are currently in prison, so it becomes difficult for them. But it's also becoming increasingly clear that there were serious concerns, we don't have the same information but it would appear that there might be some very solid information that would have led the government to that decision [to cut relations with Iran], so until we have that information it's hard to comment further."[125] In other words, the government can do what they want to Iran because they have more information on the matter. Instead of questioning Ottawa's low-level war, the NDP joined the attacks. In 2013, 2014 and 2015 Dewar cosponsored Iran Accountability Week, which was put on by Israeli nationalist MP Irwin Cotler.[126] Another repeated participant in Iran Accountability Week was Mark Dubowitz who Ynet, Israel's largest English language news site, dubbed "The Man Who Fights Iran".[127]

More recently, the NDP backed a coup in Kiev, war in eastern Ukraine and NATO military build-up in Eastern Europe. In 2014 the right-wing nationalist Euro-Maidan movement ousted Viktor Yanukovych who was oscillating between the European Union and Russia. The US-backed coup divided the Ukraine politically, geographically and linguistically (Russian is the mother tongue of 30% of Ukrainians). After Yanukovych's ouster Russia reinforced its military presence — or "seized"— the southern area of Crimea and then organized a referendum on secession. Home to Moscow's major Baltic naval base, Crimea had long been part of Russia and the bulk of the population preferred Moscow's rule to the post-coup right wing nationalist government in Kiev.[128]

The NDP echoed the US/Stephen Harper government position on Ukraine. The day after Yanukovych fled, NDP MP Olivia Chow told a Euro-Maidan Canada rally in Toronto, "we must be vigilant, we must ensure our government, our Canadian government, continues to keep an eye on the Ukraine to make sure that the Russians do not interfere."[129]

But, the NDP MP wasn't bothered by Canadian interference in that country. Eighteen months after the coup the Canadian Press reported that opposition protesters were camped in the Canadian Embassy for a week during the February 2014 rebellion against Yanukovych. "Canada's embassy in Kyiv was used as a haven for several days by anti-government protesters during the uprising that toppled the regime of former president Viktor Yanukovych," the story noted.[130]

Ottawa played a similar role during the "Orange Revolution" a decade earlier. In a story headlined "Agent Orange: Our secret role in Ukraine" *Globe and Mail* reporter Mark MacKinnon detailed how Canada funded a leading civil society opposition group, promised Ukraine's lead electoral commissioner Canadian citizenship if he did "the right thing" and paid for 500 Canadians of Ukrainian descent to observe the 2004-05 elections. "[Canadian ambassador to the Ukraine, Andrew Robinson] began to organize secret monthly meetings of western ambassadors, presiding over what he called 'donor coordination' sessions among 20 countries interested in seeing Mr. [presidential candidate Viktor] Yushchenko succeed. Eventually, he acted as the group's spokesman and became a prominent critic of the Kuchma government's heavy-handed media control. Canada also invested in a controversial exit poll, carried out on election day by Ukraine's Razumkov Centre and other groups that contradicted the official results showing Mr. Yanukovych [winning]."[131]

Boosted by its success in Ukraine's 2005 elections, Ottawa continued to push against Russian influence in Eastern Europe. Federal government documents from 2007 explain that Ottawa was trying to be "a visible and effective partner of the United States in Russia, Ukraine and zones of instability in Eastern Europe."[132] During a visit to the Ukraine that year, Foreign Minister Peter MacKay said Canada would help provide a "counterbalance" to Russia. "There are outside pressures [on Ukraine], from Russia most notably. … We want to make sure they feel the support that is there for them in the international community."[133] As part of Canada's "counterbalance" to Russia, MacKay announced $16 million in aid to support "democratic reform" in the Ukraine.[134]

Indifferent to Canada's interference in Ukrainian affairs, during the 2015 federal election leaders debate Mulcair said, "with regard to Ukraine, yes, Putin is a danger. We stand firmly with Ukraine against the aggression by Russia."[135] The NDP leader also reiterated the party's call for harsher measures against Russian officials, naming two businessmen whom he said should be added to Canada's list of Russians targeted for sanctions.[136] In March 2014 NDP foreign critic Paul Dewar released a statement calling for "travel bans against certain Russian officials and suspending trade with Russia's military sector."[137] Five months later the NDP put out a press release under the headline "Conservatives shield Russian business elite from sanctions: Toothless sanctions are out of step with Canada's closest allies."[138] In 2017 NDP foreign critic Hélène Laverdière applauded a bill modeled after the US Magnitsky Act that would further strain relations between Ottawa and Moscow by sanctioning Russian officials. NDP MPs voted for legislation Laverdière labelled an "important step to support the Global Magnitsky movement."[139]

In summer 2016 NDP defence critic Randall Garrison expressed support for Canada leading a NATO battle group to Latvia as part of a ratcheting up of tensions with Russia.[140] Four hundred and fifty Canadian troops were deployed to head up a 1,000-strong NATO force in Latvia while the US, Britain and Germany headed missions in Poland, Lithuania and Estonia. As vice-chair of Parliament's Standing Committee on National Defence, Garrison endorsed a December 2017 report titled "Canada's support to Ukraine in crisis and armed conflict." It denounced Russia's "war of aggression against Ukraine" and lauded Canada's "support of Ukraine in its fight against Russia."[141]

NDP representatives even flirted with the Ukraine's hard right. At a Toronto event NDP MP Peggy Nash shared a stage with a speaker from Ukraine's Right Sector, which said it was "defending the values of white, Christian Europe against the loss of the nation and deregionalisation."[142] For her part, Ontario NDP MPP Cheri DiNovo attended a Ukrainian parade in Toronto where some marched behind a banner titled "Right Sector Canada".[143]

In another region where the US and Russia were in conflict the NDP aligned with the Washington-Riyadh position. At the start of the Syrian conflict the NDP criticized the Harper government for failing to take stronger action against the Bashar al-Assad regime. In 2011-12 they urged Harper to recall Canada's ambassador to Syria and complained that energy giant Suncor was exempted from sanctions, calling on Canada to "put our money where our mouth is."[144]

In the midst of growing calls for the US to impose a "no-fly zone" on Syria in 2016, the NDP's foreign critic recommended Canada nominate the White Helmets for the Nobel Peace Prize. A letter NDP MPs wrote to foreign minister Stéphane Dion noted: "Canada has a proud and long-standing commitment to human rights, humanitarianism and international peacekeeping. It is surely our place to recognize the selflessness, bravery, and fundamental commitment to human dignity of these brave women and men."[145] In Spring 2018 Laverdière posted on twitter about the "honour" she had in meeting representatives of the White Helmets' and told *The Hill Times* Ottawa "must match their words of support with more funds" to the group and Syrians.[146]

Also known as the Syrian Civil Defence, the White Helmets were credited with rescuing many people from bombed out buildings. But, they also fostered opposition to Assad and promoted western intervention. The White Helmets operated almost entirely in areas of Syria occupied by the Saudi Arabia–Washington backed Al Nusra/Al Qaeda rebels. They criticized the Syrian government and disseminated images of its violence while largely ignoring those targeted by the opposition. Their members were repeatedly photographed with anti-government Jihadists and reportedly enabled some of their executions.[147]

The White Helmets were closely associated with the Syria Campaign, which was set up by Ayman Asfari, a British billionaire of Syrian descent actively opposed to Assad. The White Helmets also received at least $23 million US from USAID.[148] The British, Dutch, German and French governments have also provided the group with tens of millions of dollars.[149] In late 2016 Global Affairs Canada sponsored a five-city White Helmets tour of Canada and eighteen months later announced they "provided $12 million for groups in Syria, such as the White Helmets, that are saving lives by providing communities with emergency response services and removing explosives."[150]

In the summer of 2017, the NDP went so far down the road in supporting American imperialism that it joined Washington and right-wing Latin American governments in stoking opposition protests against Venezuela's elected government. Between 1998 and 2017 the Bolivarian Revolution won 19 of 21 elections and for most of that period it improved the lives of poor and working-class Venezuelans. But, the revolution was weakened by President Hugo Chavez' death in 2013, a huge drop in the price of oil, a shift to the right in the region as well as a failure to overcome the country's oil dependence, corruption and crime. Throughout this period it faced aggressive attacks by the country's traditional business class, opposition parties and much of the media, not to mention the US Empire.

While the NDP sometimes challenged Ottawa's hostility towards the Chavez government, between 2014 and 2017 the party's foreign critics backed renewed efforts by Washington and the opposition to undermine an essentially democratic effort to empower the poor and working class. On a number of occasions the NDP foreign critic demanded Ottawa do more to undermine President Nicolás Maduro's government. Amidst opposition protests, in August 2017 Laverdière told CBC "we would like to see the [Canadian] government be more active in … calling for the release of political prisoners, the holding of elections and respecting the National Assembly."[151]

Laverdière's statements ignored the death and destruction caused by the opposition protesters and the division of powers between the different branches of Venezuela's government. It also ignored the opposition's effort to hamstring the government after it won control of the National Assembly in 2015.

In June 2016 Laverdière put out a press release bemoaning "the erosion of democracy" and the need for Ottawa to "defend democracy in Venezuela". In it Laverdière said, "the

OAS Secretary General Luis Almagro has invoked the Inter-American Democratic Charter regarding Venezuela, and Canada, as a member of the OAS, should support his efforts."[152] But, the former Uruguayan Foreign Minister's actions as head of the OAS were highly controversial. They even prompted Almagro's past boss, former Uruguayan president José Mujica, to condemn his bias against the Venezuelan government, which had been elected.[153] (The president of Brazil, on the other hand, came to power through a questionable impeachment process and had a 5% approval rating, according to polls.[154] But, the NDP appears to have stayed mum about Vice President Michel Temer's "soft coup" in Brazil in mid-2016.)

Amidst three months of violent right wing protests in early 2014, then NDP foreign critic Paul Dewar sponsored a House of Commons resolution that asked "the Government of Canada to urge Venezuelan authorities to proactively de-escalate the conflict, protect the human and democratic freedoms of Venezuelan citizens, release all those detained during the protests, immediately cease all government interference with peaceful protesters, and ensure that those people who perpetrated the violence be brought to justice and bear the full weight of the law."[155]

While they found cause to criticize the Venezuelan government, the NDP's foreign critic staid mum when US President Donald Trump threatened to invade Venezuela in the summer of 2017.[156] Similarly, the party failed to criticize US Secretary of State Rex Tillerson's February 2018 call for a military coup in Venezuela.[157] They also failed to challenge Canadian sanctions, which followed a similar move by the US. In an effort that probably violated the UN and OAS charters, in September 2017 the elected president, vice president and 38 other Venezuelan officials had their assets in Canada frozen and Canadians were barred from having financial relations with these individuals.[158]

The NDP also ignored Canada's role in directly financing an often-unsavoury Venezuelan opposition. A specialist in social media and political transition, Canada's ambassador to Venezuela between 2014 and July 2017 Ben Rowswell told the *Ottawa Citizen* just after leaving his position: "We established quite a significant internet presence inside Venezuela, so that we could then engage tens of thousands of Venezuelan citizens in a conversation on human rights. We became one of the most vocal embassies in speaking out on human rights issues and encouraging Venezuelans to speak out."[159]

While not forthcoming with information about the groups they supported in Venezuela, Ottawa funnelled money to the U.S.-backed opposition. In 2010 the foremost researcher on US funding to the opposition, Eva Golinger, claimed Canadian groups were playing a growing role in Venezuela and according to a 2010 report from Spanish NGO Fride, "Canada is the third most important provider of democracy assistance" to Venezuela after the U.S. and Spain.[160] In "The Revolution Will Not Be Destabilized: Ottawa's democracy promoters target Venezuela" Anthony Fenton details Canadian funding to anti-government groups.[161] Among other examples, he cites a $94,580 grant to opposition NGO Asociación Civil Consorcio Desarrollo y Justicia in 2007 and $22,000 to Súmate in 2005.

Súmate leader Maria Corina Machado, who was invited to Ottawa in 2005 by Foreign Affairs, backed the "Carmona Decree" during the 2002 coup against President Chavez, which dissolved the National Assembly and Supreme Court and suspended the elected government, Attorney General,

Comptroller General, governors as well as mayors elected during Chavez's administration.[162]

Hopefully the NDP would condemn American or other foreign officials who interfered in Canadian politics in this way. So, why is it okay in a South American country? Is it because the party was blinded by relentless media propaganda against Venezuela of the sort that has long been aimed at Cuba or any country that tries to assert its independence from the US Empire? Or is something more fundamental happening? Has the desire of some in the NDP to replace the Liberals as the slightly leftish alternative to the Conservatives caused the party to move so far to the right that it agrees with Canada being a partner in enforcing imperialism? If so, what sort of home does it offer those who oppose the US Empire and all forms of imperialism? If the NDP does not criticize blatant interference in the affairs of other countries, what sort of approach does it take to the other key litmus test of a just foreign policy: opposition to the use of military might to get one's way.

MILITARISM

The NDP has staunchly defended Canadian militarism. After the 2017 federal budget NDP Leader Tom Mulcair criticized the Liberals for not spending more on the Canadian Forces. "Canadians have every right to be concerned," Mulcair said. "We are in desperate need of new ships for our Navy, we're in desperate need of new fighter aircraft for our Air Force, and there's no way that with the type of budget we've seen here that they're going to be getting them."[163]

Two months later the Liberals announced a 70 per cent increase in military spending over the next decade. The June

2017 Canadian defence policy included a significant increase in lethal fighter jets and secretive special forces, as well as enhancing offensive cyber-attack capabilities and purchasing armed drones. NDP defence critic Randall Garrison criticized the announcement for not putting up money immediately. "We were expecting a lot more from this defence review," Garrison said. "All we have is promises for future [military spending] increases."[164] In another interview he bemoaned (incorrectly) that "the money you're proposing will not keep pace with the rate of inflation."[165]

According to a Huffington Post analysis, in the three days after the funding announcement the NDP failed to devote a single one of its 33 questions in the House of Commons to the increase in military spending. "The NDP did find time though to ask about cuts to the salmon classroom education program," noted HuffPost's Althia Raj drily.[166]

In July 2012 the head of the military publicly demanded a new war. "We have some men and women who have had two, three and four tours and what they're telling me is 'Sir, we've got that bumper sticker. Can we go somewhere else now?'" General Walter Natynczyk told Canadian Press. "You also have the young sailors, soldiers, airmen and women who have just finished basic training and they want to go somewhere and in their minds it was going to be Afghanistan. So if not Afghanistan, where's it going to be? They all want to serve."[167]

It is not surprising that the head of the military would want to go to war (that's his job after all). What's troubling is that Natynczyk felt comfortable saying so in public and that the NDP failed to condemn his comments.

During the 2011 and 2015 federal elections the party explicitly supported the Stephen Harper government's large military budget. In 2011 Layton promised to "maintain the current planned levels of defence spending commitments" and the 2015 NDP platform said the party would "meet our military commitments by maintaining Department of National Defence budget allocations."[168] This wasn't the first time the party took such a stand. In 2002 the NDP endorsed a parliamentary committee's call to increase military spending 50 per cent over eight years and in 2005 the NDP supported the Paul Martin Liberal budget, which included the largest boost in military spending in two decades.[169]

In addition to backing budget allocations, the NDP criticized base closures and called on the Trudeau government to modernize the North American Aerospace Defense Command (NORAD), which is a military alliance that has drawn Canadian personnel into supporting numerous US wars. In 2017 defence critic Randall Garrison criticized the Liberals for failing to follow its defence policy review's recommendation to upgrade a multi-billion dollar early-warning radar system used by NORAD.[170] In a story headlined "Conservatives, NDP call on Liberal government to match rhetoric with action on NORAD" Garrison told the *Hill Times*, "so they put in that they are going to replace it, and that's certainly the biggest thing we need to do in terms of our cooperation with NORAD, [but] I don't see the follow through down the road on it, in terms of planning, implementation, or budgeting."[171]

The NDP aggressively promoted the National Shipbuilding Procurement Strategy, a $60 billion effort to expand the combat fleet over three decades (over its lifespan the cost is expected to top $100 billion).[172] "Our current ships have reached the end of their operational lives", said Layton in 2011. "They need to be replaced immediately."[173] In 2015, defence critic Jack Harris bemoaned, "Conservative delays" undermining "our navy from getting wanted equipment."[174] The 2015 party platform said it would "carry forward the National Shipbuilding Procurement Strategy to ensure Canada has the ships we need."[175] (In the late 1980s the NDP "agreed with the strengthening of the Navy", notes naval historian Tony German, and during the 1984 election campaign party leader Ed Broadbent "deplored the Navy's near demise."[176])

But a naval upgrade will strengthen Canadian officials' capacity to bully weaker countries. The 2000 book *Canadian Gunboat Diplomacy* details numerous interventions to exert a delicate and subtle threat short of declared war. In 1921 three vessels were sent to Costa Rica to pressure the government to repay money the Royal Bank loaned a dictator as he fled a popular revolt.[177] In 1932 a Canadian ship provided support to an El Salvadorian dictatorship as it put down an Indigenous rebellion, which ultimately led to the execution of famous revolutionary, Farabundo Marti.[178] Since 1963 Canadian warships have been used to pressure the government of Haiti on multiple occasions.[179] And it's not just history. Since the early 1990s the Canadian Navy has played an increasing role in the Middle East and off parts of Africa.

In an opportunistic appeal to militarist culture, NDP Veteran Affairs critic Peter Stoffer joined some veterans in criticizing a 2013 agreement between Target and the Royal Canadian Legion allowing red poppies to be sold outside the retailer's stores. The dissident poppy sellers wanted the right to set up inside the company's stores whenever they wanted, not only during bad weather. Stoffer called on the company "to allow them [red poppy sellers] to come into the store at all times."[180] Remembrance Day Poppies commemorate

Canadians who have died at war. Not commemorated are the Afghans or Libyans killed by Canadians in the 2000s or the Iraqis and Serbians killed in the 1990s or the Koreans killed in the 1950s or the Russians, South Africans, Sudanese and others killed before that. By focusing exclusively on 'our' side Remembrance Day poppies reinforce a sense that Canada's cause is righteous. The NDP never called on Target to allow peace organizations to set up tables and sell anti-war white poppies.

During 2014-15 the NDP campaigned to "Make Remembrance Day a Legal Holiday".[181] In a 2015 Remembrance Day statement party leader Tom Mulcair said, "we reaffirm our commitment to the values for which they fought. Lest we forget."[182] But World War I had no clear and compelling purpose other than rivalry between up-and-coming Germany and the lead imperial powers of the day, Britain and France. In fact, support for the British Empire was Ottawa's primary motive in joining the war. Nor should we celebrate "the values for which they fought" in Sudan, South Africa, Korea, Iraq, Serbia, Afghanistan or Libya. Canadian soldiers have only fought in one morally justifiable war: World War II.

ANALYSIS

Rather than challenging unjust foreign policies, the NDP has all too often made opportunistic appeals to veterans and the military. The party leadership has been happy to heed the foreign policy establishment, only challenging policy when activists force the issue or segments of the dominant media already question it. As such, the party challenged Canada's complicity in the US war in Vietnam, 1973 coup in Chile, apartheid in South Africa, Indonesia's occupation of East Timor and the Iraq wars, as well as nuclear weapons in the 1980s and Ballistic Missile Defence in the 2000s. But, even regarding some issues with substantial grassroots activism — Palestinian rights most obviously — the party's position has been lacking, to say the least.

Ignorance is part of the problem, but it isn't the primary explanation for the dearth of foreign policy criticism. Many NDP members and officials lack knowledge of global affairs and believe official mythology. At the top of the decision-making pyramid, however, it's likely a political calculation.

Party leaders have often sought to suppress critical information or positions. In the decade after World War II popular Manitoba official Berry Richards was denied positions within the party because he attacked US imperialism in Europe and "to many CCF leaders, this was an attack on the party."[183] In 1949 the party expelled two elected members of the Manitoba legislature for criticizing the Marshall Plan and NATO.[184] The federal CCF also deterred members from engaging with the Canadian Peace Congress.

During the 1950 federal convention B.C. CCF President and foreign policy expert Dorothy Steeves "was blocked from providing a full report." National Secretary David Lewis also pressured Steeves to tone down her (not particularly aggressive) challenges to the status quo in her *CCF News* column titled "A Socialist View of World Affairs".[185]

Less extreme today, the party continues to deter foreign policy criticism. During the 2015 federal election the NDP responded to Conservative party pressure by ousting as many as eight individuals from running or contesting nominations to be candidates because they defended Palestinian rights on social media.[186] In the most high-profile incident, Morgan Wheeldon was dismissed as the party's candidate in a Nova Scotia riding because he accused Israel of committing war crimes in Gaza, when it killed 2,200, mostly civilians, in the summer of 2014.[187]

Over the past two decades the party has repeatedly blocked strong Palestine solidarity resolutions submitted by riding associations "from reaching the stage of debate on the floor of the convention."[188] In 2018 the party machinery employed a slew of manoeuvres to avoid debating the "Palestine Resolution", which was unanimously endorsed by the NDP youth convention, many affiliated groups and over 25 riding associations.[189] It mostly restated official Canadian policy, except that it called for "banning settlement products from Canadian markets, and using other forms of diplomatic and economic pressure to end the occupation."[190]

At its 2011 convention "delegates at the foreign policy priorities panel succeeded in moving the Canadian Boat to Gaza resolution from very low on the list up to #2 position", noted an NDP Socialist Caucus report. "But minutes before we could vote on approval of the content of the resolution, party officials herded 30 to 40 MPs and staff into the room to vote it down."[191]

Party leaders haven't only suppressed criticism of Israel. A Haiti solidarity resolution submitted by four riding associations never made the floor of the 2006 convention.[192] Socialist Caucus leader Barry Weisleder wrote: "Former NDP leader and current External Affairs Critic, Alexa McDonough, moved to kill a high-ranked resolution on Haiti, endorsed by supporters of the Canada Haiti Action Network, which calls for an investigation into Ottawa's role in the overthrow of democratically elected Haitian President Jean-Bertrand Aristide and demands the removal of Canadian police and an end to the ongoing foreign occupation of the super-exploited Caribbean country. McDonough's attempt to substitute her own resolution, which sought to ignore the past and justify an ongoing imperialist 'aid and reconstruction' presence in Haiti, was soundly defeated following a sharp 20-minute debate. No doubt, the leftist Haiti motion would have carried, had it come to a vote — a point certainly not lost on the party brass."[193]

"To forestall debate on Libya, Gaza and NATO in 2011," wrote Weisleder about a subsequent convention, "the foreign policy panel moved up two resolutions on military and RCMP veterans' affairs, plus 'motherhood' motions on accessible medicines and conflict minerals. To the dismay of many, party icon Stephen Lewis gave a rhapsodic introduction to the foreign policy selections, during which he bestowed his blessing on the murderous NATO bombing of Libya, purportedly as an antidote to alleged mass rapes attributed to forces of the Ghadaffi regime."[194] (Amnesty and Human Rights Watch couldn't find evidence of the alleged mass rape. Amnesty senior crisis response adviser Donatella Rovera, who was in Libya for three months after the start of the uprising, said: "We have not found any evidence or a single victim of rape or a doctor who knew about somebody being raped."[195])

I've witnessed first-hand party officials ignoring critical international information. In the mid-2000s the Canada Haiti Action Network informed foreign critic Alexa McDonough of important developments in Haiti, but she largely failed to act on the information. In 2012 I gave a copy of *The Ugly Canadian: Stephen Harper's Foreign Policy* to an advisor of foreign critic Paul Dewar and told him I was open to discussing international issues. They never followed up and when I ran into Dewar on a number of occasions in Ottawa it was clear he'd decided to follow a tepid approach to the file.

The NDP has largely aligned with the foreign policy establishment or those, as long time NDP MP Libby Davies put it, who believe a "Time Magazine version" of international affairs.[196] This is another way of saying the party effectively supports the US Empire, which includes Canada's role in supporting 21st century imperialism. Whether this is a tactical calculation by those who seek to position the NDP just a little to the left of the Liberals or a reflection of the power of the "marketing" outlined in *A Propaganda System* can be debated. But Canadians who want a progressive foreign policy need to understand the NDP's international alignment. Whether one seeks to affect change from inside or outside the party, it's essential to break the media's grip over NDP foreign policy by amplifying the voices of ordinary people from around the world, who wish us to do them no harm.

Where's Labour?

BETWEEN APRIL 2012 AND JULY 2014 I worked for the Communications, Energy and Paperworkers Union, which merged with the Canadian Auto Workers during this period to create Unifor. In my position as CEP researcher I was assigned to meetings about Employment Insurance and the Canadian Pension Plan as well as Friends of Medicare and the Canadian Social Forum. The leadership also gave me considerable latitude to write articles (under the president's name) criticizing exorbitant CEO pay, master servant relations at work and the social/health impacts of inequality. Yet, even though I'd written a handful of books about Canadian foreign policy, the CEP had little use for my experience in this domain. I only did one minor project related to foreign policy.

Unifor is not the only union largely indifferent to international affairs. I've spoken at over 200 public meetings since 2005 and can only remember being invited to address two small union events. Nor can I recall any request to contribute an article about international affairs for a labour newsletter.

While they challenge corporate power on many domestic issues, unions generally remain silent on international affairs. In fact, it's often worse than that. The 'House of Labour' and individual unions have often echoed official policy.

***

Some praise before criticism. Unions have on occasion been part of international solidarity efforts. Many fought against South African apartheid and backed Central America solidarity campaigns in the 1980s. Some also opposed

Indonesia's occupation of East Timor in the 1990s and backed the movement to keep Canada out of the 2003 Iraq war. A few unions have provided meaningful support to the Palestinian struggle by endorsing the Canadian Boat to Gaza or Boycott, Divestment and Sanctions campaign. Some unions have also backed Mining Watch and the Canadian Peace Alliance.

As an important source of funds for left institutions, organized labour supports media outlets such as Rabble.ca, Canadian Dimension, Briarpatch, etc. that publish important critiques of Canadian foreign policy. But, this mostly reflects the importance of union funds for left wing initiatives rather than a commitment to challenging Canadian foreign policy.

…

Since workers began organizing unions in Canada most locals were part of so-called international US unions. Established in 1883, the Trades and Labour Congress (TLC) was highly dependent on the craft oriented American Federation of Labour (AFL). Created in 1940, the Canadian Congress of Labour (CCL) was close to the US Congress of Industrial Organizations (CIO). The AFL and CIO merged in 1955 and the TLC and CCL followed suit the next year. The international positions of US unions greatly influenced their Canadian counterparts.[197]

The AFL largely supported US foreign policy. A staunch "business unionist", AFL president Samuel Gompers backed the turn-of-the-century US occupation of Cuba, World War I and isolating Russia after the 1917 Bolshevik revolution.[198] The long-time US labour leader called World War I "the most wonderful crusade ever entered into by men in the whole history of the world."[199] Gompers' foreign policy didn't end with his 37-year tenure at the helm of the labour federation.

After World War II the AFL helped Washington divide European unions and it consistently backed US policy in the Americas. In the 1978 book *Yankee Unions Go Home*, Jack Scott writes, "support for United States foreign policy with respect to American imperialist objectives had been central to union policy since the Spanish American war of 1898."[200]

BOER WAR TO WORLD WAR II

The TLC endorsed deploying 7,000 Canadians to the Boer War, which was a brutal conflict to strengthen British colonial authority and secure control of large quantities of gold. In criticizing a bill designed to weaken US unions in Canada just after the 1899–1902 war, the TLC's lawyer told the Senate, "the recent South African war was for the recognition of a principle that this bill will deny."[201]

A decade later Canadian unions largely backed an inter-imperialist struggle that Africans experienced as the final phase in the multi-decade European conquest of their continent. In 1915 the TLC characterized World War I as a "mighty endeavour to secure early and final victory for the cause of freedom and democracy."[202] *Industrial Banner*, the leading labour newspaper in southern Ontario, called for crushing "Prussian authoritarianism" under which the "common man suffered most."[203] But, opposition to the war grew dramatically after Ottawa introduced conscription in August 1917. Many union activists argued that if labour was to be conscripted so should wealth.[204]

To undermine antiwar sentiment within the TLC Prime Minister Robert Borden invited the head of the AFL to Ottawa. Only the third public figure to ever address a joint Senate and House of Commons session, Samuel Gompers argued in favour of conscription.[205] The US labour leader also purchased a large sum of Victory Bonds on behalf of the federation.[206]

In a bid to woo the fledgling labour movement, the government offered unions greater influence. During Gompers' visit Borden appointed a workers' representative to the War Trade Board, Canada Registration Board, Labour Appeals Board, Soldiers Vocational Training Board and Canadian Railway Board and made an individual "acceptable to Ontario labour" minister of labour.[207] These measures succeeded in curtailing criticism of the war from the most powerful segments of organized labour, which were mostly in Ontario.[208]

The First World War was particularly horrific for Russians. Hundreds of thousands perished from the fighting and many more died from hunger and disease caused by the conflict. Bolshevism grew in response to this misery brought upon the country by a brutal czar. The French, English and US responded to the Bolshevik government by supporting the Russian monarchists (the whites) in their fight to maintain power. The war against the Bolsheviks was initially justified as a way to reopen the war's Eastern Front (the Bolsheviks signed a peace treaty with Germany), but 2,700 Canadian troops arrived in the eastern city of Vladivostok two months after WWI's conclusion.[209]

During the 1920s and 1930s the West worked to isolate Moscow. The TLC largely supported the anti-Soviet efforts. In 1928 "the full weight of the executive was thrown against" a union local's resolution calling on Canada to resume trade relations with Russia.[210] Two years later an editorial in the TLC's *Canadian Congress Journal* praised a European labour meeting's "universal condemnation of the communistic activities of the Red International of Moscow."[211]

WWI strengthened pacifist sentiment and interest in international affairs. Between the two world wars the TLC supported the emergence of the League of Nations, joining the League of Nations Society in Canada and promoting its journal *Interdependence*.[212]

Despite growing interest in international affairs, I couldn't find any TLC criticism of Canadian influence within the British controlled Caribbean. In fact, the *Canadian Congress Journal* pushed for a publicly owned steamship service to increase "contact" with the West Indies.[213] A 1929 editorial in TLC's *Journal* claimed, "there is every reason to believe that a considerable trade of benefit to both countries will be developed."[214] In a story the previous year titled "Development of Trade with the West Indies" the *Canadian Congress Journal* depicted ties to the former slave plantation colonies glowingly. Referring to the great wealth the Maritimes and Newfoundland generated trading with the Caribbean slave colonies, the article noted, "for well over 100 years Nova Scotia and New Brunswick traders and sailors established contact with the islands, bringing Canadian fish and produce in exchange for fruits, sugar and other products."[215] Unwilling to devote valuable sugar planting space to food crops, Caribbean plantation owners bought high-protein salty cod to keep hundreds of thousands of "enslaved people working 16 hours a day."[216] The 1928 story also noted approvingly how "Canadian trading and financial interests have become well-established throughout the islands."[217] Dating back to the 1830s, Canadian banks had become major players in the English Caribbean and US-dominated Cuba by the early 1900s.

In an indirect sign of the labour federation's attitude towards Canadian banking influence, a 1925 Royal Bank ad in its Journal showed a map of the Western Hemisphere with dots denoting their presence throughout the Caribbean and South America. The headline read, "A bank with 900 branches: at home and abroad."[218]

Further afield, I failed to uncover any criticism of Canada's economic ties to European colonialism in Africa, including the Canadians who oversaw British colonies, rising to governor of Kenya, Ghana and Northern Nigeria.[219] Instead, the TLC lauded the British Empire, attended British Labour Party conferences and developed close ties to the British Trade Union Congress.[220] A *Canadian Congress Journal* editorial quoted approvingly British Labour Party Prime Minister Ramsay MacDonald's 1924 Empire Day appeal "that the Empire does not stand for aggression but for human progress." The magazine simply said his statement was dated as "it is no longer a question of wresting land from the red Indian and living on Buffalo", but "wresting a job from some soulless corporation."[221] Three years later a Journal editorial noted, "it will not support any action which would weaken in the slightest manner the bonds which hold together the peoples who constitute the British Empire" and described a "common desire to protect British ideals and institutions."[222] In 1953 the TLC devoted a two-page editorial to "Queen Elizabeth: long may she reign." It called the new queen "the head of the world's greatest democracy ... helping to bring together the races of mankind."[223]

In the lead up to World War II TLC Secretary-Treasurer Robert Tallon said the Congress was "wholeheartedly behind the Empire".[224] The historical record shows that Nazi expansionism's threat to British interests, not opposition to fascism or anti-Semitism, led Ottawa to join WWII. (Only two years before the war Prime Minister Mackenzie King visited Hitler and in his diary King repeatedly expressed sympathy towards the Nazis.[225]) As Jack Granatstein and Desmond Morton explain, "Canada went to war in September 1939 for the same reason as in 1914: because Britain went to war."[226]

While participating in World War II was morally justifiable, the Allies often fought in ways that were not. In probably the starkest example, the US dropped atomic bombs on Japan. At the end of the war the *Canadian Congress Journal* "express[ed] their heartfelt thanks for the wonderful news that Japan has surrendered unconditionally to the Allied nations."[227] But, the editorial said nothing about the US destruction of Hiroshima and Nagasaki. On the next page a story celebrated "the tremendous contribution of American labour in making the success of the atomic bomb possible, and in keeping the project secret until the bomb was actually in use." The story quoted US Secretary of War Henry Stimson calling the atomic bomb "the greatest achievement of the combined efforts of science, industry, labour, and the military in all history."[228]

COLD WAR

After World War II unions promoted the Anglo-sphere and NATO. In 1945 the CCL described "Canada's historic role as a keystone in the arch of Anglo-American understanding, and the necessity of Canada's continuing to act in that capacity for many years to come."[229]

Unions backed the various policies and institutions of the growing US-Canada-Britain alliance. In 1947 the CCL executive and resolutions committee rejected "a large number of resolutions that were sent in by local unions" critical of Canadian foreign policy and the Truman Doctrine, which called on Washington to support countries threatened by communists.[230] Instead, the executive got the convention to support an omnibus foreign-policy resolution that criticized "rampant and militant Russian Communist imperialism, assisted by its 'fifth columns.'"[231] The resolution also described the Marshall Plan as "a symbol of the generosity of the people of the United States and Canada in giving so largely of their treasure."[232] While supporting the Marshall Plan became a sort of loyalty test for Canadian trade unionist leaders, the officially named European Recovery Plan (ERP) was highly controversial among Western European labour representatives.[233] The Marshall Plan was partly designed to counter left-wing influence, particularly in Italy and France. In *The United States and the European trade union movement, 1944–1951* Federico Romero outlines how it was used to split the Italian labour movement.[234] "Motivated by the need of moving union representation away from Communist influence", he writes, "the ERP stressed both a political realignment and a theoretical and strategic review of the European trade union movement."[235] Support for the Marshall Plan was the "rallying point" that brought European unions together to establish "a new international."[236] Claiming the World Federation of Trade Unions was communist dominated, in 1949 some Italian, French, Spanish and British unions split from the WFTU to create the International Confederation of Free Trade Unions (ICFTU).

Following the AFL's lead, the TLC never affiliated with the WFTU, which was established to unite world labour at the end of WWII. In an allusion to Soviet labour unions, the TLC Journal noted, "we took one look at it at the time of formation and decided it was not possible to mix state owned and controlled labour fronts with free and democratic trade union movements."[237]

The TLC's US parent stoked the split within the WFTU. In *The CIA, the British Left and the Cold War* Hugh Wilford calls "the destruction of the World Federation of Trade Unions" an "important ... objective of the AFL's in this period."[238] Created in 1944, the AFL's Free Trade Union Committee received Marshall Plan and CIA funds to undermine leftist (communist) unions in Western Europe. Significant sums were funnelled to the French and Italian unions that broke from the WFTU to set up the ICFTU.[239]

Once the ICFTU was created, the US State Department "initiated an impressive propaganda campaign for the new international", writes Romero. They also gave US unions assistance "to expand their offices ... especially in Asia, Africa and colonial areas."[240] In a letter to AFL leaders, the State Department wrote, "the formation of the new organization is important to us because, by working through it, American labour can support our objective in helping to change the attitude of politically-minded foreign trade unionists who are suspicious of 'capitalist' governments, especially the US."[241]

A member of several government advisory committees during World War II, TLC president Percy Bengough helped found the ICFTU. He and CCL president Pat Conroy were on its initial executive board.[242] In a 1956 speech to the Empire Club of Canada the president of the newly created Canadian Labour Congress, Claude Jodoin, said, "the word 'Free' in the name of this [ICFTU] organization is extremely important.

These are the labour organizations of the free world. Under a dictatorship there can be no free trade unions."[243] Jodoin was referring to communist dictatorships since ICFTU affiliates operated in US-backed Latin American and Asian dictatorships. Additionally, during this period the *Canadian Congress Journal* reported on British and ICFTU union activities in decidedly "unfree" British colonies in Africa and Asia.

A Canadian steelworker sent to Kenya as part of an ICFTU initiative in the early 1950s echoed racist, colonial, depictions of what became known as the "Mau Mau Uprising." In 1952, the Kikuyu, Kenya's largest ethnic group, launched an anti-colonial struggle, which the British brutally suppressed. Over the next eight years they detained most of the 1.5 million Kikuyu in camps and fortified villages.[244] Far surpassing the 32 white civilians killed by the Mau Mau, tens of thousands of Kenyans were killed by British-led forces. Yet, the British and Canadian press focused their coverage on lurid stories detailing purported Mau Mau violence. In a report to the CCL Jim Bury called the Mau Mau "terrorists" and claimed they were "generating hate and bestiality."[245] Highlighting the paternalism driving the CLC predecessor's work in colonial Africa, the CCL described Bury's objective as "giving the necessary advice on the proper running of unions."[246]

With the support of the Colonial Office, the British Trade Union Congress sent advisers to English colonies to support union organizing. But, they generally sought to de-radicalize labour activists. Not wanting the natives to get any bad ideas, the Trade Union Congress actually rewrote a history manual it used in England to downplay the intensity of the conflict in the early stages of British labour organizing.[247]

During the 1950s there was a revealing battle between Canadian unions' closest international allies. The AFL pushed the ICFTU to do more to combat "communism" in Africa and Asia while the British Trade Union Congress opposed ICFTU and AFL involvement in British colonies, which it considered its sphere of influence.[248]

Appointed regional director of the ICFTU in 1956, Charles Millard navigated tensions between the two powerful imperialist federations within the ICFTU. No. 2 in the international federation, the director of the United Steelworkers in Canada was put in charge of ICFTU foreign work by the AFL, which sought to increase its "anti-communist" efforts.[249]

The ICFTU significantly influenced CLC foreign policy. Until 1966, for instance, the Congress' international fund was known as the "ICFTU Activities Fund of the CLC".[250] Additionally, a number of CLC International Affairs Department officials were former ICFTU employees and the Canadian aid agency channeled funds to CLC projects supporting ICFTU initiatives.[251]

Designed to maintain western power in Asia, unions strongly supported Canada's first significant (non-European) allocation of foreign aid. Labour leaders, notes John Price, "heap[ed] undiluted praise on the Canadian government for its participation in the [Colombo] Plan."[252]

With Mao's triumph in China a year earlier, the 1950 Colombo Plan's primary aim was to keep the former British Asian colonies, especially India, within the Western capitalist fold. Prime Minister Louis St. Laurent explained, "in South East Asia through the establishment of the Colombo Plan not only are we trying to provide wider commercial relations but we are also fighting another Asiatic war against Communism in the interests of peace, this time with economic rather than military weapons."[253] In 1951 St. Laurent thanked the CCL for supporting the Colombo Plan writing, "the government feels that this a practical way of helping to deal with the threat of Communism in that area."[254]

In another example of their support for the Cold War, unions backed the CBC International Service (IS). According to external minister Lester Pearson, CBC-IS beamed radio abroad as part of "the psychological war against communism."[255] In 1961 CLC President Claude Jodoin criticized cuts to the "Voice of Canada" and two years later the Canadian Union of Public Employees wrote Prime Minister Pearson noting, "at a time when the radio voice of the free world is weakened by increased efforts by totalitarian countries, it would be in our view, a disaster to cut this service at this time."[256]

Unions also backed the military arm of the Western alliance. The CCL and TLC supported the formation of NATO and the CLC's inaugural convention called on the "Canadian government not to falter or fail in its support of NATO", which it described as a measure for "self-protection against aggression."[257] In 1957 the CLC "reiterated its support of NATO in the memorandum submitted to the government of Canada."[258] As part of an effort to promote the military alliance, the newly formed labour federation distributed 11,000 copies of a booklet titled "The Trade Unions and NATO". The pamphlet explained, "unfortunately we still do have to spend large sums on defence, and the responsibility for the fact rests with international communism. Canadian labour firmly supports NATO."[259] In October 1958 the CLC's director of international affairs participated in a NATO trade union conference. The General Secretary of NATO Paul

Henry Spaak, a Belgian Socialist politician, addressed the conference.[260]

Through the 1960s the CLC backed NATO. A 1962 statement noted: "Your Government's defence policies have recently been open to considerable controversy. While rejecting suggestions that Canada should withdraw from the North Atlantic Treaty Organization and regional defence agreements with the United States, we suggest that our present commitments should be carefully and critically reviewed."[261] It wasn't until 1976 that the CLC "urged the federal government to ... deemphasize the role of the North Atlantic organization."[262]

Organized labour backed the 1950-53 Korean War, which led to millions of deaths. The TLC and CCL published a joint statement expressing "full support" for the UN Security Council's effort to counter North Korea and to "re-establish peace and democratic government in Korea."[263] TLC President Percy Bengough told the Congress' 1950 convention: "Today under the banner of the United Nations we are fighting on the soil of Korea to put down an armed attack undertaken by a puppet government under the influence of Soviet Russia and the Stalinist dictatorship. We are fighting to protect a small country from armed aggression by a large and powerful army."[264] The CCL further explained: "As is now well known, the armies of Stalin's puppet government of North Korea invaded South Korea on June 25, after having resisted all efforts of the United Nations to re-unite Korea under stable democratic government."[265]

But, it is incorrect to claim North Korea was a Soviet puppet. While Washington justified its intervention by claiming Moscow pushed Pyongyang to fight, North Korea acted on its own initiative.[266] Rather than "re-establish peace", Washington expanded and internationalized a Korean civil war. Additionally, it's absurd to imply South Korean leader Syngman Rhee was "democratic". His regime killed tens of thousands in what Canadian diplomats in Washington described, in an internal cable to External Affairs, as "a fair amount of repression by the Military Government of left-wing groups." The understated diplomats added, "liberal social legislation had been definitely resisted."[267]

Union support for the Korean War was partly based on blind anti-Communism. A *Canadian Congress Journal* article titled "65th Convention Liquidates Communism" reported on President Percy Bengough's speech to the convention: "We are fighting Stalin's Russian Soviet dictatorship in South Korea. We must fight its willing dupes right here at home, and most particularly, it is our job to expose them and destroy their influence inside our own trade unions."[268]

During the Korean War the TLC barred organizers with ties to the Victoria Peace Council and Stockholm Appeal to ban the atomic bomb.[269] A joint TLC/CCL statement complained that communists and their sympathizers asked union members to sign "the phoney Stockholm Peace Pledge and to pass 'ban the A-bomb' resolutions, hoping to keep us disarmed and leave Soviet Russia free to move in on any country whenever it suits their purpose."[270]

In a sign of the political climate, a resolution from an International Chemical Workers local supporting trade with China and Eastern Europe was considered evidence of communist activities. After being made aware of the resolution, Chemical Workers' president H. A. Bradley said the 'international' union would purge itself. "I want you to know," Bradley told delegates to the 1949 TLC convention, "that of the 10,000 Chemical Workers in Canada, 9000, 900, and 90 of them are the finest, loyal citizens that your country can claim. The other 10 we will take care of ourselves. We will take care of them good."[271]

International issues were a big part of the post-World War II witch-hunt against leftist labour activists. In *Cold War Canada: The Making of a National Insecurity State, 1945–1957*, Reg Whitaker and Gary Marcuse write: "By the time of the Korean War, the Canadian Labour Congresses were in step with their American counterparts. Radicals were purged from the conventions or reduced, as one left-winger recalled, to a caucus that could meet in an elevator. Moreover, the unions established political tests for membership in the labour congresses, based on delegates support for the pillars of the Cold War. NATO, the Marshall Plan, the rearmament of Germany, and non-recognition of communist China were among the credos. Belief in a communist conspiracy was required and unquestionable; the unions thus became part of the culture of the Cold War, and an effective means of disseminating it."[272]

The demonization of "communism" led unions "to oppose various liberation struggles" in Asia, writes John Price.[273] Speaking to the Empire Club in 1956, CLC President Claude Jodoin echoed the justification employed by the colonial powers' to violently reassert control over Vietnam, Malaysia, etc. He said: "The men in the Kremlin look to these areas for further extensions of the Soviet Empire. The extent to which they have already extended the clutches of Soviet colonialism is seldom realized. Since the communists took control in Russia, Red domination has spread over 5,000,000 square miles and 732,000,000 people. And this has taken place at a time when the western powers, and particularly Great Britain, has been giving independence to peoples who were once under a colonial status."[274]

In another independence struggle Washington and the colonizer sought to portray as a battle against 'communism', the CLC backed Canada and the UN's destruction of the Congolese independence struggle and its leader Patrice Lumumba. According to the CLC's 1962 Executive Council Report, Jodoin sent a telegram to External Affairs "in which he expressed support of the Secretary General of the United Nations, then under attack because of the Congo crisis. A press statement was issued on February 17 [1961], based on this telegram."[275]

But, UN head Dag Hammarskjold worked to undermine the Congolese independence leader. When President Joseph Kasavubu dismissed Lumumba as prime minister — a move of debatable legality and opposed by the vast majority of the country's parliament — the UN Secretary General publicly endorsed the dismissal of a politician who a short time earlier had received the most votes in the country's election.[276] UN forces also blocked Lumumba from responding to his dismissal on the country's main radio station.[277]

To get a sense of Hammarskjold's antipathy towards the Congolese leader, the head of the UN privately told officials in Washington that Lumumba should be "broken".[278] In response to Hammarskjold's efforts to undermine his leadership, Lumumba broke off relations with the Secretary General.[279]

The CLC's executive committee explicitly endorsed Canada's role in the UN mission that undermined Lumumba. Its 1962 convention report noted: "We support the United

Nations in the belief that only through a world organization of this kind, through the common discussion of problems, through the establishment of a strong supranational organization, can world order be established and maintained. For all the difficulties encountered by the United Nations in the Congo, we feel nonetheless that the very fact of UN intervention has been a major step forward in the development of such a supranational force. We are proud that Canadians are playing a part in this affair."[280]

While alluding to "difficulties", the labour federation's executive seems to have believed Lumumba's assassination was worth the "development of such a supranational force". In other words, Congolese aspirations could be sacrificed in the name of strengthening the UN.

During this period in Latin America, Canadian unions echoed US policy. The TLC applauded a military coup against nationalist, social democratic, president Juan Peron in Argentina. "The free trade union movements all over the world hails the fall of Peron", *Canadian Congress Journal* editorialized after the ouster of an elected president who significantly expanded workers' rights. "The news of the fall of general Peron has been hailed with great satisfaction by all workers of the free world … The Trades and Labour Congress of Canada, as a member of the International Confederation of Free Trade Unions, fully endorses and congratulates the ICFTU for this timely statement" celebrating Peron's ouster.[281]

In 1957 the former head of the Steelworkers in Canada and director of the ICFTU led a delegation to observe workers' rights under the pro-US Fulgencio Batista dictatorship in Cuba. According to Jack Scott in *Yankee Unions Go Home*, "[Charles] Millard voiced high praise for the Cuban unionists, and claimed that the movement was a non-political organization. He asserted that trade union freedom existed, and that union rights were fully observed and respected by Batista."[282] But, Batista was highly repressive and anti-worker.

In *A Journalist's Life on the Left* Ed Finn describes the collapse of a paper he helped establish in the early 1960s. The *Newfoundland Examiner* went under after the CLC abruptly cut off financial support because Finn's colleague "wrote a blistering column denouncing the United States for its unprovoked but foredoomed Bay of Pigs invasion." The piece criticized the Kennedy Administration for "financing and equipping a mercenary army with the aim of overthrowing the Castro government and giving the island back to the corrupt Batista regime, the crooked casino operators, and the brutally anti-labour American fruit plantation owners."[283] In a letter rescinding its funding, CLC Secretary-Treasurer Donald McDonald said the AFL-CIO supported the 1961 US-orchestrated invasion of Cuba and so did the CLC.[284]

At the time of independence in British Guiana CCL policy was "explicitly aligned with the interests of Canadian capital", notes Katherine Nastovski in *Towards Transformative Solidarities: Wars of Position in the Making of Labour Internationalism in Canada*.[285] CCL executive member Charles Millard argued that aid to Guiana and other former British colonies in the Caribbean was "in the interests of Canadian security", stating bluntly that Alcan Canada "gained much from the mining of bauxite in British Guiana over the past thirty years."[286] In reference to the 1953 election of Cheddi Jagan, who sought to nationalize the Alcan dominated bauxite industry before the British ousted him the next year, Millard pointed out that the "recurrence of the events that took place in British Guiana may be more detrimental to Canadian interests than to British."[287]

Millard argued that a Canadian aid program was important since this country was better placed than Britain to fight communism in the Caribbean. In a 1954 memo to external affairs he noted: "Despite their satisfactory record in certain territories, the British are still associated with the evils of colonialism … Moreover, because of our commonwealth relationships, common British traditions and similar political institutions, the Caribbean colonies are much closer to us than to the United States. Taken together, these factors give us the opportunity of playing an important role in the Caribbean … [and Canada can help] lighten the load which the British Government is now carrying."[288]

As part of its anti-communism the CLC supported the Organización Regional Interamericana de Trabajadores (ORIT), which subverted radical Latin American unions. Former CIA agent turned whistleblower Philip Agee labeled ORIT "a principal mechanism for CIA labor operations in Latin America."[289]

In 1958 international affairs director Kalmen Kaplansky noted, "although Communist influence is on the decline, it still remains a formidable threat to the free trade union movement. In spite of all these obstacles, Orit has made a tremendous contribution to the welfare of the workers in Central and South America." In the late 1960s the CLC entered into a formal relationship with CIDA to support ORIT projects.

The two decades after World War II were a low point in union support for ordinary people's struggles for liberation around the world and a time when unions largely fell in step behind the Canadian/American/British ruling classes on foreign affairs. "It was not until the late 1960s," note Whitaker and Marcuse, "when union criticism of America's conduct of the war in Vietnam was voiced publicly, that the Canadian union movement was able to re-establish an autonomous position in relation to the wider world."[290]

In an example of that breakdown of stifling anti-communism, during the late 1970s and 1980s important sectors of the union movement criticized the CLC's work in South Africa and Nicaragua. Representatives of the anti-apartheid South African Congress of Trade Unions and its Canadian supporters condemned CLC international director John Harker's opposition to those doing the heavy lifting against apartheid. During the 1980s CIDA funded CLC projects in South Africa that needed to be okayed by the Canadian Embassy in Pretoria and External Affairs, which were ambivalent/sympathetic to white rule.[291] One CIDA project form stated, "we have been assured by CLC that these unions have no links with the African liberation movements."[292]

At the behest of South African conglomerate Barlow Rand, Harker approached the ICFTU-affiliated International Metalworkers Federation to help organize a mine after bargaining rights were extended to black workers in 1980.[293] Alluding to unions actively campaigning against apartheid, Harker said the company didn't want "to leave a vacuum which could be filled by political agitators."[294]

After the Anastasio Somoza dictatorship fell in 1979 the CLC organized "operation solidarity" for Nicaragua. CIDA, the military and Air Canada helped the Congress deliver tons of goods to the Central American country.[295] But, the goods were mostly directed to the Confederation de Unificacion Sindical "a tiny, and discredited, ICFTU affiliate in Nicaragua."[296] The CUS never joined the armed struggle against the four-decade long Somoza family dictatorship and only turned antagonistic after employers' organizations did so.[297] Supported by the AFL-CIO and operating out of the US embassy, the CUS was one of two unions allowed to operate under Somoza.[298] With allies among the US-backed, Honduras-based, Contra paramilitaries, the CUS was involved in "active opposition against the Sandinistas."[299]

Important sectors of the union movement backed more progressive forces in Nicaragua and the CLC tried to prevent Canadian unions from inviting pro-Sandinista union representatives to Canada.[300] A 1983 international affairs department report, complained one CLC delegate, "could have been written by the Canadian government."[301] Incredibly, the CLC accused the US media of seeing Nicaragua's leftist government "through a romantic haze."[302]

Opposition to the international department's Cold War attitude prompted the Ontario Federation of Labour, the CLC's largest provincial affiliate, to publish a report and pass a resolution criticizing the Congress' foreign policy. The 1989 report said, "the CLC should play a major role in promoting progressive workers' causes in other countries. It should be challenging often regressive Canadian government positions."[303] But, the OFL's criticism included a nationalist bent. It called for a "Made in Canada policy" — instead of at the ICFTU headquarters in Brussels — and described Canada's "special role to play in Latin, central and South America."[304]

In so far as unions and labour federations have widened the scope of "what we wish for ourselves, we want for all" to include people everywhere, it's due to internationalist education and activism. In the 1970s and 80s Latin American and African solidarity groups arose and they often had ties with union activists. In many instances it was relatively easy to overcome corporate and government propaganda by simply giving voice to the stories of working people from another corner of the world. But, not always. Sometimes it has taken decades of organizing for grassroots campaigns to achieve significant success.

PALESTINE

Despite growing progress towards an independent foreign policy, on certain issues the union movement remained proponents of the Western perspective. Until recently most Canadian unions supported Israel's dispossession of Palestinians and bullying in the region (Israel has bombed Syria, Jordan, Egypt, Palestine, Sudan, Lebanon, Tunisia and Iraq).

Prior to Israel's creation TLC President Percy Bengough and CCL President Aaron Mosher were members of the Canada Palestine Committee.[305] In 1944 they participated in a meeting between that Zionist lobby group and Prime Minister Mackenzie King.[306]

Histadrut representatives regularly spoke at CLC conventions, addressing all but two of them between 1956 and 1982.[307] Its representatives were granted a status nearly on par with the US, British and ICFTU federations. At its 1964 convention the Histadrut speaker was introduced thusly: "Brother Ilan was in the Defence Army of Israel and was very well known."[308] Excluding non-Jewish workers for much of its history, the Histadrut "was a great colonizing agency", in the words of former Israeli Prime Minister Golda Meir.[309] In 1920 the Histadrut founded the Haganah, an armed Zionist militia, which later became the Israeli armed forces.[310] The country's second largest employer into the 1980s, the "labour federation" owned a quarter of Israel's industry.[311]

At its inaugural convention in 1956 the CLC called on the "government to lend sympathetic support to Israel's request for defensive armaments, in order that Israel may match, in quality if not in quantity, the constant flow of Soviet bloc armaments into the Arab countries, and further appeals to our government to use its good offices in urging other free Western countries to do likewise."[312] The resolution was passed just before Israel invaded Egypt alongside colonial powers France and Britain. At the time Canada had been selling Israel weapons for a number of years and was under (private) pressure from Washington to send Israel advanced fighter jets.[313]

The CLC vigorously opposed admitting the Palestinian Liberation Organization (PLO) to the International Labour Organization.[314] CLC President Joe Morris used his position as ILO committee chairman to block the PLO's admission as an observer to the organization.[315] Two years later the CLC passed a resolution demanding Ottawa enact anti-boycott legislation against Arab countries boycotting companies doing business with Israel to pressure that country to return land captured in the 1967 war. When the UN General Assembly passed a resolution (72 votes to 35 with 32 abstentions) in 1975 calling Zionism a form of racism CLC President Joe Morris complained vociferously. He stated, "by this act, it can justifiably be argued the UN has 'legitimized' anti-Semitism and pogroms against Jews. Canadian labour will fight all moves to implement such a resolution and will exercise its influence to prevent further extensions of the resolution."[316]

In 1985 CLC president Dennis McDermott denounced a Canadian Senate report that rebuked Israel's 1982 invasion/occupation of Lebanon and provided mild support for the PLO. McDermott, who referred to himself as a "Catholic Zionist," said the Senate report, which stopped short of calling the PLO the legitimate voice of Palestinians, was an "exercise in bad judgment and, even worse, bad taste."[317] (A portrait of McDermott hangs in a library named after him at the trade school of the Histadrut.[318])

Anger at decades of unwavering support for Israeli expansionism prompted a resolution to the CLC's 1988 convention, which never made the floor. It noted: "Whereas in the past both the Federation and Congress have often been reluctant to allow debate on resolutions critical of Israel, often scheduling them so that they will not reach the floor. Therefore be it resolved that in light of the extensive killing and violation of Palestinian human rights by Israel, that the resolutions committee for the Canadian Labour Congress convention schedule resolutions so that the delegates can have the opportunity to debate this issue."[319]

Labour unions have also offered Israel financial support. With the new state having difficulty raising money on Wall Street, Israel Bonds were launched in 1951 to pay for infrastructure. According to a 2005 estimate, Canadian unions purchased $20 million worth of Israel Bonds annually.[320] Economics was the main motivation for acquiring Israel Bonds but there was also "a historical bond between Israel and the unions," said Lawrence Waller, executive vice president of State of Israel Bonds Canada, which has a Canadian labour division that organizes annual dinners.[321] In 2000 Hamilton's Jewish National Fund dedicated its Negev Dinner to Enrico and Joe Mancinelli from the Laborers' International Union of North America (LIUNA). The union's pension fund began investing in Israel Bonds in the early 1980s and in 1999 Joe Mancinelli visited Israel to see the construction and infrastructure projects financed by Israel Bonds. "They have a longstanding relationship with and support for the state of Israel," said JNF Hamilton chairperson Tom Weisz to the *Hamilton Spectator.*[322]

In this century Canadian Auto Workers' president Buzz Hargrove was the most prominent anti-Palestinian labour leader. Amidst a 2004 campaign by Israeli nationalist groups, the CAW published a press release calling for professor Mohamed Elmasry to resign as head of the Canadian Islamic Congress.[323] Elmasry had suggested all Israelis over 18, because of the country's mandatory military service, were legitimate targets during an interview on the Michael Coren Show. In contrast, when B'nai Brith official Adam Aptowitzer told the same program: "when Israel uses terror to go and, I say, uses terror to destroy a home and convince people to be terrified of what the possible consequences are, I'd say that's acceptable use to terrify someone," there was no response from the CAW.[324]

Hargrove criticized the Canadian Union of Public Employees (Ontario) 2006 vote in favour of the Boycott, Divestment and Sanctions movement, which calls for non-violent pressure on Israel to respect international law and offer Palestinian citizens equal rights. In a *Toronto Star* column Hargrove attacked unions' "claim that Israel is equivalent to the former South African apartheid regime." He added:

"Supporters of a two-state solution to the conflict must recognize the genuine progress that has been made — even, surprisingly, under the leadership of the old warhorse, Ariel Sharon. Israel withdrew from the Gaza Strip and proposed relocating more than 80,000 settlers from the West Bank, sparking a huge controversy within Israel."[325]

During Israel's 33-day war on Lebanon in 2006 the CAW issued a release "calling on Prime Minister Harper to take a leadership role in trying to bring the parties to the table to find a resolution to the conflicts in the Middle East."[326] Blaming both sides for the conflict, a CAW resolution ignored Israel's responsibility for provoking the war and the right of the Lebanese and Palestinians to self-defence. The first three demands of the CAW motion put the onus on the Lebanese and Palestinians, calling for: "the immediate return, unharmed, of captured Israeli soldiers", "an end to the shelling of Israeli cities by Hamas militants" and "an end to the shelling of Israeli cities by the Hezbollah militants."[327] Fifteen times more Lebanese civilians than Israelis were killed during the 33-day war.[328]

In *Laying It On The Line: Buzz Hargrove* he devotes a couple of pages to berating CUPE Ontario President Sid Ryan for defending Palestinian rights. In his 2009 biography Hargrove also notes, "I never gave a Council report without referring to events in the Middle East."[329]

In 2006 Hargrove traveled to Israel with his friends Heather Reisman and Jerry Schwartz.[330] The pro-Israel billionaire couple created the Heseg Foundation to support non-Israelis who joined the country's military and were one of a half-dozen rich right-wing donors that scrapped the hundred-year-old Canadian Jewish Congress in 2011 and replaced it with the Centre for Israel and Jewish Affairs. As the name change suggests, this move represented a shift towards ever greater lobbying in favour of Israeli nationalism (as well as alignment with the Conservatives).

Not until recently have Canadian unions (including Unifor the successor to Hargrove's CAW) been willing to condemn Israeli discrimination against Palestinians and call for non-violent pressure to ensure Palestinian human rights. But while many unions have improved their positions regarding Canadian colonialism and supported "truth and reconciliation" campaigns towards First Nations, some still support the final frontier of European settler colonialism. While some do so for fear of being labelled anti-Semitic, others follow the ruling class consensus on most international policies in the hopes of winning official respectability. But the fact that even Palestinians now receive support from Canadian unions proves that grassroots education and activism works.

HAITI

In a more recent example of labour organizations siding with the ruling class against the interests of ordinary people in another country, Québec unions assisted the February 29, 2004, coup in Haiti that saw President Jean-Bertrand Aristide and thousands of other elected officials driven from office. At the height of the US-orchestrated campaign to destabilize Aristide's government, the Fédération des travailleurs et travailleuses du Québec (FTQ) forcefully opposed a government elected by the poor majority. On February 12, the province's largest union federation sent out a press release condemning Aristide's government.[331] A few days later, Fernand Daoust, the former head of the FTQ, along with representatives of two other Québec union federations, participated in an international union delegation critical of Haiti's government. The delegation garnered significant media attention in Haiti and after returning from that country, Daoust was quoted throughout the Québec media denouncing Aristide. A day after the elected president was removed by US marines, the FTQ sent out a press release celebrating the release of detained union activists and calling on the international community to "help Haitians build democracy in their country."[332]

The FTQ's condemnations of Haiti's elected government took place while a CIA-backed paramilitary invasion (led by well-known thugs such as Jodel Chamblain and Guy Philippe) terrorized the country. The FTQ's criticism of Haiti's government helped justify Canada's participation in a coup designed to further subjugate the country's poor majority.

To the best of my knowledge, the FTQ did not comment on the transport union destroyed after the coup, the Confédération de travailleurs haitiens (CTH) offices attacked in September 2004, the death threats by the police against CTH leader Lulu Cherie in December 2004 or the massive increase in human rights violations in the two years after the coup. In 2008 the FTQ issued a 59-page report on Haiti that ignored the coup and its aftermath.[333] The closest thing in the report to a mention of the 2004 coup was a criticism of the CTH for its purported sympathy towards Aristide's Lavalas party.

At least some FTQ officials were informed of developments in Haiti. A number of Haiti solidarity activists and Haitian community members discussed the issue with their international representative Denise Gagnon. But, it was easy for union leaders, who have many structural ties to Québec's ruling class, to ignore these voices and follow the dominant media narrative regarding Canadian actions in Haiti. While they are willing to fight the prevailing business class orthodoxy on matters directly affecting their members, unions failed to do the same for the vast majority of Haitians. Supporting imperialism is usually easier than international solidarity, especially when there is little grassroots union activism on the subject.

UKRAINE

Demonstrating a striking lack of solidarity with their Ukrainian brethren, Canadian unions were silent when more than 30 were killed in a fire at the headquarters of the Odessa federation of trade unions on May 2, 2014. Neo-Nazi "Right Sector" militants sequestered pro-Russian "anti-Maidan" demonstrators inside and at least 31 people choked to death on smoke or died jumping from the building.[334]

I searched in vain for a Unifor, CUPE, United Steelworkers, UFCW or PSAC statement on the fire at the union office. Six weeks earlier Unifor released a statement about the upheaval in the Ukraine, noting "we watched with horror as the political protesters demonstrating in the main square of Kiev, Ukraine were met with deadly violence."[335] But, unlike those in Kiev, the victims in Odessa were considered "pro-Russian" so the dominant media barely covered their killings. As a result, Canadian union officials ignored them as well.

Again unions are frequently willing to go along with the ruling class narrative of what is happening in the world because it is easy, garners positive attention in the dominant media and legitimizes their status inside a system of vastly unequal power relations. And when an alternative story isn't easily accessible this is the safest route to travel.

UNDER THE INFLUENCE

In a reflection of its international outlook, the CLC works with various establishment foreign policy organizations. While generally on the liberal end of the international affairs discussion, these CLC allies often depend heavily on Ottawa.

When it existed the CLC president was on the board of directors of the Canadian Institute for International Peace and Security.[336] Associated with peace researchers, CIIPS was created by an act of Parliament in 1984. The organization's first chair was long-time External Affairs official William Barton, its founding director was Brigadier-General George Gray Bell and its initial executive director was Geoffrey Pearson, son of Lester Pearson and former ambassador to the Soviet Union and Mongolia.[337]

The CLC was also represented on the Canadian Institute of International Affairs (CIIA).[338] The CCL became a corporate member in 1954 and CIIA representatives participated in the CLC predecessor's educational conferences.[339] The CLC's first director of international affairs was a former CIIA executive member.[340] Renamed Canadian International Council in 2007, CIIA received substantial External Affairs and Department of National Defence funding, as well as money from corporations and the Rockefeller and Carnegie foundations.[341] Upon leaving office external ministers Lester Pearson, Paul Martin Senior and Mitchell Sharp all took up honorary positions with the CIIA.[342] In 1999 former foreign minister Barbara McDougall took charge of the CIIA and many chapters continue to be dominated by retired diplomats.[343]

In the late 1960s the CLC contributed $3,000 ($20,000 today) to the Parliamentary Centre for Foreign Affairs and Foreign Trade. According to the CLC, "its primary function has been to promote greater understanding of world problems among the Members of Parliament and other interested groups in Canadian society."[344] But, the Parliamentary Centre was the brainchild of a long-time member of the foreign service and was government funded.[345]

The CLC has long-standing ties to the Canadian Council for International Cooperation and is represented on the CCIC board.[346] An umbrella group representing dozens of major development NGOs, the CCIC was created in 1968 with financing from the Canadian International Development Agency.[347] The aid agency expected it to coordinate relations with the growing NGO network and build domestic political support for the aid program.[348] While it has challenged government policy on occasion, the CCIC is highly dependent on government funds. Shortly after it publicly complained the government created a "chill" in the NGO community by adopting "the politics of punishment … towards those whose public views run at cross purposes to the government," the CCIC's $1.7 million CIDA grant was cut in 2012. This forced it to lay off two thirds of its staff.[349]

Modeling their operations on CCIC member organizations' international activities, a number of major unions operate internationally focused "humanities funds". These funds mostly act like and work with development charities.

Established in response to a high-profile famine in Ethiopia, the Steelworkers' Humanity Fund started the ball rolling in 1985.[350] Canada's then ambassador to the UN, Stephen Lewis, was on hand for its launch.[351]

Union members generally donate a few cents each hour of work to their "humanity" or "solidarity" funds and often bargain to have employers match their contribution. With tens, even hundreds, of thousands of members working full-time, these funds generate significant sums of money. The Steelworkers Humanity Fund raised $2 million in 2015 while the Unifor Social Justice Fund had a bigger budget.[352]

In 1995 the Steelworkers, Canadian Union of Public Employees, Communications, Energy and Paperworkers and Canadian Auto Workers humanities' funds established the Labour International Development Program (LIDP).[353] The LIDP was set up as part of a co-funding agreement with the Canadian International Development Agency, which provided $1.7 million annually to the union solidarity funds in the early 2000s.[354]

Unifor, Steelworkers, Elementary Teachers' Federation of Ontario, Manitoba Government and General Employees' Union, BCGEU and CUPE funds are all registered charities. Able to provide tax credits to donors, registered charities are forbidden from engaging in any partisan political work and are only permitted to devote 10 percent of their resources to "political activities".[355]

In 2015 the Canada Revenue Agency audited the Steelworkers Humanity Fund over its political activities. The presumed reason was that in 2013 the Steelworkers Humanity Fund gave about two per cent of its revenue to the Canadian Network on Corporate Accountability, which challenges mining companies' international abuses. The Network on Corporate Accountability is not a registered charity.[356]

Acceding to the constraints of charitable status reflects a narrow view of international affairs. It also contradicts unions' positions on domestic issues. On domestic affairs organized labour opposes attempts to constrain their political activities. In fact, the CLC helped found the NDP and continues to have formal relations with that party. Unions also channel resources into election campaigns, lobbying, political action committees, etc. On domestic affairs they recognize that legislative change, won through political struggle, is generally the best way to correct social problems. But, they don't take the same position towards Canada's relations with the Global South.

While the status of registered charity offers humanities funds certain tax benefits, unions receive many of these anyhow. Unions are exempt from paying certain taxes and members' dues are deductible from income tax.[357] Charitable status constrains an organization's ability to effectively challenge government policy.

Humanities funds rarely educate members about Canadian foreign policy. In mid 2017, I searched the six projects Unifor's Social Justice Fund listed online and the only one that mentioned Canada was an initiative to support an oil workers union in Columbia. The three-page write-up mentioned that Toronto–based Pacific Rubiales suppressed the activities of the national petroleum union of Colombia.[358]

Another project listed was a partnership with War on Want to help individuals who lost limbs during the 2010 earthquake in Haiti.[359] While undoubtedly welcome by its beneficiaries, the Unifor description of the project said nothing about Canada's violent, anti-democratic, policies in that country. That's akin to a union offering money to strikers, but failing to mention the company's attempt to cut their wages.

A charity orientation to international affairs partly flows from unions' ties to the official Canadian aid agency. Soon after the CLC was established in 1956 it began selecting students from Southeast Asia to visit Canada through the Colombo (assistance) Plan.[360] By 1966 the External Aid office was providing $200,000 ($1.5 million today) for 80 students to attend the Labour College of Canada.[361] Not long after CIDA was created the CLC began receiving funds through its Voluntary Agencies Program.[362] In 1969 the aid agency agreed to contribute three dollars for every dollar the Congress raised for international projects supporting the ICFTU and ORIT (Organización Regional Interamericana de Trabajadores).[363] As a result of this agreement, the CLC's international affairs department expanded substantially.[364] By 1983 six out of nine CLC international affairs positions were funded by CIDA.[365] That year the aid agency approved 17 new CLC projects costing $1.8 million ($4 million today).[366] Over the next decade government funding continued to flow and in the early 1990s CIDA covered two thirds of all CLC international staff and project costs.[367] Through the 1990s and 2000s the CLC received tens of millions of dollars from CIDA.[368]

Federal funding greatly shaped the Congress' international operations. A CIDA commissioned evaluation of the CLC's International Affairs Department in 1988 noted, "the current core program is as much a response to the availability of CIDA funding and to CIDA funding categories as it is to the CLC's perception of the needs of trade unions in developing countries."[369]

The Congress all but admitted as much on a number of occasions.[370] In 2012 CLC International Program Administrator Monique Charron highlighted how the labour federation shaped its policies to acquire government funding: "Alignment with the Canadian International Development

Agency (CIDA)'s pro-poor growth strategy has been an enormous challenge for the LIDP [Labour International Development Program] of late, in particular as the program attempts to position itself for future CIDA funding."[371]

As discussed in *Paved with Good Intentions: Canada's Development NGOs on the Road from Idealism to Imperialism,* Canadian aid officials have frequently withdrawn funding to organizations that challenge their policy. A resolution submitted to the CLC's 16th Constitutional Convention in 1986, which didn't make the convention floor, recognized the danger of receiving government aid. It explained: "Whereas in order to properly implement the policies of the Congress, it is essential that the International Affairs Department of the Canadian Labour Congress be independent of government influence; and whereas the Canadian International Development Agency (CIDA) is an agency of government designed to promote government objectives in international affairs; and whereas the CLC receives substantial financial support from CIDA for its international work; therefore be it resolved that the CLC make full disclosure of the amount of funds received from CIDA, including any amount used for staff persons in Canada and abroad; and be it further resolved that the CLC take action to become independent from financing from CIDA."[372]

Along with ties to the aid agency, union officialdom collaborated with External Affairs. In a 1982 article on "Canadian Trade Unions and Palestine" Mordecai Briemberg refers to "the intimate linkages and interchanges between IAD [International Affairs Department] and External Affairs."[373] In the post-World War II years, explains John Price, labour leaders "developed close ties with the Canadian government and to some extent became an appendage of state foreign policy. ... [Union leaders] Millard, Conroy and Mosher were all willing to collaborate with the Canadian government in the same fashion that the AFL was collaborating with the CIA and U.S. State Department."[374]

In a 1949 letter to Israel's foreign minister external minister Lester Pearson describes CCL Vice President Pat Conroy in glowing terms and notes that he travelled with him to Israel.[375] After lobbying for the creation of this position, Conroy was appointed labour attaché to the Canadian embassy in Washington in 1952, where he remained for two decades.[376]

When first CLC President Claude Jodoin and international affairs director Kalmen Kaplansky met new external minister Sidney Smith in 1957 they called for the "establishment of personal contact between our International Affairs Department and heads of division in [the] External Affairs department."[377] Building on earlier relations, there would be significant "contact". Kaplansky was part of government delegations to UNESCO, the UN and ILO.[378] A mid-1960s CLC international affairs committee included government representatives and "Canadian Trade Commissioners in Training" visited the CLC's headquarters.[379] During this period the CLC invited Canada's ambassador to Mexico to present certificates to graduates of an education program it operated at a labour institute in Mexico (former CIA agent Philip Agee described the labour school in Cuernavaca as being "financed and controlled by the CIA."[380]). Speakers from External Affairs also led CLC international affairs seminars.[381] In 1971 external minister Mitchell Sharp spoke to a CLC foreign policy conference and in 1981 the CLC sponsored a national tour with the director of CIDA's Cooperatives,

Unions and Professional Associations Program.[382] A 1980 CLC executive council report noted that the deputy director of the international affairs department, Bruce Gillies, was "on secondment to the CLC from the Department of External Affairs of Canada."[383] The CLC Director of International Affairs at the time, John Harker, worked previously as Executive Director of the Professional Association of Foreign Service Officers, which represents Canada's diplomats.[384] In a 1980 journal article on the CLC's international policies John Clark writes, "there are periodic communications between Harker (of the CLC) and Allan Gotlieb, Undersecretary of State for External Affairs. Neither of the two is reluctant to call the other on special issues. Regular contacts are maintained with External Affairs desk officers who sometimes use the CLC network of contacts to obtain information on special areas. Relationships with CIDA are good and some contacts are maintained with the department of Industry, Trade and Commerce."[385]

After a decade at the CLC, Harker would oversee a number of foreign affairs-initiated projects.[386] CLC Development Education Animator and Project Officer for Asia in the 1980s, Alan Amey previously worked at CIDA.[387] An External Affairs employee based at the Canadian Embassy in Santiago, Chile, in the mid 1970s, Rick Jackson, later became a CLC Development Education Officer and Project Officer for Latin America.[388]

Other labour leaders were appointed to government posts after leaving the CLC. After a decade as international affairs director Kaplansky was appointed head of the Canadian branch of the ILO and the Congress' international director in the early 1970s, Romeo Maione, was made head of CIDA's NGO section.[389] For his part, CLC President Dennis McDermott was appointed ambassador to Ireland.[390]

Organized labour's failure to forthrightly challenge foreign policy decisions is one element in the multifaceted, self-reinforcing, dynamic that yields popular ignorance of international affairs. Links to Foreign Affairs, the aid agency and government-backed institutes/NGOs, along with the policies of the CCF/NDP, have formed unions' international policies and statements. Below I discuss how nationalism has also shaped these policies.

But, it's important to reiterate the importance of the dominant media in shaping both unions and the NDP's international positions. That media is structurally biased in favour of the corporate and state perspective. As I outline in *A Propaganda System*, vast resources are poured into convincing us to view the world through the lens of the ruling-class rather than of ordinary people across the planet. If union activists and leaders only hear the story told by state and corporate shills, how can we expect better?

The next chapter will explore largely unsuccessful attempts to create alternative narratives through think tanks and individual "left" critics.

Think Tanks and Critics

WE ARE ALL FAMILIAR WITH THE QUESTION: Does it begin with the chicken or the egg? In the realm of left wing foreign policy we might ask: Does it start with the information provided or the requirements of the organization receiving the information? Political parties and unions can only take positions on issues they've heard about. If politicians, union leaders and members are only exposed to issues raised by corporate-dominated media or military-funded think tanks why would they question the status quo? Recognizing this problem within domestic politics, unions and individuals donate money to "left wing" think tanks and provide resources to "left wing" critics through jobs, contracts, speaking fees, etc. While difficult to compete with the propaganda produced by corporations, governments and wealthy individuals, there is at least an attempt to develop alternative voices. Unfortunately, in the realm of foreign affairs these alternative voices are deeply flawed or fail to challenge the status quo.

Is that because unions, political parties and individuals with resources do not want to challenge the foreign policy status quo or because they haven't heard a persuasive competing narrative? The chicken or the egg?

In this chapter I will look at the "left wing" think tanks and individual left-wing critics who receive resources from the union movement, either directly or indirectly. The focus will be on whether or not these institutions and individuals promote a "first do no harm" and "Golden Rule" foreign policy for Canada. Some of the important criteria to measure this are: Do they promote war as a way of settling international disputes? Do they generally support imperialism and the American Empire? Do they assume foreign policy is good just because it is Canadian? How tied in are they to the foreign policy propaganda machinery of the Canadian or American governments? Do they question capitalism outside Canada in the same way they question corporate power inside Canada?

Of necessity in a short book, much of what follows is negative. This does not mean I am arguing that everything these institutions and individuals write or do is bad. Rather, I am pointing out shortcomings based on the criteria above. If we are to build better Canadian foreign policy it will start with a better left.

RIDEAU INSTITUTE

The Rideau Institute (RI) is Ottawa's leading "left-wing" foreign policy think tank. But, it spurns demilitarization and anti-imperialist voices and the "independent research and advocacy group" is headed by a long-time foreign affairs insider. It generally promotes the views of the liberal end of the military establishment.

In 2014 Peggy Mason became president of the RI, a position she held when this book went to print. Mason worked in Canadian foreign policy circles for three decades. Between 1984 and 1989 Mason was a lead adviser to Progressive Conservative MP and foreign minister Joe Clark.[391] During this period she attended all NATO Council meetings.[392] In 1989 Mason was appointed Canadian Ambassador for Disarmament at the UN. She held that position for six years and in this capacity Mason headed the Canadian delegation to numerous diplomatic conferences.[393] In 1996 Mason became a faculty member at the military run and funded Pearson Peacekeeping Centre (see *A Propaganda System*).[394] At the start of the 2000s Mason was an advisor to Foreign Affairs on the control of small arms and light weapons.[395]

During the mid-2000s Mason helped found and chaired the board of Peacebuild. In 2007 the Canadian International Development Agency gave Peacebuild $575,000, which was in addition to money from Foreign Affairs and the government-run International Development Research Centre.[396] Largely focused on Afghanistan, Peacebuild was a network of NGOs some viewed as a less-left-wing counterweight to the Canadian Peace Alliance, which campaigned against Canada's occupation of Afghanistan.[397]

Through her positions at the UN Mason worked with NATO. During a 2012 National Defence Committee parliamentary meeting she noted, "I'm talking as someone who has spent the better part of the last 10 years working with NATO."[398] The head of RI trained NATO commanders for peace and crisis stabilization operations and, according to Mason's LinkedIn profile, continued in this role after taking over RI. In mid 2018 it noted, "she is frequently an exercise developer, trainer and role player of Senior UN positions (Special Representative of the Secretary-General – SRSG) in NATO and EU peacekeeping training exercises including all of the NATO 'Steadfast' series joint exercises for the certification of the NATO Response Force (NRF)."[399] During the aforementioned parliamentary committee discussion Mason noted, "I was happy ... General Bouchard [who oversaw NATO's 2011 bombing of Libya] was the first Canadian commander I was involved in training with. This was before he ended up as the head of that very important mission."[400]

Mason made a number of other significant revelations to the parliamentary committee. During the 2012 meeting NDP MP Christine Moore asked: "While NATO always turns to the UN for a mandate to conduct expeditionary operations, the alliance does not need a UN mandate to undertake a mission, particularly in defence of an ally. Knowing that, and in that context, what should NATO do when the UN Security Council is paralyzed?" Mason responded to this question by saying it is okay to break international law, but NATO shouldn't do it too often. "I will say right now that it doesn't mean there might not be some exception in the future where we say, oh, the [UN security] council is so blocked, and we really believe we have to act even without it. But that should be seen as an extraordinary exception in extraordinary circumstances, because you're making your chances of success that much more difficult."[401]

At another point during the parliamentary discussion Mason ignored rural Manitoba Conservative MP Robert Sopuck's racist outburst. Sopuck said, "I think, however, in less developed countries tribalism is almost innate; tribalism is almost genetically in us. That's why the development of functioning institutions took centuries, because we have to overcome our tribal nature. When you throw in endemic corruption and tribalism, I become less optimistic all the time. One of my roles in Parliament is as chair of the Canada-Ukraine Parliamentary Friendship Group. That is a European country that, of any country, should have developed into a functioning democracy, and yet it's not even happening there. When you look at where Afghanistan is, I don't know ... Help me out here." Mason helped Sopuck out by simply responding: "You're wise to be very concerned and cautious."[402]

Presumably, Mason was chosen to head the Rideau Institute because of her establishment credentials. With three decades of experience working in Canadian foreign policy circles, she no doubt has a standing on Parliament Hill and within the dominant media. But, it's hard to imagine Mason has the sort of background to forthrightly challenge the foreign policy status quo.

**

In a 2016 email to its 25,000-person list RI working group Ceasefire.ca outlined, "key steps towards building sustainable peace and common security." The first demand was a motherhood statement about "giving top priority to war prevention, peaceful conflict resolution and building the United Nations envisaged by the UN Charter." The second point was a call for "greater participation in UN peacekeeping missions and international peacekeeping training."[403]

Premised on the specious notion that UN missions are by definition socially useful, Ceasefire.ca's position aligned with the Justin Trudeau government's plan at the time to dispatch 600 peacekeepers to Africa. Cheerleading all "peacekeeping" is a way to align with Canadian mythology and evade confronting military power. Proponents of peacekeeping are remarkably uninterested in investigating the strategic calculations driving this aspect of their foreign policy vision. Invariably, they fail to dissect why Ottawa initiates specific peacekeeping missions.

Historically, peacekeeping was Canada's contribution to the Cold War. In *Canada and UN Peacekeeping: Cold War by Other Means – 1945-1970* right-wing historian Sean Maloney asserts, "during the Cold War, the United States, the United Kingdom and France, all permanent members of the Security Council, remained aloof in several difficult circumstances as a sort of plausible deniability. Canada was the West's champion in the Cold War UN arena."[404]

Canada's sizable contribution to UN missions in Egypt and Cyprus were largely designed to reduce tensions within NATO. In Egypt (1956) the US opposed the British/French invasion while in Cyprus (1964) NATO members Turkey and Greece were on opposite sides. Through UN missions in Korea (1950) and Congo (1960) Ottawa contributed to US imperial crimes.

Contrary to what some leftist commentators claim, Canadian internationalism has rarely been at odds with American belligerence. As far as I can tell, major Canadian peacekeeping missions have always received support from Washington. Ignoring the power politics often driving peacekeeping missions has resulted in (unwitting?) support for western imperialism.

Overt militarist commentators are often clearer about the motives behind UN interventions than those on the nationalist left. Having constructed a Canadian identity in opposition to US imperialism, many nationalists are forced to mythologize foreign policy history. Responding to the myth that Canada has primarily been a defender of peaceful, internationalism, pro-US/militarist commentators argue Canada's "peacekeeping" interventions were not merely benevolent. According to the militarists, they have been designed to further this country's interests, particularly maintaining close relations to Canada's largest trading partner.

The nationalist left remained largely silent during two years of Canadian-backed killing in Haiti. After constructing a framework that idolized the UN, and Canada's history within the organization, it became difficult to criticize the UN occupation and Canada's role in overthrowing Haiti's elected government in 2004. In fact, some generally sensible leftists praised Canada's role in Haiti. In a 2006 Council of Canadians position paper titled "Marching Orders: How Canada abandoned peacekeeping – and why the UN needs us now more than ever" RI founder Steven Staples complained the war in Afghanistan deprived Haiti (and Sudan) of Canada's humanistic military resources.[405] Discussing the use of the C-17 Globemaster cargo plane to airlift troops to Haiti after the 2010 earthquake, Staples told the *Globe and Mail*, "I was skeptical of this purchase, these are very expensive aircraft. But, I will have to admit this it's good to see this kind of equipment being spent in this way."[406]

(To police Haiti's traumatized and suffering population 2,000 Canadian troops were deployed alongside 12,000 US soldiers and 1,500 UN troops (8,000 UN soldiers were already there). Confirming what I and other Haiti solidarity activists said in the days after the terrible earthquake, officials in Ottawa sent soldiers because they feared a post-earthquake power vacuum could lead to a "popular uprising." According to an internal briefing note the Canadian Press examined a year after the disaster, "political fragility has increased the risks of a popular uprising, and has fed the rumour that ex-president Jean-Bertrand Aristide, currently in exile in South Africa, wants to organize a return to power."[407] Though the Conservative government rapidly deployed 2,000 troops they ignored calls to dispatch this country's Heavy Urban Search and Rescue Teams, which are trained to "locate trapped persons in collapsed structures."[408])

Three months after the earthquake, prominent BC-based progressive author Murray Dobbin wrote a piece contrasting

Canadian violence in Afghanistan with the more noble UN mission in Haiti (after a wave of criticism Dobbin, to his credit, wrote a "Mea culpa on Haiti").[409] More significantly, RI promoted the views of Walter Dorn (more below) who worked for and lauded the UN mission in Haiti. After I criticized a 2016 RI report in an article titled "Do Black (Haitian) lives matter to Canada's leading 'left-wing' foreign-policy think tank?" RI President Peggy Mason responded by distancing the organization from the actions of the UN mission in Haiti. She wrote, "Haiti is almost a text book example of a deeply flawed political process, imposed from the outside, and which has consistently denied the majority a chance to choose the government they want. ... UN peacekeeping in Haiti has been hugely problematic. ... The people of Haiti need good peacekeeping, not an abandonment of the field."[410] To the best of my knowledge, this wishy-washy statement was RI's first critical comment about Haiti since the 2004 Canada-backed coup.

***

In 2011 Ceasefire.ca asked its supporters "Is Remembrance Day too much about war, and not enough about peace?"[411] While this is a legitimate question, the opening paragraph of its email contained troubling historical distortions. It explained: "Remembrance Day is changing as the veterans of the First and Second World Wars, and the Korean War, pass away. More attention is being paid to current and more controversial conflicts, such as those in Afghanistan and Libya."[412]

The claim that Canadian participation in World War I or Korea was, and is, not controversial is a striking example of a purportedly progressive organization accepting the establishment's version of history. Canada definitely should not have participated in these wars. Both were wars fought to advance imperial and geopolitical aims of the rich and powerful against the interests of the majority of people.

Ceasefire.ca's acceptance of the elite version of history is harmful because it obscures the imperial interests that have motivated Canadian foreign policy. It also erases decades of international solidarity and anti-war activism that has, to some extent, civilized the Canadian military. The 2011 bombing of Libya and 2001–14 war in Afghanistan help illustrate the point. These conflicts caused significant suffering, but they weren't nearly as destructive as the Korean War, which resulted in as many as four million dead. The Canadian military didn't simply discard their most violent methods. Instead their actions have been constrained (to some extent) by anti-war and international solidarity movements.

Perpetuating ignorance of our military's history has the effect of weakening the movements that have struggled valiantly to civilize Canadian foreign policy. It is akin to erasing the role of union struggles in restricting child labour, dangerous working conditions, long working hours, etc. The labour movement points to gains in these areas to build strength and the same should be done by anti-war and solidarity organizations.

Instead of promoting a sanitized version of Canadian military history, anti-war groups should help the public understand the role that struggle and protest have played in lessening the military's worst excesses. This knowledge will help fuel campaigns to build a sense of collective humanity.

WALTER DORN

The Rideau Institute has worked with an individual backed by leading figures within Canada's "natural governing party" and who aggressively supported Canada's worst foreign policy crime of the first decade of the 21st century. Walter Dorn is a senior RI advisor and regularly contributes to the organization's reports and public events.

A military website describes Dorn as a "professor at the Canadian Forces College and Chair of the Master of Defence Studies programme at RMC [Royal Military College]."[413] In 2001 he received Foreign Affairs' first Human Security Fellowship and has received research funding from Canada's Permanent Mission to the United Nations and Defence Research and Development Canada.[414] "With financial support from the Department of Foreign Affairs and International Trade", Dorn wrote, "the United Nations sent me on research trips to the UN missions in Haiti" and elsewhere in 2006.[415] During a sabbatical that year Dorn served as a consultant to the UN Department of Peacekeeping Operations and later briefed the "Military Directors of the UN Mission in Haiti (MINUSTAH)" on "Technologies for Peacekeeping".[416] In a 2009 report on MINUSTAH Dorn writes, "UN officials there [Haiti] and at New York headquarters provided many useful documents and comments on drafts of this paper."[417]

Dorn was a strong proponent of the UN occupation of Haiti. After briefing its leaders, he wrote a report titled "Intelligence-led Peacekeeping: The United Nations Stabilization Mission in Haiti (MINUSTAH), 2006–07." In it he claimed the foreign intervention to overthrow Haiti's elected government in 2004 was designed "to create basic conditions for security and stability."[418] Focused on UN intelligence activities in the large Port-au-Prince slum of Cité Soleil, the report ignored MINUSTAH's political role.

After helping oust Aristide and thousands of other elected officials, 500 Canadian soldiers were incorporated into a UN mission that backed up a coup government's violent crackdown against pro-democracy protesters between March 2004 and May 2006.[419] The UN force also killed dozens of civilians directly when it pacified Cité Soleil, a bastion of support for Aristide. The worst incident was early in the morning on July 6, 2005, when 400 UN troops entered the densely populated neighbourhood.[420] Eyewitnesses and victims of the attack claim MINUSTAH helicopters fired on residents throughout the operation.[421] The cardboard and corrugated tin wall houses were no match for the troops' heavy weaponry, which fired "over 22,000 rounds of ammunition", according to a US embassy file released through a Freedom of Information request.[422] The raid left at least 23 civilians dead, including numerous women and children.[423] The UN initially claimed they only killed "gang" leader Dread Wilme. (Graphic footage of victims dying on camera can be viewed in Kevin Piña's Haiti: We Must Kill the Bandits.[424])

Dorn delivered a number of lectures in favour of the UN force. In 2010 he made a presentation on "The Protection of Civilians: The United Nations Stabilization Mission in Haiti."[425] The next year he told CBC Radio the world is "crying for Canada" to expand its role in UN military missions, noting "we have a long-standing police contribution in Haiti but we could easily contribute to the military side."[426]

Dorn also rebuked critics of the UN occupation. In 2012 the author of a Council on Hemispheric Affairs report, Courtney Frantz, told IPS that MINUSTAH "perpetrated acts of violence" and had "become an instrument of the U.S., France and Canada in terms of their economic interests (including privatisation in Haiti)."[427] Countering Frantz in the article, Dorn said UN forces delivered "law and order".[428] The next year he told Canadian Press that adding 34 Canadian soldiers to MINUSTAH was a "positive development. It helps Haiti. It helps the United Nations, the United States and Brazil."[429]

While dispatching Canadian soldiers may have helped the US and Brazil, most Haitians saw the UN as an occupying force responsible for innumerable abuses.[430] Aside from its role in the coup and subsequent political repression, the UN's disregard for Haitian life caused a major cholera outbreak, which left over 10,000 dead and one million ill.[431] In October 2010 a UN base in central Haiti recklessly discharged sewage, including the feces of newly deployed Nepalese troops, into a river where people drank.[432] This introduced the water-borne disease into the country. Even after the deadly cholera outbreak, UN forces were caught disposing sewage into waterways Haitians drank from.[433]

Haiti represents but one example of Dorn's support for UN violence. In writing about the early 1960s UN mission in the Congo he ignores that mission's role in the assassination of elected Prime Minister Patrice Lumumba. He also fails to mention that Canadian soldiers worked to undermine the Congolese independence leader and how Prime Minister John Diefenbaker privately called Lumumba a "major threat to Western interests".[434] Lumumba's death dealt a significant blow to that country and the continent's post-independence aspirations.

Similarly, Dorn provides a one-sided account of a war that left as many as four million dead. According to the RI advisor, "Canada sent a large contingent of troops to Korea in 1950 to fight in a UN 'police action' to protect the elected South

Korean government."[435] Ottawa's actions weren't so pure. At the end of World War II the Soviets occupied the northern part of Korea, which borders Russia. US troops controlled the southern part of the country. According to Noam Chomsky, "when US forces entered Korea in 1945, they dispersed the local popular government, consisting primarily of antifascists who resisted the Japanese, and inaugurated a brutal repression, using Japanese fascist police and Koreans who had collaborated with them during the Japanese occupation. About 100,000 people were murdered in South Korea prior to what we call the Korean War, including 30-40,000 killed during the suppression of a peasant revolt in one small region, Cheju Island."[436]

In sharp contrast to its position on Japan and Germany, Washington wanted the (Western dominated) UN to take responsibility for Korea in 1947. The Soviets objected, claiming the international organization had no jurisdiction over post-WWII settlement issues (as the US had argued for Germany and Japan). Instead, Moscow proposed that all foreign forces withdraw from Korea by January 1948.[437] Washington demurred, convincing member states to create the United Nations Temporary Commission on Korea (UNTCOK) to organize elections in the part of Korea occupied by the US. Left-wing parties boycotted the poll and the Soviet bloc refused to participate in UNTCOK.[438] Canada joined UNTCOK even though Prime Minister Mackenzie King noted privately, "the [US] State Department was simply using the United Nations as an arm of that office to further its own policies."[439] The UN-sponsored election in South Korea led to the long-term division of that country and Canada's involvement in a conflict that would cause untold suffering.

Dorn fails to criticize any Canadian foreign-policy decisions except (from what I read) to call for increased participation in UN missions. He writes regularly about the need for more UN military engagement but doesn't mind if this takes place alongside US/NATO led wars. In March 2015 Dorn wrote: "The two approaches can coexist. It's not one or the other and nothing in between. We can excel in combat and excel in peacekeeping."[440]

Sympathetic to Washington's worldview, Dorn isn't troubled by UN forces standing in for NATO. In a February 2016 RI/CCPA report he writes, "in the post-Afghanistan period, the burden of addressing emerging international crises is increasingly shifted towards the United Nations, with NATO limiting its intervention primarily to air strikes such as those used in Libya in 2011."[441]

In the case of the 2011 Canada/France/Britain/US war in Libya, Dorn called for a UN force to mop up a conflict he deemed, even four years after, "justified ... easily passing a Just War threshold."[442] Five months into that war the *Independent* reported him saying, a "peacekeeping mission in Libya would present the UN with an opportunity to overcome its surprisingly outmoded attitude to new military technology."[443]

Dorn campaigned for improved UN military capacity and enthused about the Barack Obama administration's commitment to strengthening UN military capacity. "The U.S. effort is genuine", he said in March 2015. "I've been to Washington three times in recent months to talk with the (U.S.) Department of Defense on helping bring United Nations peacekeeping technology into the 21st century."[444]

Dorn's push to improve UN military capacities led him to promote controversial military technologies. In an article about a conference hosted by the US government's Defense Advanced Research Projects Agency on solutions to the war in Syria, Dorn said, "you need the technology such as Radarsat or other systems to corroborate the Information coming in from local sources."[445] But, the taxpayer funded RADARSAT is a billion-dollar Canadian contribution to weaponizing space. It provides crucial satellite imagery data for first strike theatre missile defence.[446] (It's called "missile defence" because it is designed to defend US missiles used in offensive wars.)

Leaving aside military extremism, Dorn's positions align with those of Canadian foreign policy decision makers. In an indication of his place among the establishment, Dorn's 2011 book received a blurb from then Liberal foreign critic Bob Rae and he's repeatedly spoken alongside former Liberal foreign minister Lloyd 'let's bomb Yugoslavia' Axworthy.

In 2010 Dorn launched the RI/Ceasefire.ca "campaign to make Canada a UN peacekeeper again." At the event televised by CPAC, prominent *Globe and Mail* reporter Gloria Galloway interviewed Dorn on "Will Canada Be a UN Peacekeeper Again?"[447] Dorn attracts corporate media interest, which presumably explains RI's interest in collaborating. But, his establishment standing is mostly due to his position at the Royal Military College and Canadian Forces College. Dorn survives, even thrives, at the military-run colleges because elements of the CF have long viewed "peacekeeping", which demands a military force, as a way to maintain public support for its budget.[448] According to Steven Staples, "some [in the military] view peacekeeping as generating a positive image that can build public support for the Canadian Forces and its large budget, which ... is really used to pay for non-U.N. combat missions."[449] Additionally, UN operations can be a boon to arms manufacturers. A June 2016 *Hill Times* article about Canada's potential reengagement with UN peacekeeping was titled "Greater Role in International Crises Could Bolster Domestic Defence Manufacturers."[450]

As a sign of his opinion towards military spending, iPolitics reported on a 2014 interview in which Dorn "said he is satisfied with the current size of the military. He said anything smaller would mean Canada is spending less than 1 per cent of GDP on its Armed Forces – and, as a professor of defence studies, that's not something he could support."[451]

MICHAEL BYERS

To denote his critical stance the *Globe and Mail*'s Michael Valpy called Michael Byers the "angry academic voice of Canadian foreign policy."[452] Despite the label, the RI Board member concedes a great deal to the foreign policy establishment. He mostly criticizes the allocation of military spending, not the size of the armed forces. Byers has also promoted a benevolent Canada mythology.

In 2015 the UBC professor published "Smart Defence: A Plan for Rebuilding Canada's Military" which begins: "Canada is a significant country. With the world's eleventh largest economy, second largest landmass and longest coastline, one could expect it to have a well-equipped and capable military. However, most of this country's major military hardware is old, degraded, unreliable and often unavailable. When the Harper government came to power in 2006, it pledged to rebuild Canada's military. But for nine long years, it has failed to deliver on most of its promises, from new armoured trucks and supply ships to fighter jets and search-and-rescue planes."[453]

Byers peppers the RI/CCPA report with various other militarist claims. Canada "faces challenges at home and abroad that require a well-equipped and capable military," he writes. At another point he says, "the Canadian Army cannot deploy large numbers of troops overseas because of a shortage of armoured trucks."[454] Smart Defence was partly an attack against the Harper government's supposed lack of military commitment. Byers writes, "Prime Minister Stephen Harper has reduced defence spending to just 1.0 percent of GDP — the lowest level in Canadian history."

Byers co-published another militarist paper two years earlier. "Stuck in a Rut: Harper Government Overrides Canadian Army, Insists on Buying Outdated Equipment" argued against the Conservatives' plan to spend $2 billion to buy tanks since the US military shifted its counterinsurgency tactics. The 2013 RI/CCPA report invoked the Petraeus Doctrine, which is named after General David Petraeus, who was in charge of US forces in Iraq and Afghanistan. It noted, "the doctrine calls for soldiers to engage with and support local people so as to erode any incentive they might have to side with insurgents."[455]

Stuck in a Rut said nothing about the thousands of Iraqis and Afghans killed by the US-led forces implementing the Petraeus Doctrine. Nor did the report call for a reduction in Canada's military spending – which was 13th highest in the world at the time.[456]

In a chapter in *Living with Uncle: Canada-US relations in an age of Empire*, edited by the CCPA's Bruce Campbell and Ed Finn, Byers notes that "the defence budget, roughly 1.2% of GDP, is a bit low by comparable standards."[457] He describes writing a 2004 paper for NDP defence critic Bill Blakey that called for a $2-3 billion per year increase in military spending. "A defence budget increase", it noted, "essentially repairs some of the damage that was done by a decade and a half of neglect."[458] But, the military budget was $15 billion and represented 10% of federal government outlays at the time (and a much higher percentage of discretionary spending).[459]

In op-eds Byers regularly cites benevolent Canada mythology. In a 2016 *Toronto Star* piece he wrote, "the country that 'gave the world Lester Pearson's peacekeeping and Brian Mulroney's stand against apartheid' now had to struggle 'with Stephen Harper's apparent blindness to compelling evidence of Afghanistan prisoner abuse.'"[460] In another op-ed Byers noted, "Canada used to stand tall for human rights. Lester Pearson won the Nobel Peace Prize because he devised a new mechanism — UN Peacekeeping — for preventing death and suffering. Lloyd Axworthy built on that reputation."[461]

But, Pearson designed the 1956 peacekeeping force to extricate London from an invasion of Egypt that Washington opposed. The principal objective of the UN force was not to protect Egyptian civilians or sovereignty, but to overcome the division within NATO between the US and Britain/France.[462] Additionally, Brian Mulroney's sanctions against apartheid South Africa were only partial measures (trade was cut in half) and Ottawa never severed diplomatic ties unlike a number of other countries.[463] For his part, Axworthy supported Indonesia's occupation of East Timor, backed Talisman Oil despite its contribution to violence in southern Sudan and had Canada join NATO's bombing of the former Yugoslavia.[464]

Byers is not ignorant of this history. A number of books available at the UBC library detail these issues and after presenting to his class in 2012 Byers told me he'd read my

Black Book of Canadian Foreign Policy, which touches on all of the above.

When Byers lauds Pearson's foreign policy I don't believe it reflects his personal conviction, but rather a mix of careerist and tactical considerations. As discussed further below, if you seek to publish or be quoted in the dominant media it is best to avoid directly confronting military power and foreign policy mythology. At the tactical level Byers is probably calculating that if one seeks to shape policy he needs to remain close to power (in the political party, academic or media spheres). Additionally, he likely believes the best way to marshal public concern about an international issue distant from people's lives is to speak to Canadians' sense that their country usually does good in the world. Whether it is effective or not in the short term, this strategy contributes to confusion about Canadian foreign policy history.

***

Leftists often reinforce Canadian exceptionalism when challenging specific policy. Researching the *Black Book of Canadian Foreign Policy* I discovered numerous articles that started off by stating, Canada usually does good internationally except for whatever the subject that particular article was criticizing. Obviously when repeated over and over again the 'usually good but not this time' formulation is incorrect.

Linking criticism of current policy to a mythical 'Golden era' is motivated by ideology and tactical considerations. Many leftists simply can't think outside the benevolent foreign policy box. At the tactical level, it isolates the issue and is supposed to elicit a "this isn't the Canada I know" reaction. But, structuring criticism in this way downplays the structural character of the problem and distorts history.

In another important concession to Canadian mythology and vested interests, commentators/politicians regularly oppose wars by calling for the military to be redirected. Indifferent to the morality of the occupation, many called for the troops to be withdrawn from Afghanistan so they'd be available for an alternative moral crusade. RI advisor Walter Dorn noted, "the first consequence of our current deployment in Afghanistan is that Canada is currently at a historic low in its UN peacekeeping contribution."[465]

The NDP's leader echoed this theme on a number of occasions. In 2006 Layton said, "the New Democrats have not written a blank check so that this government, or any other government, can drag Canada still farther into war, so that it can remove us farther from our role as international peacekeepers."[466] In an article titled "Take lead in Darfur, Layton urges Canada", the *Globe and Mail* reported NDP defence critic Dawn Black commenting, "it's unlikely the Armed Forces can make the necessary commitment to a Darfur mission and still maintain its forces in Afghanistan at current levels."[467] Also citing Sudan, NDP leader Jack Layton described Afghanistan as "not the right mission for Canada."[468]

Criticizing military missions in this manner sets the stage for future interventions. In a schoolyard context it would be akin to telling Billy to stop harassing Johnny because Freddie hasn't been bullied for a while.

Why can't the NDP or left-wing commentators simply say they don't support a military mission? Just criticize the ineffectiveness or, even better, immorality of the deployment. Why present an alternative deployment for Canadian troops?

"Shift the deployment" criticism is less threatening because it upholds 'world needs more Canada' ideology. It is also a sop to the military and its associated industries. Promoting an alternative deployment doesn't call the military or its massive budget into question.

CCPA

After I complained privately about their report titled "Unprepared for Peace? The decline of Canadian Peacekeeping Training (And What to Do About It)" *CCPA Monitor* editor Stuart Trew asked me to write a response for the magazine. A call for the Canadian Forces to offer its members more peacekeeping training, "Unprepared for Peace?" is premised on the erroneous notion that UN missions are by definition socially useful. As mentioned above, lead author Walter Dorn worked with and publicly lauded the UN Stabilization Mission in Haiti (MINUSTAH) and the report repeatedly implies that Canada's contribution to that mission was something to be proud of.

A not-so-subtle cover image of "Unprepared for Peace?" included a white Canadian soldier with an M-16 strapped to his shoulder bent over and extending a hand to a young black boy. Canadian and UN colours feature prominently in the background. Criticizing the report, Nik Barry-Shaw, an Institute for Justice & Democracy Haiti voting rights advocate, wrote: "Please lay off the colonial imagery of benevolent white men lending a hand to small, vulnerable black children. This is the 21st century, people."

I submitted a piece Trew called a "fair critique" and "edited it down to a point where it will fit on one page." A week later Trew wrote, "the Monitor board, including E.D. [Executive Director] Peter Bleyer, feel that at the least we should put your letter alongside responses from Dorn and Byers, which will take a bit more time. I've slotted in a section to deal with this in the July-August issue."

Unsurprisingly, Dorn and Byers refused to respond to my criticism. When I inquired about my piece two months later Trew said they couldn't publish it. "We've since reconsidered running your rebuttal in the Monitor", he wrote. "Since we didn't feature the peacekeeping report in the Monitor and your critique has appeared elsewhere the editorial board preferred not to devote the two pages we would need to for the back-and-forth." But, the Monitor imposed the "back-and-forth" stipulation. While it is true that part of the critique appeared elsewhere, this was known when he accepted my piece and my submission dissected two additional CCPA reports published by Michael Byers (see above).

While Trew buckled to institutional prerogatives, he's less of a nationalist than the Monitor editor between 1994 and 2014. Ed Finn described himself "as an ardent nationalist" and wrote in the preface to *After Harper*, "let's make Canada the great country it could be … the authors of this anthology fervently hope their advice will help Canadians find their way back to the path that leads to true national greatness."[469]

Finn seemed largely indifferent to Canada's international abuses.[470] Not one of 20 chapters in the Finn edited *After Harper* focused on foreign policy.

Though I asked, Finn didn't review any of my first four books on Canadian foreign policy in the Monitor (*Canada in Haiti —Waging War on the Poor Majority*, The *Black Book of Canadian Foreign Policy, Canada and Israel: Building Apartheid*, or *Lester Pearson's Peacekeeping: The Truth May Hurt*). The only text he accepted for review was the *Ugly Canadian: Stephen Harper's Foreign Policy*, which didn't upend the dominant liberal nationalist ideology. Finn described Harper as "bent on transforming Canada into a US colony with all its flaws and inequities."[471]

According to two insiders, Bruce Campbell was the individual responsible for the CCPA co-publishing reports with RI by Dorn and Byers. Executive Director of the CCPA between 1994 and 2015, Campbell received an MA from Carleton's Norman Paterson School of International Affairs, which has close ties to, and is basically a training ground for, Global Affairs Canada (see *A Propaganda System*). Describing Canada as a "colonial supplicant", Campbell also worked as a researcher with the North South Institute, an organization instigated and funded by CIDA (see *A Propaganda System*).[472]

In *Living with Uncle: Canada-US relations in an age of Empire* editors Bruce Campbell and Ed Finn describe the book's aim as "to advance … an agenda that builds on a social democratic–just society vision that emerged after World War II."[473] While the dominant economic ideology after World War II was preferable to neoliberal capitalism, their statement disregards Canada's role in creating post-World War II, US-centered multilateral institutions such as the IMF/World Bank, International Trade Organization (the WTO's predecessor) and NATO, as well as waging war on Korea, backing colonialism in Africa and helping assassinate Patrice Lumumba.

But, it's not simply historical revisionism that is the problem. With the exception of a two-sentence mention in a chapter by Avi Lewis, *Living with Uncle* avoided any discussion of Canada's role in overthrowing Haiti's elected government in 2004. Published at the height of the post-coup violence, the 2006 book says nothing about Canada's role in plotting and executing the coup. It is a particularly odd omission for a book titled *Living with Uncle* since Canada participated in the coup partly to make good with Washington after (officially) declining to participate in the Bush administration's "coalition of the willing" that invaded Iraq in 2003. Former foreign minister Bill Graham later explained: "Foreign Affairs view was there is a limit to how much we can constantly say no to the political masters in Washington. All we had was Afghanistan to wave. On every other file we were offside. Eventually we came on side on Haiti, so we got another arrow in our quiver."[474]

While Campbell and Finn mostly failed to challenge foreign-policy moves, Finn did provide Asad Ismi space in the Monitor to write about Canadian corporate malfeasance abroad. Current Monitor editor Stuart Trew also seems open to publishing some critical foreign policy articles. If one were to summarize the CCPA's foreign policy, it would be that serious challenges are published on the back pages of the Monitor while resources/profile are devoted to reports calling for more "peacekeeping" and questioning military procurement decisions.

LINDA MCQUAIG AND THE PEARSON DISEASE

"The liberal intellectuals (and not just in the United States) are typically the guardians at the gates: we'll go this far, but not one millimeter farther; and it's terrifying to think that somebody might go a millimeter farther"
— *Noam Chomsky*[475]

No political figure elicits more nonsense from generally sensible and progressive Canadians than Lester Pearson. As I detail in *Lester Pearson's Peacekeeping: The Truth May Hurt*, the former external minister and prime minister staunchly backed the US-led world order. Among many dubious distinctions, the ardent cold warrior played a part in creating NATO and aiding US-led wars in Vietnam and Korea.

Despite a foreign-policy record dripping with blood, individuals such as Jack Layton, Stephen Lewis, Noah Richler, Michael Byers, Naomi Klein, Tom Woodley, Steven Staples, Svend Robinson and Elizabeth May have, at one time or another, cited Pearson's name glowingly. But none more shamefully than well-known left-wing author Linda McQuaig.

In a May 2008 *Toronto Star* column titled "Keep Pearson out of it" McQuaig took exception with "[former Liberal minister] John Manley, head of the government's advisory panel on Afghanistan, defend[ing] the mission by invoking the name of Canadian peacekeeping hero Lester Pearson."[476] Author of a 2007 book that devoted a chapter to his foreign policy, McQuaig quoted an academic who called this a "real desecration of [Pearson's] memory and his monumental achievement for world peace." But, it is McQuaig who "desecrates" the historical record in her bid to style Pearson a "peacekeeping" hero.

In *Holding the Bully's Coat* McQuaig claims Pearson had a "keenness to reduce Cold War tension with Moscow and Beijing."[477] There's little basis for this statement and a great deal of evidence to suggest the Nobel Peace Prize winner was a determined cold warrior. Before making his famous Iron Curtain speech, which some consider the opening salvo in the Cold War, former British Prime Minister Winston Churchill asked Canada's then ambassador to Washington to look it over. Calling the March 1946 talk "one of the most impressive things that Churchill has done", Pearson made a correction and added a line he thought would be popular with the Missouri audience.[478] This was one of Pearson's many contributions to Cold War hysteria. In a 1951 speech to Parliament Pearson said the CBC International Service was "playing a useful part in the psychological war against communism."[479]

Pearson also played a part in creating NATO, which contributed to Cold War hysteria. NATO planners feared a weakening self-confidence in Western Europe and the widely held belief that communism was the wave of the future. In March 1949 Pearson told the House of Commons: "The power of the communists, wherever that power flourishes, depends upon their ability to suppress and destroy the free institutions that stand against them. They pick them off one by one: the political parties, the trade unions, the churches, the schools, the universities, the trade associations, even the sporting clubs and the kindergartens. The North Atlantic Treaty Organization is meant to be a declaration to the world that this kind of conquest from within will not in the future take place amongst us."[480] Tens of thousands of North American troops were stationed in Western Europe to deter any "conquest from within".

At the end of his career Pearson described his role in the "formation of NATO", not peacekeeping, as the "most important thing I participated in."[481] To square his admiration of NATO with her desire to portray Pearson as a peace promoting, anti-American internationalist, McQuaig claims the North Atlantic alliance challenged Washington. "There were even fears at the outset that Washington would retreat back into isolationism and decline to participate ... In supporting NATO, Canada [Pearson] was also promoting an internationalist vision of collective security, rather than simply tying itself and its security to Washington."[482]

First, to claim NATO was about "security", at least defined in a humanistic sense, is absurd. The organization was designed to advance the US-led order. Second, why would McQuaig oppose US isolationism? The world would be a better place if there had been no US-backed coups in Chile, Iran, Guatemala, Haiti, etc. or US-led wars in Korea, Vietnam, Iraq, etc. Finally, it's incorrect to imply that Washington was not immediately supportive of NATO. The US government convened top-secret talks in March 1948 with British and Canadian officials on the possibility of creating a North Atlantic alliance.[483] Implying that NATO was not part of expanding the US-centered imperial order distorts 70 years of Canadian foreign policy, including the organization's more recent wars in Afghanistan, Serbia and Libya.

When Britain, France and Israel invaded Egypt in 1956 Pearson's actions undermined the former European colonial powers position. As a result, McQuaig claims, "Pearson's distaste for colonialism played a role in what ended up being a significant diplomatic and foreign policy triumph: his handling of the 1956 Suez Crisis."[484] But, there's little evidence to suggest he was motivated by any "distaste for colonialism".

On November 29, 1956, Pearson declared: "I do not for one minute criticize the motives of the governments of the United Kingdom and France … I may have thought their intervention was not wise, but I do not criticize their purposes."[485] The invasion's primary aim was to re-establish European control over the Suez Canal and weaken Arab nationalism. For France the goal was also to end Egyptian support for Algeria's independence movement.

Pearson supported the colonial status quo. With anticolonial sentiment spreading across Africa, in 1953 the external minister lauded the United Kingdom's "big contribution" to "the defence of freedom generally" and in 1957 Pearson told the House of Commons "no people in the world have proved themselves more 'dependable defenders of freedom' than have the British."[486] In that speech he added: "Those countries which still have direct responsibilities for non self-governing territories [colonies] should not be made to feel at the United Nations or elsewhere that they are oppressors to be deprived arbitrarily of their rights or indeed their reputations."[487]

Pearson also backed France's brutal suppression of the independence struggle in Algeria. In *Towards a Francophone Community* Robin Gendron explains: "Increasingly concerned for France's political stability, in January 1957 [External Affairs Undersecretary] Jules Leger again tried to persuade Lester Pearson that the time had come to get the French government to accept the eventual independence of Algeria as the basis for a negotiated end to the war. Pearson was not convinced, arguing that no country could exert enough pressure to change France's Algerian policy and that any attempt to do so would run afoul of the strength of French national feeling."[488] Canada gave France tens of millions of dollars in military equipment while it had hundreds of thousands of troops in Algeria.[489] During his time as external minister Ottawa donated over $1 billion ($5 billion today) in NATO Mutual Assistance Program weaponry to the European colonial powers.[490]

Pearson's main concern during the Suez Crisis was the disagreement between the US and UK over the intervention, not Egyptian sovereignty or the plight of that country's people. The minister explained at the time that Canada's "interest is prejudiced when there is division within the Commonwealth or between London, Washington or Paris."[491] Maintaining the seven-year-old NATO alliance was Pearson's priority when he intervened in Egypt in the fall of 1956.

In the annals of Canadian foreign policy, the Suez Crisis represents Ottawa's decisive break from London. While McQuaig says Pearson "managed to create a role for Canada outside the U.S. sphere of influence," he's actually the individual most responsible for Ottawa's post-World War II shift away from British imperialism and towards the US version.[492]

Supporting the US war in Southeast Asia is a shameful example of his pro-Washington position. Despite offering various forms of support, Pearson is often portrayed as an opponent of the US war in Vietnam. An April 1965 speech he delivered at Temple University in Philadelphia is probably the most often cited example of a Canadian leader (supposedly) opposing US militarism. McQuaig, for instance, claims "one could argue that Pearson's urgings may have, in some small way, contributed to ending the U.S. war effort in Vietnam."[493] (To be precise, McQuaig's quote refers to Pearson's Temple speech and a private meeting he had with President Lyndon B. Johnson two years later.)

If similar statements had not been made elsewhere, McQuaig's comment would be hard to fathom. Here's part of what Pearson said in Philadelphia: "The government and great majority of people of my country have supported wholeheartedly the US peacekeeping and peacemaking policies in Vietnam." In *Quiet Complicity: Canadian involvement in the Vietnam War,* a book McQuaig cites, Victor Levant puts Pearson's Temple speech (available online) in proper context: "In his Temple speech, the Prime Minister did accept all the premises and almost all the conclusions of US policy. The chief cause of the escalation of the war in Vietnam, in Pearson's view, was North Vietnamese aggression. 'This situation cannot be expected to improve,' he said, 'until North Vietnam becomes convinced that aggression, in whatever guise, for whatever reason, is inadmissible and will not succeed.' This had wider implications, since 'no nation ... could ever feel secure if capitulation in Vietnam led to the sanctification of aggression through subversion and spurious wars of national liberation.' If peace was to be achieved, the first condition was a cease-fire, and this could happen only if Hanoi recognizes the error of its ways: 'aggressive action by North Vietnam to bring about a Communist liberation (which means Communist rule) of the South must end. Only then can there be negotiations.' Since US military action was aimed at resisting Hanoi's aggression, the measures taken so far, including the bombing of the North, were entirely justified: 'the retaliatory strikes against North Vietnamese military targets, for which there has been great provocation, aim at making it clear that the maintenance of aggressive policies toward the south will become increasingly costly to the northern regime. After about two months of airstrikes, the message should now have been received loud and clear.'"

Levant continues: "On the other hand, Pearson argued that continued bombing, instead of weakening Hanoi's will to resist, might have the effect of driving it into an even more intransigent position. He therefore suggested, as a tactical move, that the United States consider a carefully timed 'pause' in the bombing: 'there are many factors which I am not in a position to weigh. But there does appear to be at least a possibility that a suspension of such airstrikes against North Vietnam, at the right time, might provide the Hanoi authorities with an opportunity, if they wish to take it, to inject some flexibility into their policy without appearing to do so as the direct result of military pressure. If such a suspension took place for a limited time, then the rate of incidents in South Vietnam would provide a fairly accurate way of measuring its usefulness and the desirability of continuing. I am not, of course, proposing any compromise on points of principle, nor any weakening of resistance to aggression in South Vietnam. Indeed, resistance may require increased military strength to be used against the armed and attacking Communists. I merely suggest that a measured and announced pause in one field of military action at the right time might facilitate the development of diplomatic resources which cannot easily be applied to the problem under the existing circumstances. It could, at the least, expose the intransigence of the North Vietnam government.'"[494]

Let's further dissect Pearson's "anti-war" position. Approximately three million people died during the US war in Indochina, about 100,000 of whom were killed during the US bombing of the North.[495] To put Pearson's Temple speech in the crassest terms possible, opposing the bombing of the North was a call to end 3.3% of the death toll.

The day after he spoke in Philadelphia President Johnson privately berated the Canadian prime minister, a story McQuaig and other Pearson supporters describe in (probably exaggerated) detail. Johnson was mad because senior US foreign-policy planners were debating a pause in the bombing of North Vietnam. By speaking out Pearson effectively sided with Johnson's opponents in the US administration. Pearson told friend and journalist Bruce Hutchison that a highly placed US government official asked him to speak out on the bombing of North Vietnam.[496] Johnson felt betrayed partly because the prime minister had previously enabled the bombing campaign through Canada's role on the International Control Commission.[497] Supposed to enforce the implementation of the Geneva Accords and the peaceful reunification of Vietnam, Canadian International Control Commission officials delivered US bombing threats to the North Vietnamese leadership under Pearson's orders.[498] This is the reason Noam Chomsky has called Pearson a war criminal.

McQuaig and many other progressive intellectuals have stood Pearson's policy record on its head. By lauding the lead figure in post-World War II Canadian foreign policy they've greatly confused our understanding of global affairs. We cannot build a decent foreign policy on a foundation of mythology and outright lies. Rather, in order to move forward we must understand the truth about our past in order to reconcile with its victims.[i]

STEPHEN LEWIS

"Those who, like me, have long wondered when, if ever, Canada will produce another international statesman and diplomat in the mould of Lester Pearson need wonder no more. In Stephen Lewis, the Canadian tradition of ground-breaking international statesmanship is assured"
— *Bonny Ibhawoh, McMaster history professor*[499]

During the tour for my *Canada in Africa: 300 Years of Aid and Exploitation* I came across an iPolitics interview with

---

i For anyone who feels I've been unfair to McQuaig I suggest you read her chapter on Pearson in Holding the Bully's Coat and my Lester Pearson's Peacekeeping: The Truth May Hurt.

Lewis on Prime Minister Stephen Harper's policies in Africa. In it the former UN Special Envoy for HIV-AIDS in Africa said Harper's government was not doing enough to fight the disease in Africa and decried Canada's withdrawal from the continent. "It's heartbreaking. You know what Canada could do. You know the difference we could make," said Canada's former Permanent Representative to the UN.[500]

But criticizing Harper's failure to 'do more' in Africa was an affront to the victims of Canadian policy on the continent. The Conservatives worked aggressively to increase Canadian mining profits at the expense of local communities and in 2011 they waged an illegal war on Libya, destabilizing that country and surrounding states. Most troubling of all, Harper's promotion of heavy carbon emitting tar sands and sabotage of international climate change negotiations was tantamount to a death sentence to ever-growing numbers of Africans.

Angered by Lewis' interview I spent an overnight bus ride from Lethbridge to Nelson researching everything I could find online about someone prominent CBC journalist Paul Kennedy described as a "spokesperson for Africa".[501] On Africa no Canadian is more revered than Lewis. Though he's widely viewed as a champion of the continent, the standing of the former Deputy Executive Director of the United Nations Children's Fund (UNICEF) reflects the dearth of critical discussion about Canada's role in Africa. In fact, rather than advancing African liberation, the long-time member of Canadian and UN policy-making circles represents the critical end of an establishment debate oscillating between neo-conservatives who advocate aggressive, nakedly self-interested, policies and those who promote the "Responsibility to Protect", "do more" worldview.

Recipient of 37 honorary degrees from Canadian universities, Lewis has been dubbed "one of the greatest Canadians ever and certainly one of the greatest, if not the greatest, living today."[502] Recipient of the Pearson Peace Medal, Lewis has also been described as the preeminent "advocate for international development and the ideal of Canadian traditional values."[503]

But, "traditional values" don't seem to include serious criticism of Canadian government policies. Lewis has long bemoaned the lack of "support" for Africa all the while ignoring Ottawa and corporate Canada's contribution to the continent's impoverishment. "There's also a tendency just to discard Africa as no longer of geopolitical value in the world or to engage in the vile slander that Africa is too corrupt to support," Lewis told a Canadian Club of Toronto lunch in 2006.[504] During his speech the former head of the Ontario NDP called on the business crowd, some of whom led companies extracting the continent's natural resources, to 'do more' for Africa. "The big multinational corporations, whether in Canada or abroad, have been reluctant to make financial contributions [to fight HIV-AIDS]," Lewis said. "The multinational corporations seem to need additional incentives over and above the central prescriptive of corporate social responsibility."[505]

In *Race Against Time,* based on his 2005 CBC Massey lectures, Lewis fails to criticize any Canadian policy measure in Africa except for Ottawa's insufficient aid. Bestowing almost divine like power on Western "aid", Lewis writes that "if the [aid] promises of the G8 summit fall apart, Africa falls apart with them."[506]

But the staunch advocate of "aid" appears remarkably uninterested in the often self-interested and harmful character of "aid". He ignores how Ottawa initially began dispersing aid to African countries as a way to dissuade newly independent countries from following wholly independent paths or falling under the influence of the Communist bloc.[507] A big part of Canada's early assistance went to train militaries, including the Ghanaian military that overthrew (with Ottawa's backing) pan-Africanist independence leader Kwame Nkrumah in 1966.[508] Since the 1980s hundreds of millions of dollars in Canadian aid money has gone to support pro-corporate structural adjustment policies and other initiatives benefiting Canada's rapacious mining industry in Africa.[509]

While only criticizing Canadian policy-makers for not "doing enough" in Africa, Lewis is often withering in his indictment of other countries. Describing South Africa's poor rollout of AIDS treatments as "obtuse, dilatory and negligent", Lewis told the *New York Times* in 2006 "the government has a lot to atone for" and "I'm of the opinion that they can never achieve redemption."[510]

He levelled even stronger criticism against the Zimbabwean president. In 2009 Lewis described Robert Mugabe as "a man who has sanctioned murder and rape and totalitarianism and economic disintegration; watched a nation haunted by cholera, a country where people living with AIDS now die without access to drugs, more human misery than Shakespearean tragedy could summon, and we tell him, Repent or leave, and you're off the hook?"[511] While Mugabe was a repressive autocrat, he was re-elected in 2013 and, notwithstanding the Western media uproar, Zimbabwe's early 2000s land reform broadly succeeded in overturning a historical injustice.[512]

Lewis also aggressively criticized Chinese policy in Africa, claiming its investments fuelled corruption and rights violations. "There is no justification in the world for Darfur continuing as it has been", Lewis proclaimed in 2008. "It's just beyond the pale. The critical thing here is to go after the government of China and to make sure that they understand that this is going to be the Genocide Olympics, as it has been termed. What China is doing is sustaining the government of Sudan in an unholy alliance, wrecking the lives of the people in Darfur." (As part of Israeli lobby group Hillel's 2004 Holocaust Education Week, Lewis delivered a lecture at the University of Toronto titled "Never Again: The Crisis in Sudan".[513])

While Beijing backed a regime in Khartoum responsible for substantial human rights violations (though less than some claim), I searched in vain for a similar comment from Lewis about US/Britain/Canada support for Paul Kagame in Rwanda. More dependent on Washington/London/Ottawa than Sudanese president Omar al-Bashir was on Beijing, Kagame's invasions of the Congo triggered several times more deaths than the highest estimates of those killed in Darfur.

Lewis' tendency to fire rhetorical bombs at geopolitical competitors and verbal pellets at Canadian policymakers reflects the long-time politician's deference to the Ottawa/West perspective. So does his claim that Ottawa led the charge against apartheid South Africa. Compared to whom? African countries? Asian states? Latin America? When Nelson Mandela died in 2013 Lewis was widely quoted as saying South Africa's first democratically elected president was struck by "the intensity of our opposition to apartheid" and "the extraordinary role that Canada had played in fighting apartheid."[514]

But African countries began calling for the isolation of apartheid South Africa in the late 1950s, with many

Canadians adding their voice to these calls through the 1960s, 70s and early 80s. Yet, the Brian Mulroney government only brought in (partial) economic sanctions against South Africa in 1986. From October 1986 to September 1993, the period in which economic sanctions were in effect, Canada's two-way trade with South Africa totalled $1.6 billion — 44 percent of the comparable period before sanctions (1979-1985).[515] Ottawa never cut off diplomatic relations as did Norway, Denmark, New Zealand, Brazil, Argentina, etc.[516] To the extent the federal government deserves praise it is that it took a more principled position towards the apartheid regime than erstwhile allies London, Israel and Washington. Or, to put it differently, it was the best of a bad lot.

His response to Mandela's death is but one example of Lewis celebrating Canadian foreign policy. *Race Against Time* is peppered with praise for Canadian diplomats, lauding Canada's role in fighting for gender equality at the UN, dubbing businessman-turned diplomat Maurice Strong "the ultimate ubiquitous internationalist" and exalting in "our own Lester Pearson ... who negotiated with other Western governments the benchmark of 0.7% of GNP as the legitimate level of foreign aid for all industrial countries."[517]

Asked "who was the best on African AIDS policy?" by the *National Review of Medicine* in 2008 Lewis responded: "Paul Martin, overwhelmingly. Chrétien, I got the impression he felt for Africa but I don't think it was around AIDS more than a pro forma commitment, but Paul Martin had a very genuine and intense commitment and, had he had more time, I think that commitment would have continued to show itself. I don't get any sense from Harper — none whatsoever. The prime minister who cared most about Africa and did the most in development systems and foreign aid was unquestionably Brian Mulroney and he gets insufficient credit for his very real commitment to the continent."[518]

Surely Lewis knows that the Mulroney government, which he represented as Canadian ambassador to the UN for four years, pressed African countries to follow neoliberal economic prescriptions and spent tens of millions of dollars in "aid" to promote International Monetary Fund/World Bank structural adjustment programs across the continent.[519] As Lewis correctly points out in *Race Against Time* structural adjustment policies devastated the health and education sectors of many African countries. But, Ottawa's extensive support for structural adjustment is ignored in Lewis' book.

Lewis endorsed the Canadian promoted Responsibility to Protect doctrine used to justify the 2011 NATO war in Libya, which he publicly backed, and the 2004 overthrow of Haiti's elected government. In *Race Against Time* Lewis describes R2P as a "particularly Canadian contract", claiming that if it had been in place in the 1990s there "might not have been a genocide" in Rwanda.[520] In another speech Lewis describes R2P thusly: "It simply means that when a government is unable or unwilling to protect its citizens from egregious violations of human rights, then the international community has the responsibility to protect. That responsibility can be exercised through diplomatic or political pressure, or economic boycott or, in extreme cases, military intervention. But something has to trigger. It would be a great boon if the United States were to insist on the implementation of R2P in instances like the Congo and Zimbabwe."[521]

Lewis expressed trust in US military interventions on other occasions. When criticizing Washington for not intervening in Rwanda he highlighted "the moral legitimacy of the United States ... at many times in its history."[522]

While Lewis generally crafts his positions to fit the dominant discourse, a 2000 *Globe and Mail* opinion piece provides a strikingly direct sop to a major media outlet's anti-Africanism. Responding to the Globe editors' criticism of a report they published on Rwanda, Lewis and his "close friend and alter ego of nearly 50 years", Gerald Caplan, write: "We agree that Africa too often and too blithely has blamed its problems on external factors."[523]

If Africans are too quick to blame others for their problems Lewis is guilty of a much worse offense — overlooking his own country's role in subjugating the continent. I failed to find any comment on the many thousands of Canadian soldiers and missionaries who helped conquer the continent or undermine African cultural ways at the turn of the 19th century. Nor does Lewis seem to have mentioned official Ottawa's multi-faceted support for European colonial rule or Canada's role in overthrowing progressive post-independence leaders Patrice Lumumba, Milton Obote and Kwame Nkrumah.

While ignoring his own country's destructive role on the continent, he portrays himself as challenging power. "I am a Canadian speaking in my own country, delivering the Massey lectures," Lewis declares towards the end of *Race Against Time*. "I'm putting the self-imposed muzzle aside."[524]

Lewis' effort to "muzzle" any question of the official version of the Rwanda genocide and ideological support for Paul Kagame's regime is what history will judge most harshly (in 2009 a Rwandan media outlet described Lewis as "a very close friend to President Paul Kagame."[525]). In 2014 he signed an open letter condemning the BBC 2 documentary Rwanda's

Untold Story. The 1,266 word public letter refers to the BBC's "genocide denial", "genocide deniers" or "deniers" at least 13 times.[526] Notwithstanding Lewis and his co-signers' smears, which gave Kagame cover to ban the BBC's Kinyarwanda station, Rwanda the Untold Story includes interviews with a former chief prosecutor at the International Criminal Tribunal for Rwanda (ICTR), a former high-ranking member of the United Nations Assistance Mission in Rwanda and a number of former Rwandan Patriotic Front (RPF) associates of Paul Kagame.[527] In "The Kagame-Power Lobby's Dishonest Attack on the BBC 2's Documentary on Rwanda", Edward S. Herman and David Peterson write: "[Lewis, Gerald Caplan, Romeo Dallaire et al.'s] cry of the immorality of 'genocide denial' provides a dishonest cover for Paul Kagame's crimes in 1994 and for his even larger crimes in Zaire-DRC [Congo]. ... [The letter signees are] apologists for Kagame Power, who now and in years past have served as intellectual enforcers of an RPF and U.S.-U.K.-Canadian party line."[528]

As Deputy Executive Director of UNICEF in the late 1990s Lewis was appointed to a Panel of Eminent Personalities to Investigate the 1994 Genocide in Rwanda and the Surrounding Events. Reportedly instigated by US Secretary of State Madeleine Albright and partly funded by Canada, the Organization of African Unity's 2000 report, "The Preventable Genocide", was largely written by Lewis recruit Gerald Caplan.[529]

While paying lip service to the complex interplay of ethnic, class and regional politics, as well as international pressures, that spurred the Rwandan Genocide, the 300-page report is premised on the unsubstantiated claim there was a high level plan by the Hutu government to kill all Tutsi.[530] It ignores the overwhelming logic and evidence pointing to the RPF as the most likely culprit in shooting down the plane carrying Rwandan Hutu President Juvénal Habyarimana and much of the army high command.[531] This event sparked the mass killings of spring 1994.

The report also rationalizes Rwanda's repeated invasions of the Congo, including a 1,500 km march to topple the Mobutu regime in Kinshasa and subsequent re-invasion after the government it installed expelled Rwandan troops. That led to millions of deaths during an eight-country war between 1998 and 2003.

In a Democracy Now interview concerning the 2000 Eminent Personalities report Lewis mentioned "evidence of major human rights violations on the part of the present [Kagame] government of Rwanda, particularly post-genocide in the Kivus and in what is now the Democratic Republic of the Congo." But, he immediately justified the slaughter, which surpassed Rwanda's 1994 casualty toll. "Now, let me say that the [Eminent Personalities] panel understands that until Rwanda's borders are secure, there will always be these depredations. And another terrible failure of the international community was the failure to disarm the refugee camps in the then-Zaire, because it was an invitation to the *génocidaires* to continue to attack Rwanda from the base within the now-Congo. So we know that has to be resolved. That's still what's plaguing the whole Great Lakes region."[532]

An alternative explanation of "what's plaguing the whole Great Lakes region" is US/UK/Canada backed Ugandan/RPF belligerence, which began with their invasion of Rwanda in 1990 and continued with their 1996, 1998 and subsequent invasions of the Congo. "An unprecedented 600-page investigation by the UN high commissioner for human rights", reported a 2010 *Guardian* story, found Rwanda responsible for "crimes against humanity, war crimes, or even genocide" in the Congo.[533]

Fifteen years after the mass killing in Rwanda in 1994 Lewis was still repeating Kagame's rationale for unleashing mayhem in the Congo. In 2009 he told a Washington D.C. audience that "just yesterday morning up to two thousand Rwandan troops crossed into the Eastern Region of the Congo to hunt down, it is said, the Hutu *génocidaires*."[534]

A year earlier Lewis blamed Rwandan Hutu militias for the violence in Eastern Congo. "What's happening in eastern Congo is the continuation of the genocide in Rwanda ... The Hutu militias that sought refuge in Congo in 1994, attracted by its wealth, are perpetrating rape, mutilation, cannibalism with impunity from world opinion."[535]

If, according to Lewis, the South African government "can never achieve redemption" for its AIDS policies in the mid-2000s the same must be said of his ideological support for Kagame whose repeated invasions of the Congo have left millions dead.

Contrasting the 'left' reputation of Lewis in international affairs with his contentious history inside the domestic left reveals a great deal about the state of foreign policy discussion. As head of the Ontario NDP, Lewis purged the Waffle (or Movement for an Independent Socialist Canada) from the provincial party in 1972. At the time many leftists criticized his role in expelling the Waffle from the party and some activists remain critical of Lewis for doing so to this day. In an article titled "On the 40th anniversary of the expulsion of the Waffle" Michael Laxer eviscerates Lewis for driving activists from the NDP.[536] While his move to expel the Waffle continues to be debated, criticism of Lewis largely dried up as he shifted towards the international scene (as Canada's ambassador to the UN, UNICEF Deputy Executive Director and UN Special Envoy for HIV-AIDS in Africa). Yet, I believe most progressives, if they understood the implication of his positions on Africa, would find more common ground with Lewis' domestic positions. On domestic policy Lewis has at times forthrightly criticized Canada's power structures, broadly supports labour against capital and would largely reject charity as a model of social service delivery/poverty alleviation. But, there's at least some culture of holding politicians/public commentators accountable for their concessions to the dominant order on domestic issues so Lewis has faced some criticism. On Africa the situation is quite different. When it comes to the 'dark continent' any prominent person's charitable endeavour, call for increased "aid" or criticism of a geopolitical competitor is sufficient to win accolades.

In an article titled "Africa in the Canadian media: The Globe and Mail's coverage of Africa from 2003 to 2012" Tokunbo Ojo provides an informative assessment of the paper's coverage of Lewis. Ojo writes, "built into this moralising media gaze is the 'white man's burden' imagery, and the voice of Canadian Stephen Lewis, a campaigner against HIV/AIDS, effectively symbolised this imagery in the coverage. Metaphorically, Lewis was framed as the iconic [19th century liberal missionary] 'David Livingstone' in campaigns against HIV/AIDS in Africa. About 20 per cent of the 109 HIV/AIDS stories published between 2003 and 2008 featured quotes from him or featured him as the subject of the story."[537] (The *Globe and Mail's* Stephanie Nolen won the 2004 National

Newspaper Award for international reporting in recognition of her coverage of Lewis' campaign against HIV/AIDS in Africa.)[538]

I found only one other comment critical of Lewis' role in Africa. In the rather tame book *Canada and Africa in the New Millennium: The Politics of Consistent Inconsistency* Dalhousie professor David R. Black writes, "in so far as Lewis continues to attract and hold the support of those who might otherwise be inclined toward a more radical challenge to their own government, and to the global order it contributes to and benefits from, he can perhaps be seen to alleviate the possibility of such a challenge and in this sense contribute, paradoxically, to the persistence of the very order he is so elegantly critical of."[539]

While I don't share Black's characterization of Lewis' criticisms of the dominant "order", the broader point is correct. Lewis' positions are generally an obstacle to those who believe Canadians have a responsibility to challenge their institutions contribution to African subjugation. They also hinder people's understanding of Canadian policy on the continent.[ii]

***

The above is not simply a criticism of individuals who deliver rousing social democratic speeches, but an effort to expose an obstacle to shifting the foreign policy discussion. If Lewis, McQuaig, Byers, Dorn, the CCPA or Rideau Institute are the alternative voices to the foreign policy status quo we will not achieve a justice-oriented international policy. We need voices that question the foundations of Canada's foreign

---

ii *For anyone who believes I've been unfair to Lewis I suggest reading his* Race Against Time *and my* Canada in Africa: 300 Years of Aid and Exploitation.

policy, rather than accepting the existing political and economic world order as inevitable. We need voices that cut through the propaganda and mythology, telling the truth about what has been done in our name.

Just as fledgling hockey players must understand their weaknesses in skating, passing and shooting to improve, so too must the Canadian Left understand our foreign policy deficiencies if we are to become effective players in international solidarity.

Ties that Bind and Blind

THE FIRST THREE CHAPTERS of this book have been about positions taken by "left" organizations and individuals that have failed the Golden Rule test, harmed ordinary people around the world or misconstrued Canada's bad behaviour. In order to build a just foreign policy we must ask why so much of the left would accept — even promote — policies that do harm to ordinary people across the planet.

Part of the problem is that much of the Canadian left supports a capitalist economic system built on exploitation, which leads to accepting foreign policies that beggar thy neighbour. But, at least some of the individuals and organizations discussed above support change, or an alternative economic system. So, why have they taken anti-human international positions? What has tied them to the existing foreign policy order and blinded them to the harm done to ordinary people around the world?

TIES THAT BIND

As the only substantial left-wing institution required to take foreign policy positions as part of its parliamentary mandate, the federal NDP's position is highly influential. Part of the explanation for its failure to apply the same standards on foreign policy as domestic affairs is immediate self-interest.

Ties between the NDP leadership and foreign affairs establishment partly explain the dearth of opposition from Canada's social democratic opposition. Prominent early CCF backers Frank Scott, Escott Reid and Frank Underhill were members of the influential Canadian Institute for International Affairs, which was close to External Affairs and funded by leading Canadian capitalists and the US-based Rockefeller, Carnegie and Ford foundations (see *A Propaganda System*).[540] Underhill and Reid contributed to writing the Regina Manifesto.[541]

A number of party officials have worked in External Affairs or been part of the military. The party's foreign critic when this book went to print, Hélène Laverdière, held a number of Foreign Affairs positions over a decade and a half, even winning the Foreign Minister's Award for her contribution to Canadian foreign policy.[542] "Before I was elected in 2011," she wrote in the *Ottawa Citizen*, "I was a diplomat for 15 years, and I saw how Canada made a difference by lending its political capital and its good name to causes that struggled to get a hearing."[543] Laverdière was chummy with Stephen Harper's foreign minister. John Baird said, "I'm getting to know Hélène Laverdière and I'm off to a good start with her" and when Baird retired CBC reported that she was "among the first to line up in the House on Tuesday to hug the departing minister."[544]

Canadian ambassador to Ukraine between 2008 and 2011, G. Daniel Caron ran for the party in Québec City in 2015. An NDP spokesperson told *La Presse* Caron would "consolidate a team already very experienced in foreign affairs to advise [party head] Thomas Mulcair."[545]

Leader of the Alberta CCF and failed federal candidate in 1945, Chester Ronning later held diplomatic postings in China, Norway, India and at the UN.[546] In between heading the Alberta CCF and running federally, Ronning joined the Royal Canadian Air Force.[547]

A veteran, Doug Fisher was thrice elected CCF/NDP MP and was the party's deputy leader while retired Army General Leonard Johnson ran for the NDP in 1988.[548] Son of a general and grandson of the 'father of Canada's army', prominent military historian Desmond Morton was an advisor to Tommy Douglas in the mid-1960s.[549] The Royal Military College graduate and captain in the army was also assistant secretary of the Ontario NDP and helped David and Stephen Lewis counter the Waffle.[550]

In *The Blaikie Report: An Insider's Look at Faith and Politics* long time NDP external and defence critic Bill Blaikie details his militarist background. As a Scout growing up Blaikie received piping lessons from a pipe major who played during the World War II raid at Dieppe.[551] Blaikie's father was in the Navy during WWII and was active in the Royal Canadian Legion.[552] A militarist outlook remained with Blaikie throughout his political career. In 1995 Bill and his dad traveled to Victoria to christen HMCS Winnipeg and he passed a private members bill to award medals to those who participated in the Allied raid on Dieppe.[553]

Blaikie's biography shines light on the intersection between MPs' backgrounds and their international outlook. It also reveals how Parliament Hill draws politicians into the foreign policy establishment. With a foreword from former Liberal foreign minister Lloyd Axworthy and a blurb from former Conservative foreign minister Joe Clark, *The Blaikie Report* describes his travels to Namibia with Clark and visiting Russia with the governor general.[554] He writes, "thanks to Tory defence minister Gerry Merrithew, I was privileged to play the lament at the Canadian Cemetery in Dieppe when I represented the NDP on the 1992 pilgrimage to mark the

75th anniversary of the battle of Vimy Ridge and the 50th anniversary of the Dieppe raid."[555]

Blaikie was active in the NATO Parliamentary Association for a couple of decades.[556] A presentation at a NATO meeting convinced him to support the organization's bombing of the former Yugoslavia. "I myself", he writes, "had been affected by the presentation at a 1998 NATO parliamentary meeting in Barcelona of an Albanian woman from Kosovo, who tearfully pleaded for an intervention to stop the anticipated wholesale slaughter of Kosovar Albanians."[557]

NDP MPs are drawn into the military's orbit in a variety of ways. The social democratic party's members in the House joined their colleagues in the Canadian Forces Parliamentary Program, which the *Globe and Mail* labeled a "valuable public-relations tool."[558] Set up by DND's Director of External Communications and Public Relations in 2000, the Parliamentary Program embedded MPs in military training (Army in Action or Experience the Navy). According to the Canadian Parliamentary Review, the MPs "learn how the equipment works, they train with the troops, and they deploy with their units on operations. Parliamentarians are integrated into the unit by wearing the same uniform, living on bases, eating in messes, using CF facilities and equipment."[559] As part of the program, the military even flew MPs to the Persian Gulf to join a naval vessel on patrol.[560] Military officials regularly brief Members of Parliament. Additionally, the slew of "arms-length" military organizations/think tanks discussed in *A Propaganda System* speak at defence and international affairs committees.

NDP MPs are absorbed into the foreign policy establishment as well as the military. At the start of 2017 B.C.

MP Wayne Stetski participated in a House of Commons Standing Committee on Foreign Affairs and International Development mission to Ukraine, Latvia, Poland and Kazakhstan while at the end of the year Tom Mulcair went on a committee mission to Beijing, Hong Kong, Hanoi and Jakarta.[561] In 2014 NDP foreign critic Paul Dewar joined foreign minister John Baird and Liberal MP Marc Garneau on a visit to Iraq while NDP leader Tom Mulcair joined the government's official delegation to Nelson Mandela's funeral in 2013.[562] In 1945 then CCF leader M.J. Coldwell was part of Canada's delegation to the founding conference of the UN in San Francisco.[563]

Representing Canada internationally often reinforces nationalist sentiment (see below). Blaikie writes, "it often fell to me to speak up on various matters. Ironically, at a variety of international parliamentary gatherings I found that it was the New Democrat who had to take to the microphone to defend or explain the Canadian position, sometimes when I didn't necessarily agree with it."[564] In Ottawa NDP MPs attend events and parties put on by diplomats. Blaikie describes "enjoying many fine evenings" at the home of the British High Commissioner.[565] Diplomats from wealthier countries, of course, have greater capacity to organize events promoting their country's international positions.

Sometimes connected to diplomatic postings in the capital, country-specific bodies also influence NDP MPs. They have joined the Canada-Israel Parliamentary Group, Canada-Japan Inter-Parliamentary Group, Canada-US Inter-Parliamentary Association and others. The parliamentary association system reflects inequities in global power and wealth with nearly half the 17 official associations focused on Europe.[566]

NDP MPs regularly travel on international trips organized by third parties. NDP MPs went on 22 all-expense paid trips in 2013.[567] Israel and Taiwan (which Canada does not officially recognize) have long been the principal destinations. A 2015 calculation found that 20 NDP MPs, including then leader Tom Mulcair, had been to Israel with a Zionist lobby organization.[568]

Alongside country-focused efforts, corporations with international interests lobby MPs. Some NDP MPs succumbed to industry pressure concerning An Act Respecting Corporate Accountability for the Activities of Mining, Oil or Gas Corporations in Developing Countries (Bill C300), which would have restricted public support for firms found responsible for significant abuses abroad. Registered lobbyists representing Barrick Gold, Vale Canada, IAMGOLD and the Prospectors and Developers Association of Canada launched a ferocious campaign to derail Liberal MP John McKay's private members bill.[569] On Oct. 27, 2010, the House voted 140 to 134 against Bill C300. The voting ran along party lines with almost every Conservative MP voting against it and the opposition parties voting in favour. But, the bill failed because four NDP MPs, six Bloc members and 13 Liberal MPs failed to show up for the vote (one independent opposed the bill and another abstained).[570]

Sometimes labour unions pressure the NDP to back internationally oriented sectors of corporate Canada. During the French language election debate in 2015 Tom Mulcair criticized the government for selling $15 billion worth of light armoured vehicles to Saudi Arabia. In response the union representing 500 workers at the General Dynamics Land Systems plant in London, Ontario, where the vehicles are manufactured, pressured the party. "We have contacted the NDP about this issue," said Fergo Berto, Unifor director in London.[571] Mulcair failed to raise the issue during two subsequent debates and London-Fanshawe NDP MP, Irene Mathyssen, called it "a signed contract and we [an NDP government] will honour that contract."[572]

Labour unions' relative indifference to challenging foreign policy is another explanation for the NDP's policy on the subject. An important force within the NDP, unions rarely take on the foreign policy establishment. In fact, as outlined above, they sometimes endorse unjust international policies. When unions engage in international affairs, it's usually through aid initiatives, relatively apolitical international labour confederations or by helping set up unions in the Global South, which can be done in a solidaristic or paternalist manner.

Links to aid agencies, foreign affairs and government-backed institutes/NGOs shape unions' international policies and statements. But, these ties also reflect unions' nationalism and ties to a political party that rarely challenges the substance of international policy.

Unfortunately, union leaders face limited pressure from members to take more strident international positions. Nor does the leadership generally see it as serving their personal or institutional interests to do so.

On many domestic issues organized labour represents a countervailing force to the corporate agenda or state policies. While dwarfed by corporate Canada, unions have significant capacities. They generate hundreds of millions of dollars in annual dues and have thousands of full-time employees. Unions fund and participate in a wide range of socially progressive initiatives such as the Canadian Health Coalition,

Canadian Council for Refugees and Canadian Centre for Policy Alternatives. But, unions rarely extend their broader (class) vision of society to international affairs. As such, the state/corporate nexus operates largely unchallenged in the Global South.

Peace and international solidarity groups have but a fraction of the resources available to organized labour. The cost of a single Unifor National Representative probably exceeds the Canadian Peace Alliance, Canadian Peace Congress and Coalition to Oppose the Arms Trade's combined annual budgets! (Unifor has over 100 national representatives and hundreds of other staff.) At its height after the 2003 invasion of Iraq the Canadian Peace Alliance had the funds to hire one employee on a meagre salary. Other groups involved in challenging elements of Canadian foreign policy don't have much more. Mining Watch has five staff while Central America focused Rights Action has one. Independent Jewish Voices has two employees while Canadians for Justice and Peace in the Middle East has another two.

The vast majority of Haiti, Palestine, peace, demilitarization and mining injustice activism is volunteer work. Few of those engaged in it are compensated financially. Nor are there future employment prospects, which exist with labour and green activism as well as some feminist, anti-racist and other types of social justice campaigning. (Some workers, for instance, remain active in their union partly in the hopes of eventually obtaining a paid position.)

While someone who volunteers with their union can expect to attend an all-expenses-paid (including lost work hours) out-of-town conference at some point, it is often difficult for those challenging Canadian foreign policy to find funds for basic materials. To give an extreme example, when Haiti Action Montréal helped defeat foreign minister Pierre Pettigrew we barely had money to print black and white posters. (During the 2006 federal election a small group of us put up 2,000 posters featuring Pettigrew's image with the words "WANTED FOR CRIMES AGAINST HUMANITY IN HAITI" and handed out over 12,000 flyers in his riding.) After barrelling through a small printing budget at Concordia's Public Interest Research Group I would go to Bureau en Gros (Staples) and print 300+ poster or leaflet pages and present the clerk with a dozen of them. Unbeknownst to Bureau en Gros, they subsidized the defeat of the foreign minister!

Organized labour's failure to forthrightly challenge foreign policy decisions partially explains why left-wing think tanks mostly ignore international affairs or present highly circumscribed opposition. Influencing their priorities, the CCPA and Broadbent Institute have both received substantial funding from labour.

Many left-wing intellectuals take their cues from think tanks and unions. Some authors garner a significant share of their income from speaking to left institutions, mostly labour unions, able to pay thousands of dollars for speeches. But, these organizations rarely seek out presentations critical of Canadian foreign policy.

It's not simply a question of subject matter. Those paid to speak at major labour, think tank or academic events are invited largely based on their corporate media profile. Since few (or no) radical critics of Canadian foreign policy have a corporate media profile none even crosses these institutions' radar. This is an indirect manifestation of the dominant media's power over the foreign policy discussion.

Leftist intellectuals mythologize Canadian foreign policy for a number of other reasons. Laziness is a simple, though not unimportant, reason why left intellectuals concede to the establishment outlook. Buried amidst a mass of state and corporate generated apologetics, critical information about Canada's role in the world takes more effort to uncover. And the extra work is often bad for one's career.

A thorough investigation uncovers information tough to square with the narrow spectrum of opinion permitted in the dominant media. It's nearly impossible to survive if you say Canadian foreign policy has always been self-serving/elite-driven or that no government has come close to reflecting their self-professed ideals on the international stage. Almost everyone with a substantial platform to comment sees no problem with Canadian power, finding it expedient to assume/imply Canada's international aims are noble.

The accumulation of ties and pressures outlined here, together with the ideological factors outlined below, combine to produce a powerful barrier to understanding what largely drives Canadian foreign policy: support for corporate interests and the US-led order. Only through building grassroots movements can we create a counterweight to the forces that bind "left leaders" to the current system.

CANADIAN NATIONALISM

Nationalism is a powerful ideological force. An "our team" attitude permeates foreign policy discussions and blinds otherwise reasonable people to the historical harm that nationalism has wrought upon the world.

As outlined in *A Propaganda System*, Ottawa has created countless nationalist ideological institutions. During World

War I Ottawa helped establish the Canadian Press to increase pro-war coverage and strengthen national identity. Two decades later CBC and the National Film Board were set up largely to strengthen nationalist sentiment.

The Canadian War Museum is another prominent ode to nationalist mythology. One of innumerable state-funded monuments to Canadians who have died in war, the $136 million museum is designed for light to shine on the headstone of the Unknown Soldier at 11 a.m. on Remembrance Day.[573] In *Imagined Communities* Benedict Anderson calls "tombs of Unknown Soldiers ... saturated with ghostly national imaginings."[574]

Influenced by these and many other nationalist ideological institutions, the Canadian left has promoted liberal nationalist mythology. Many leftists claim peacekeeping is an important part of the Canadian identity. Calling it a "stereotypical, iconic Canadianism", Michael Byers told *Adbusters* in 2007 that it "meant something to Canadian identity that our men and women went between opposing forces in blue helmets to try to stabilize a situation and ensure that ceasefires could continue."[575] For his part, Rideau Institute advisor Walter Dorn has called "the image of the peacekeeper ... key to the Canadian identity" and dubbed peacekeeping "a celebrated part of what Canada is as a nation and even who Canadians are as a people."[576]

Leftists who unthinkingly promote "peacekeeping" align, consciously or not, with a powerful nationalist ideological apparatus. In *Creating Canada's Peacekeeping Past* Colin McCullough writes, "those who lived in Canada from 1956 to 1997 were exposed to a great volume of political speeches, news reports, and editorial cartoons about peacekeeping. Even if they were not attuned to Canada's foreign policies through these channels, they would have also likely learned about peacekeeping in their high school history textbooks, perhaps watched some of the fourteen NFB films that had peacekeeping as either their primary focus or a major component, visited a monument to peacekeeping located somewhere in the country, viewed one of the three Heritage Minutes about peacekeeping, or purchased something with either the one-dollar coin, the loonie, or the ten-dollar bill, both of which have been emblazoned with a peacekeeper. There have also been songs by Canadian cultural icon 'Stompin' Tom Connors, public buildings and parklands named for peacekeeping and its key figures, a mention in the Molson Canadian 'Joe Canada' beer advertisement, dramatic plays, and national days of recognition for peacekeeping. The combined effect of all these was a saturation of Canadian life with peacekeeping."[577]

Peacekeeping is a central element of liberal nationalist ideology. In *Warrior Nation* Ian McKay and Jamie Swift write, "lacking many of the ingredients to forge a strongly imagined community within Canada — a common language, shared myths and symbols testifying to the necessity and goodness of 'the nation,' and a tightly integrated economy — the Ottawa men developed a nationalist myth-symbol complex about an imagined community outside Canada in which Canadians played an indispensable, indeed world-reshaping role, placing them at the heart of the great Crusade for peace and democracy."[578]

A claim to righteousness in international affairs is fundamental to Canadian exceptionalism, the idea that this country is morally superior to other nations. Co-founder of the 1970 Committee for an Independent Canada, prominent

Liberal journalist Peter C. Newman explained, "one of Canada's sustaining myths is that we are a peaceable kingdom, and that even when our armed forces are dispatched on gruesome missions abroad, they will be recognized as spreading goodwill."[579]

A major part of the Canadian left has long been highly nationalistic. The zenith of left nationalist activism was probably the Waffle, which promoted the manifesto for "an independent socialist Canada". Between 1969 and its expulsion from the NDP in 1972, the Waffle received the backing of four in ten party members.[580]

The manifesto described the "reduction of Canada to a colony of the United States. ... The most urgent issue for Canadians is the very survival of Canada. The major threat to Canadian survival today is American control of the Canadian economy. The major issue of our times is not national unity but national survival, and the fundamental threat is external, not internal."[581]

The Waffle was influential among the student, feminist and antiwar New Left of the late 1960s. But, other left groups have expressed a similar perspective. Through the 1980s and 90s the Council of Canadians was highly nationalistic. It was "instrumental in founding" the Pro-Canada Network and its late 1980s fight against the US Free Trade Agreement took a nationalist tone.[582]

For a long time the Communist Party advocated nationalist slogans. In the 1930s the Communist International (Comintern) criticized the slogan "Canadian independence", directing the Communist Party of Canada to denounce "Canadian imperialism" and the capitalist class as the main enemy of Canadian workers.[583] But, after World War II the party's position shifted. "References to 'Canadian imperialism' seldom appeared after 1946", notes a critical history of the party published in 1974, "From 1948 on the Communists insisted with increasing shrillness that the US had taken over Canada."[584] In 1953 the Communist Party took up the slogan "Put Canada First! Stop the Sell-Out of Canada to the USA" while in 1964 they called for "an anti-imperialist struggle that would unite a broad stratum of Canadian society, including non-comprador elements of the capitalist class, against US imperialism."[585]

While this language may be removed from today's political discourse, left nationalist thinking has long dominated Canadian political economy. In *Escape from the Staple Trap: Canadian Political Economy after Left Nationalism* Paul Kellogg labels the notion that Canada is "the richest dependent developed industrialized country ... nearly hegemonic" on the Canadian Left.[586] The idea, explains Greg Albo, is that Canada is "a 'rich dependency', skewed in its industrial development by a weak manufacturing base and massive staples exports to the US market."[587] As such, left nationalists generally believe it's necessary to develop "an industrial strategy backed by an alliance between national capitalists and Canadian workers" rather than simply promote socialist measures to democratize the economy.[588]

Left nationalism is less influential among those politicized during the turn of the 21st century anti-corporate globalization movement or Indigenous and environmental struggles. But, left nationalism retains adherents. Active in the Pro-Canada Network of the 1980s, long time Rabble.ca publisher and columnist Duncan Cameron tweeted in 2016 the "Leap [Manifesto] could learn from Waffle 2/3 of oil sands ownership and profits are foreign."[589] Leaving aside the exaggerated percentage of foreign ownership, wherever the profits end up tar sands' carbon emissions threaten humanity.[590]

A half-century earlier Cameron was drawn to left nationalist thinking by Liberal finance minister Walter Gordon.[591] This prominent businessperson was educated at the Royal Military College and Upper Canada College where, notes Stephen Azzi in *Walter Gordon and the Rise of Canadian Nationalism*, he "was exposed to the ideas of Canadian imperialists who believed that a strong tie with Britain would prevent the United States from absorbing Canada."[592] Born "into a world of privilege, into a family that was a member of Canada's economic elite", Gordon also influenced another prominent left nationalist.[593] A *This Magazine* columnist, Straight Goods board member and CCPA research associate, Mel Watkins led the 1968 Gordon-promoted Task Force on Foreign Ownership and the Structure of Canadian Investment.[594]

The Progressive Economics Forum promoted Watkins' staple trap theory. In 2013 it ran an 18-part series "marking the 50th Anniversary of the publication of Mel Watkins' classic article, 'A Staple Theory of Economic Growth.'" Simultaneously, Progressive Economics Forum stalwart Jim Stanford edited a 136-page CCPA report titled "The Staple Theory @ 50."

Looking at the world through a left nationalist lens generally leads individuals to ignore, or downplay, the destruction wrought by Canadian corporations abroad and Canada's power on the international stage. Kellogg writes, "those who apply the simple 'staple trap' analogy to Canada almost always fail to interrogate the analogy from the standpoint of Canada's hugely privileged place in the world economy — a world economy that is extremely hierarchical."[595]

Canada is a G-7 nation with among the highest GDP per capita.[596] In their summer 2017 ranking of the most important capitals of finance the Global Financial Centres Index had Toronto in seventh, Montreal in 12th and Vancouver in 17th place.[597] In 2014 Canadians had $830 billion invested abroad (though the corporate oligarchy re-routing money through tax havens inflates this figure).[598] With a net export of $100 billion, Bill Burgess notes, "what most characterizes Canada is not inward foreign investment but outward foreign investment."[599]

Canadian companies are global players in various fields. The world's largest privately held security company, GardaWorld had 50,000 employees operating across the globe while another Montréal-based firm, SNC Lavalin, is among the largest engineering companies with projects in half the countries of the world.[600] Based in the same city, Bombardier and CAE are among the world's largest aerospace and flight simulation firms. With operations across the globe, Canadian banks are major international players. The five major Canadian banks are all ranked among the world's top 63.[601]

The mining sector provides the starkest example of Canadian capital's international prominence. With 0.5% of the world's population, more than half of the world's mining companies are based in Canada or listed on Canadian stock exchanges.[602] Present in most countries, Canadian corporations operate thousands of mineral projects abroad.

Focused on Canadian subservience to US corporate power, left nationalists generally ignore Canadian power and abuses abroad. In *Canada: A New Tax Haven: How the Country That Shaped Caribbean Tax Havens is Becoming One Itself* Alain Deneault criticizes left academics for ignoring Canada's destructive influence in the region, which includes dominating its banking sector and multiple military interventions.[603] At the end of a book detailing the work of Canadian politicians, businessmen and Bank of Canada officials in developing taxation and banking policies in a number of Caribbean financial havens, Deneault notes: "How is it that Canadian intellectuals with a background in political economy and the critical tradition have not noticed the troubling nature of Canadian influence in the Caribbean as exerted by MPs, banks, development agencies and experts of all shades and stripes? Even when they have information that ought to lead them in this direction, Canada's 'critical' intellectuals do not feel that this is their responsibility ... The problem is not that they are blind to the involvement of foreign states in Caribbean development; rather, they suffer from a specific form of blindness to Canada's agency. Canada's political culture is the issue here, including, first and foremost, the political culture of its left-wing academics. A critique of their own state seems to be beyond their capacity."[604]

Deneault highlights Kari Polanyi Levitt, author of *Silent Surrender: The Multinational Corporation in Canada* and a prominent member of the Waffle. An economics professor in Jamaica and Trinidad for many years, Levitt ignores Canada's pernicious role there. Deneault writes: "While it is impossible for her not to see the domination of Canadian financial institutions such as Scotia Bank or the Royal Bank of Canada in cities in which she spends time such as Kingston or Port of Spain, Levitt manages to make them arbitrarily into symbols of — Canadian commitment to the development of the Caribbean! The same denial comes into play when she looks at the role of Alcan in Jamaica. Of course, nothing in the behaviour of this multinational sets it apart from its

American counterparts, but Levitt in 2012 stubbornly persists in viewing it as a company that, had it not been bought by Rio Tinto, would have been in the vanguard of a possible Canadian response to American domination in the countries of the South."[605]

(In fact, Alcan's operations in Jamaica were highly controversial. When "a battalion of 850 Canadian troops landed in the mountainous Jamaican interior to conduct a tropical training exercise" in the early 1970s, *Abeng*, a leftist Jamaican paper, cried foul.[606] The paper's editors claimed Ottawa was preparing to intervene to protect the Montréal-based company's bauxite facilities in the event of civil unrest and/or in case a socialist government took office. While numerous books dealing with Canadian-Caribbean relations scoff at *Abeng*'s accusations, the archives confirm the paper's suspicions. "Subsequent [to 1979] planning for intervention seems to bear out the Abeng accusations," notes right wing military historian Sean Maloney. Code-named, NIMROD CAPPER, "the objective of the operation revolved around securing and protecting the Alcan facilities from mob unrest and outright seizure or sabotage."[607] Later, Canadian military planning resumed from where NIMROD CAPPER began with an exercise titled "Southern Renewal" beginning in 1988. Maloney explains: "In this case a company from two RCR [Royal Canadian Reserves] was covertly inserted to 'rescue' Canadian industrial personnel with knowledge of bauxite deposits seized by Jamaican rebels and held hostage."[608])

Deneault continues in his criticism of Levitt: "If she had pursued her work in a more critical frame of mind, she would have seen the very un-tourist-like demeanour of the Canadian state, its agencies, and the private institutions with which it is associated in the Caribbean. … She would have appreciated to what extent Canada, far from embodying some kind of potential protection against the IMF and the World Bank in the region, is in fact their enthusiastic agent. She might even have seen that Canadian multinationals participate in the domination of the Caribbean economy."[609]

Sometimes left nationalists make their desire for Canadian capital to expand its international tentacles explicit. In the 2008 book *Mission of Folly: Why Canada Should Bring its Troops Home From Afghanistan* the late Waffle leader James Laxer complains that corporate Canada is not more expansionist. "One might imagine that Canadian business would want real power for itself", he writes. "[Instead] Canadian business moguls have usually been full of bluster but highly derivative in their ambitions, wanting little more for themselves than acceptance from their British and U.S. counterparts. The consequence is that they have been quite prepared to concede the genuine power that could have been theirs in return for a comfortable seat in someone else's vehicle."[610]

***

George Grant's 1965 book *Lament for a Nation* greatly influenced left nationalism. James Laxer called it "the most important book I ever read in my life. He was a crazy old philosopher of religion at McMaster and he woke up half our generation."[611] Lament remains influential. The book is in its fourth edition, including a 40th anniversary release, and, in a play on its title, Michael Byers called his 2007 book *Intent for a Nation*.

Nothing in Grant's book is critical of Canadian foreign policy. Rather, the book praises prime ministers Sir John A. Macdonald and Robert Borden as "great politicians who believed in this connection" to the British Empire.[612] Grant describes "the wisdom of Sir John A. Macdonald, who saw plainly more than 100 years ago that the only threat to nationalism was from the South, not from across the sea."[613] In fact, Macdonald was a raving racist who deliberately starved Indigenous people on the Canadian Prairies as part of an effort to extend British power westward.[614] For his part, Borden introduced conscription to send young men to World War I's trenches. Lament lauds British imperialism. Grant bemoans "the collapse of British power and moral force", calling it "the chief centre from which the progressive civilization spread around the world."[615]

Grant was from a prominent Anglophile family who descended from United Empire Loyalists. Grandfather George Munro Grant was long time principle of Queen's University and another grandparent, George Parkin, led Upper Canada College and the Imperial Federation Movement.[616] (In 1891 George Munro Grant explained, "the work that the British Empire has in hand is far grander than the comparatively parochial duties with which the [United] States are content to deal. ... already our sons are taking their part in introducing civilization into Africa under the aegis of the flag, and in preserving the Pax Britannica among the teeming millions of India and Southeastern Asia.") His uncle Vincent Massey was an owner of the Massey Ferguson company and the first Canadian-born governor general.[617] In the introduction to the 40th edition of Lament Andrew Potter points out that the 'Canada as victim of imperialism' storyline underpinning Grant's book wouldn't have made sense to his forefathers. "Grant's grandfathers would [not] have found [this portrayal], remotely comprehensible, since they were fond of Empire and more apt to see themselves as the colonizers, not the colonized."[618]

Grant's grandfathers were correct. At first Canada was an arm of the British Empire, conquering the northern part of the Western hemisphere by dispossessing First Nations. After 1867 Ottawa regularly argued it "was looking after British imperial interests in North America and that the country's material growth reinforced the British Empire," writes Norman Penlington in *Canada and Imperialism: 1896–1899*. "The construction of the Canadian Pacific Railway was especially justified as a British military route to the East."[619] It greatly increased the speed in which British troops stationed in the Atlantic could be deployed to the Pacific.[620] Canada helped connect Britain to the Far East in a number of ways. In 1887 a graving dock capable of holding the largest British war ships in the Pacific was opened in Esquimalt, British Columbia. Sandford Fleming, who represented Canada at the 1887 Colonial Conference in London, wanted the Dominions and Britain to build a state-owned Pacific Ocean cable from British Columbia to East Asia and to secure a mid-Pacific Island as a way station. "He [Fleming] hired a retired naval officer living in Ontario and sent him to Hawaii to raise the Union Jack over nearby Necker Island," explains Barry Gough in *Britain, Canada and the North Pacific: Maritime Enterprise and Dominion, 1778–1914*.[621] Hawaii nearly became Canadian property as part of this endeavour.

A number of Canadian military institutions were established in large part to expand the British Empire's military capacity. Opened in 1876, the Royal Military College was largely designed to train soldiers to fight on behalf of British colonialism. In 1897 Sir Adolph Caron, an MP and former minister of militia and defence, explained the Kingston, Ontario, based institution's usefulness for Canada: "there was a time, I remember, when Canada did not stand in the proud position which she occupies today in Great Britain. Our present position is due to the fact that our Royal Military College Cadets were able to take their places side by side with the men who had been trained in the [British] military service … Great Britain in her Canadian subject found men who were prepared to take their share in fighting her battles and who were able to fight these battles side by side with the best men that England could send to the front."[622]

Usually trained at the RMC, Canadians helped conquer Kenya, Nigeria and Ghana.[623] Four hundred Canadians traveled halfway across the world to beat back anti-colonial resistance in the Sudan in 1885 while a decade and a half later thousands more fought to advance British imperial interests in the southern part of the continent.[624] This is the foreign policy reality at the root of Canadian nationalism.

***

A proponent of an early version of the staple theory in Canadian political economy, famed historian Harold Innis remarked that Canada had gone "from colony to nation to colony."[625] Rather than looking at Canadian history through the "colony to nation to colony" lens, a more apt framework to understand this country's place in the world is that the Canadian elite has had a privileged position with the two great powers over the past two centuries. Or, Canada progressed from an appendage of the Imperial Centre to appendage of the Imperial Centre.

Between 1867 and 1931 Canadian foreign policy was officially determined by London. But, describing this as a "colonial" relationship ignores the Canadian elite's access to British capital, universities, armaments, etc., as well as Canada's role in extending British power westward and, to a lesser extent, in Africa, Asia and the Caribbean.

While technically accurate, employing the term "colony" to describe both Canada and Kenya makes little sense. British, French and other settlers in Canada were not dispossessed of their land, but rather dispossessed the First Nations of theirs. Additionally, they faced no repression comparable to that experienced by the Maasai or Kikuyu. Calling Canada a "colony" is akin to describing the European settlers in Kenya as "colonized". While tensions existed between the whites in Kenya and the Colonial Office in London, the settlers also had privileged access to British arms, technology and capital.

The second part of Innis' "colony to nation to colony" parable is also misleading. Has Canada been colonized by Washington in a similar way to Haiti? Among innumerable examples of domination, on December 17, 1914, US Marines marched to Haiti's treasury and took the nation's entire gold reserve — valued at $12 million US— and between 1915 and 1934 Washington formally occupied Haiti (they retained control of the country's finances until 1947).[626]

Facilitated by racial, linguistic and cultural affinity, Canada has long had privileged access to the US business and political elite. Long-time speaker of the House of Representatives and Democratic Party nominee for President in 1912, Champ Clark, highlighted Canada's prized place within US ruling circles. "They are people of our blood", Champ expounded. "They speak our language. Their institutions are much like ours. They are trained in the difficult art of self-government."[627]

During the 1898-1902 occupation of Cuba the Royal Bank was the preferred banker of US officials.[628] (National US banks were forbidden from establishing foreign branches until 1914.[629]) Canadian capitalists worked with their US counterparts in Central America as well. In the early 1900s Canadian Pacific Railway President Sir William Van Horne helped the Boston-based United Fruit Company, infamous for its later role in overthrowing elected Guatemalan president Jacobo Arbenz, build the railway required to export bananas from the country.[630] In the political realm there were also extensive ties. For instance, Canada's longest serving prime minister, Mackenzie King, worked for the Rockefeller family while the mother of long-time US Secretary of State Dean Acheson was from a wealthy Canadian family.[631]

Today, the ties are closer than ever. In a post US election exposé titled "A look inside Palm Beach, where wealthy Canadians are one degree of separation from Donald Trump" the *Globe and Mail* detailed a slew of prominent Canadians (Brian Mulroney, Charles Bronfman, George Cohon, Gerry Schwartz and Heather Reisman, Paul Desmarais' family, etc.) with winter homes near the US president's exclusive property.[632] A number of these individuals, the Globe reported, could get "Trump's ear" if he turned on Canada.

While there is a power imbalance between the two countries and differing interests at times, the Canadian elite sees the world and profits from it in a similar way to their US counterparts. The idea of Canada as a colony to be overcome through a left nationalist political program ignores our ruling class's immense power in the world. To 'do no harm' internationally we must understand this, not get sucked into nationalist mythology.

THE CASE OF ROMÉO DALLAIRE

Nationalism is dangerous in powerful states, Canada included. Left nationalists often ignore, or downplay, Canada's power on the international stage and the destruction wrought by Canadian corporations abroad. They also promote the myth of a benevolent Canada, which obscures the corporate and geostrategic interests driving foreign policy.

In an extreme example, the left nationalist prism has contributed to distorting global understanding of an important historical event, which has paved the (ideological) path to enormous suffering in eastern Africa. In their haste to promote Roméo Dallaire as a Canadian saviour, progressives have echoed a highly simplistic account of the Rwandan genocide used to legitimate a brutal dictatorship in Rwanda and its bloodletting in the Congo.

According to the official version of the Rwandan tragedy, ethnic enmity erupted in a pre-planned genocidal rampage by Hutus killing Tutsis that was only stopped by Paul Kagame's Rwandan Patriotic Front (RPF). A noble Canadian general tried to end the bloodletting but a dysfunctional UN refused resources. Washington was caught off guard by the slaughter, but it apologized for failing to intervene and has committed to never again avoid its responsibility to protect. But, this story is a fairy tale, designed to legitimate Kagame, the US, British and Canadian elite's geostrategic ally. In fact, the real story should be this country's role in promoting and protecting a war criminal. (What follows will explain the massive departure from the dominant narrative.)

A *Monthly Review* article I discovered in 2016 highlights left Canadian nationalist ideological contribution to Kagame's crimes in Rwanda and the Congo. The third paragraph of the venerable New York-based Marxist journal's 2003 review of *When Victims Become Killers: Colonialism, Nativism, and the Genocide in Rwanda* and *A People Betrayed: The Role of the West in Rwanda's Genocide* begins: "A Canadian, General Roméo Dallaire, is the hero of the Rwandan tragedy."[633]

Canadian reviewer Hugh Lukin Robinson's main criticism of Ugandan scholar Mahmood Mamdani's *When Victims Become Killers* is that he downplays the importance of the Canadian commander of the UN military force. "[Mamdani's] disinterest in the international betrayal of Rwanda is illustrated by his single reference to General Dallaire, whose name he misspells and whom he refers to as 'the *Belgian* commander in charge of UN forces in Rwanda'. In contrast, Linda Melvern marshals the evidence which amply justifies the title of her book."

But Melvern is a leading advocate of the Kigali-sponsored fairy tale about the 1994 genocide. Drawing on Dallaire's purported "genocide fax," she promotes the 'long planned genocide' narrative. Simultaneously, Melvern ignores (or downplays) the role of Uganda's 1990 invasion, structural adjustment policies and the October 1993 assassination of the first-ever Hutu president in Burundi played in the mass killing of 1994. Melvern also diminishes RPF killings and their responsibility for shooting down the plane carrying Hutu President Juvénal Habyarimana and the Rwandan military high command.[634] This event sparked the genocidal killing of Tutsi and paved the way for the RPF's rise to power.

A prominent British journalist, Melvern spearheaded public criticism of the 2014 BBC 2 documentary *Rwanda's Untold Story*, which questioned the official version of the Rwandan tragedy. An open letter she instigated refers to the

BBC's "genocide denial", "genocide deniers" or "deniers" at least 13 times.[635] In 2017 Kagame personally gave Melvern the Igihango National Order of Friendship medal and labeled her an "archaeologist of the truth" for "producing meticulously researched accounts of the 1994 Genocide against the Tutsi."[636]

A Waffle supporter and founder of the Progressive Economics Forum, Robinson was impressed with Melvern's praise for Canada's military man. "Dallaire had trained and risen through the ranks of an army proud of its tradition of peacekeeping", Robinson quotes from Melvern's writing. "He was a committed internationalist and had first hand experience of UN missions. He was a hard worker. And he was obstinate."[637] But, the "committed internationalist" admits he didn't know where Rwanda was before his appointment to that country.[638] Nor did Dallaire have much experience with the UN. "Dallaire was what military people call a NATO man," explained CBC journalist Carole Off in a biography of the general. "His defence knowledge was predicated almost exclusively on the needs of the NATO alliance."[639]

More significantly, a number of the UN officials involved in Rwanda — the head of UNAMIR troops in Kigali Luc Marchal, intelligence officer Amadou Deme, UN Secretary General Boutros Boutros-Ghali, etc. — have challenged Dallaire's interpretation of events, contradicted his claims or criticized his actions. Gilbert Ngijo, political assistant to the civilian commander of UNAMIR, outlined Dallaire's biased actions: "He let the RPF get arms. He allowed UNAMIR troops to train RPF soldiers. United Nations troops provided the logistics for the RPF. They even fed them."[640]

Dallaire's civilian commander in UNAMIR published a book accusing the Canadian general of bias towards the

Uganda/US/Britain-backed RPF. In his 2005 book *Le Patron de Dallaire Parle: Révélations sur les dérives d'un général de l'ONU au Rwanda* (Dallaire's boss speaks: Revelations about the excesses of a UN General in Rwanda), Jacques-Roger Booh Booh, a former Cameroon foreign minister and overall head of UNAMIR, claims Dallaire had little interest in the violence unleashed by the RPF despite reports of summary executions in areas controlled by them. RPF soldiers were regularly seen in Dallaire's office, with the Canadian commander describing the Rwandan army's position in Kigali. This prompted Booh Booh to wonder if Dallaire "also shared UNAMIR military secrets with the RPF when he invited them to work in his offices."[641] Finally, Booh Booh says Dallaire turned a blind eye to RPF weapons coming across the border from Uganda and he believes the UN forces may have even transported weapons directly to the RPF.[642] Dallaire, Booh Booh concludes, "abandoned his role as head of the military to play a political role. He violated the neutrality principle of UNAMIR by becoming an objective ally of one of the parties in the conflict."[643]

Washington and London's support for the RPF, as well as Kagame's more than two-decade long control of Kigali, explains the dominance of a highly simplistic Rwandan Genocide story. According to Edward Herman and David Peterson in *Enduring Lies: The Rwandan Genocide in the Propaganda System, 20 Year Later*, "[US and British] support, combined with the public's and the media's distance from and unfamiliarity with central African affairs, made the construction and dissemination of false propaganda on Rwanda very easy."[644]

But, a tertiary reason for the strength of the Rwandan fairy tale is it aligns with the nationalist mythology of another G7 state. Left/liberal Canadians have pumped out innumerable articles, books, songs, plays, poems, movies, etc. about our noble general's effort to save Rwandans. Yet the Dallaire saviour story promoted by left/liberals is based on a one-sided account of Rwanda's tragedy.

Famed left nationalist Mel Watkins described the general and son of a military man, whose son and father-in-law are also military men, as a "great Canadian elder."[645] While the hierarchical and authoritarian character of the military is usually associated with the right wing of the political spectrum, left weekly *Toronto Now* dubbed an individual who campaigned for increased military spending a "Canuck hero".[646] Rideau Institute board member Michael Byers put the former general, who opposed calls to withdraw Canadian soldiers from Afghanistan and endorsed the overthrow of Haiti's elected government in 2004, on a small list of Canadians "at the forefront of efforts to protect human beings during times of both peace and war."[647] In an article titled "Does Canada Still Stand for Something?" Vancouver-based *Adbusters* described a man who regularly speaks to Israeli nationalist groups and repeated their claims about the "genocidal intent of the Iranian state", as the "archetypal soldier of conscience … a patriot. A humanist."[648] For her part, former governor general Adrienne Clarkson labeled an individual who backed the 2011 bombing of Libya "one of the finest Canadians alive."[649] In what may be the oddest source of praise, Ceasefire.ca founder Steven Staples lauded Dallaire as "esteemed" — a former general who is a strong proponent of Canada joining US Ballistic Missile Defence (Staples campaigned against BMD).[650] The Canadian Auto Workers, Ontario Public Service Employees' Union and Unifor have given awards or a platform to a man who has repeatedly attended events with and spoken alongside Kagame, who runs a brutal dictatorship.[651]

"Canadianizing" Dallaire's purported humanitarianism in Rwanda is remarkably common. Michael Ignatieff claimed Dallaire's "struggle to contain interethnic war" was because as a member of a "multiethnic, multinational community, Canadians have looked with a particular premonitory horror at what happened in" Rwanda (and Yugoslavia). But, Rwanda is among Africa's most homogenous nations. Basically everyone speaks the same language and practices the same religion and customs. The country's "ethnic" divide is historically a caste-type distinction the Belgians racialized. "Prior to colonization," explains Ann Garrison, "the Tutsi were a cattle owning, feudal ruling class, the Hutu a subservient peasant class. Belgian colonists reified this divide by issuing ID cards that labeled Rwandans and Burundians as Hutu, Tutsi, or Twa [1% of the population]."[652]

One of Canada's preeminent nationalist philosophers has aped the official Dallaire/Rwanda story. After noting that Dallaire considers himself "a man of honour and a man of action", John Ralston Saul writes: "He reported that all the warning signs of a catastrophe were present. To be precise, on January 11, 1994, he faxed his superiors that a mass killing was being planned."[653]

But the much-celebrated January 11 "genocide fax" Saul mentions is not titled "'genocide' or 'killing' but an innocuous 'Request For Protection of Informant'", reports International Criminal Tribunal for Rwanda lawyer Christopher Black. The two-page "genocide fax", as *New Yorker* reporter Philip Gourevitch dubbed it in 1998, was probably doctored a year after the mass killings in Rwanda ended. In a chapter devoted to the fax in *Enduring Lies* Herman and Peterson argue two paragraphs were added to a cable Dallaire sent to Canadian General Maurice Baril at the UN Department of Peacekeeping Operations in New York about a weapons cache and protecting an informant (Dallaire never personally met the informant).[654] The two added paragraphs said the informant was asked to compile a list of Tutsi for possible extermination in Kigali and mentioned a plan to assassinate select political leaders and Belgian peacekeepers.

Mission head Booh-Booh denies seeing this information and there's no evidence Dallaire warned the Belgians of a plan to attack them, which later transpired.[655] Finally, a response to the cable from UN headquarters the next day ignores the (probably) added paragraphs. Herman and Peterson make a compelling case that a doctored version of the initial cable was placed in the UN file on November 27, 1995, by British Colonel Richard M. Connaughton as part of a Kigali-London-Washington effort to prove the existence of a plan by the Hutu government to exterminate Tutsi.[656]

Even if the final two paragraphs were in the original version, the credibility of the information would be suspect. Informant "Jean-Pierre" was not a high placed official in the defeated Hutu government, reports Robin Philpott in *Rwanda and the New Scramble for Africa: From Tragedy to Useful Imperial Fiction.* Instead, "Jean-Pierre" was a driver for the MRDN political party who later died fighting with Kagame's RPF.[657]

Incredibly, the "genocide fax" is the primary source of documentary record demonstrating UN foreknowledge of a Hutu "conspiracy" to exterminate Tutsi, a charge even the victor's justice at the International Criminal Tribunal for Rwanda failed to convict anyone of.[658] According to Herman and Peterson, "when finding all four defendants not guilty of the 'conspiracy to commit genocide' charge, the [ICTR] trial chamber also dismissed the evidence provided by 'informant Jean-Pierre' due to 'lingering questions concerning [his] reliability.'"[659]

Tellingly, Dallaire didn't even initially adhere to the "conspiracy to commit genocide" version of the Rwandan tragedy. Just after leaving his post as UNAMIR force commander Dallaire replied to a September 14, 1994, Radio Canada Le Point question by saying, "the plan was more political. The aim was to eliminate the coalition of moderates. … I think that the excesses that we saw were beyond people's ability to plan and organize. There was a process to destroy the political elements in the moderate camp. There was a breakdown and hysteria absolutely. … But nobody could have foreseen or planned the magnitude of the destruction we saw."[660]

At the end of their chapter tracing the history of the "genocide fax" Herman and Peterson write, "if all of this is true, we would suggest that Dallaire should be regarded as a war criminal for positively facilitating the actual mass killings of April-July, rather than taken as a hero for giving allegedly disregarded warnings that might have stopped them."[661]

In one of two footnotes Robinson ended his *Monthly Review* article on a nationalist note that, unbeknownst to the author, reveals an important contradiction of left nationalism. The former Canadian labour researcher writes: "There is another account of the Rwanda tragedy for which two Canadians can take a great deal of credit. In 1997, the Organization for African Unity (OAU) appointed an International Panel of Eminent Persons to report on what had happened. Stephen

Lewis was a member of the Panel and Gerald Caplan was its principal writer and author of the report, *Rwanda — The Preventable Genocide*. It confirms all the main facts and conclusions of Linda Melvern's book."

While paying lip service to the complex interplay of ethnic, class and regional politics, as well as international pressures, that spurred the Rwandan Genocide, the 300-page report is premised on the unsubstantiated claim there was a high-level plan by the Hutu government to kill all Tutsi. It ignores the overwhelming evidence (and logic) pointing to Kagame's RPF as the culprit in shooting down the presidential plane, which sparked the genocidal killings. It also emphasizes Dallaire's perspective. A word search of the report finds 100 mentions of "Dallaire", five times more than "Booh-Booh", the overall commander of the UN mission. Rather than a compelling overview of the Rwandan tragedy, the OAU report highlights Canada's power within international bodies. Or to ask a question left nationalists have ignored: why would Canadians write a major Organization of African Unity report?

In a *Walrus* story Caplan described "waiting for the flight back to Toronto, where I would do all my reading and writing" on a report "I called ... 'The Preventable Genocide'".[662] He was commissioned to write the OAU report by close friend Stephen Lewis, who was appointed a member of the OAU's Panel of Eminent Personalities to Investigate the 1994 Genocide in Rwanda & the Surrounding Events. Lewis was made a panel member through his position as Deputy Executive Director of UNICEF. Partly funded by Canada, the entire initiative was instigated by US Secretary of State Madeleine Albright.[663]

Caplan and Lewis are staunch advocates of the noble Canadian general story. In 2017 Caplan, who started an organization with Kagame's long-standing foreign minister Louise Mushikiwabo, called Dallaire "surely among Canada's most admired citizens, if not the most admired."[664] The previous year the former NDP national secretary wrote another article posted on Rabble.ca claiming, "the personal relationship so many Canadians feel with Rwanda can be explained in two words: Roméo Dallaire."[665]

(In addition to publishing his over-the-top praise of the former general, Rabble.ca has run articles by Caplan attacking critics of Dallaire and Kagame. In one piece he called on the University of Toronto's president to remove a program from the university's radio station because it "so blatantly promoted genocide denial."[666] In criticizing the Taylor Report Caplan complained that host Phil Taylor gave a platform to Dallaire-critic Robin Philpott and a "tiny band that constitutes North America's most notorious deniers of the Rwanda genocide." But Philpot, who has written a number of books on Rwanda, countered with an impressive list of individuals who disagree with Caplan and Dallaire's pro-RPF version of Rwandan history, including the former Secretary General of the United Nations Boutros Boutros-Ghali, head of the UN mission in Rwanda Jacques-Roger Booh-Booh, head of Belgian troops in Kigali Colonel Luc Marchal, intelligence officer for the UN mission in Rwanda Amadou Deme, Hotel Rwanda's Paul Rusesabagina, Belgian historian Filip Reyntjens, etc.

In another Rabble story Caplan described demanding the US Holocaust Museum "immediately remove" an article from its website he said "played directly into the hands of those malevolent forces that deny the genocide in Rwanda ever happened."[667] Caplan was offended that museum director Michael Dobbs wrote, "whether the genocide was planned, and was thus foreseeable, has been hotly debated by scholars, politicians and lawyers." For Caplan "only supporters of the Hutu *génocidaires* and a small gang of cranks question the essential nature of the genocide in Rwanda."[668]

While publishing Caplan's attacks against critics of Dallaire and Kagame, Rabble supressed a number of my blogs challenging Dallaire, Caplan and the official story of Rwanda's 1994 tragedy. While they did publish a few of my blogs on Dallaire/Rwanda, they've refused to publish at least four more on the same subject. In the most egregious case Rabble refused to print a story I titled "Dallaire does not deserve accolades from progressive organizations", which listed numerous positions the general had taken on international issues that were hard to align with championing international human rights.)

As Robinson's praise of Lewis and Caplan's contribution to the OAU report highlights, left nationalists ignore Canada's international diplomatic influence. They also ignore Canada's international ideological power. Diplomatic initiatives to promote Canada date to the late 1800s and in 1945 the CBC International-Service ("Voice of Canada") began beaming radio abroad.[669] Created as part of the government's World War II propaganda arsenal, the 1950 National Film Board Act calls for it to "promote the production and distribution of films in the national interest" and to "interpret Canada to Canadians and to other nations."[670] In the 1970s Ottawa started funding Canadian Studies programs at universities abroad and today Global Affairs Canada has over 10,000 personnel spread across 270 embassies, high commissions, consular offices, trade offices and its Ottawa headquarters who promote this country's international positions.[671] Every year DND, GAC,

Veterans Affairs and Canadian Heritage spend hundreds of millions of dollars articulating a one-sided version of Canada's place in the world.[672]

Beyond state initiatives, Canada's wealthy and educated population represents a sizable information/cultural market. Speaking the world's two major colonial languages, Canada's vast intelligentsia is well placed internationally. It's even able to insert nationalist platitudes into a discussion of a small East African nation published by a US Marxist magazine (Monthly Review)! Certainly compared to the countries directly affected by the Rwandan tragedy, Canada's international media/cultural apparatus is gigantic.

Canadian media influence and nationalist mythology has shaped international understanding of the Rwandan tragedy. In their haste to promote a Canadian saviour in Africa, left/liberals have promoted a one-sided version of the Rwandan tragedy that serves a brutal dictatorship in Kigali responsible for significant violence in the Congo.

Dallaire's name, and the highly simplistic account of the Rwandan tragedy more broadly, have also been invoked to justify imperialist interventions and the Responsibility to Protect (R2P) doctrine. On January 31, 2003, Liberal Secretary of State for Latin America and Minister for La Francophonie Denis Paradis organized the "Ottawa Initiative on Haiti" to discuss that country's future.[673] No Haitian officials were invited to this two-day assembly where high-level US, Canadian and French officials discussed removing Haiti's elected president, re-creating the dreaded army and putting the country under UN trusteeship. To justify the government's plans in Haiti, Paradis cited purported inaction in Rwanda and Dallaire's personal breakdown thereafter. The minister told the March 15, 2003, issue of *l'Actualité*, which brought the "Ottawa Initiative on Haiti" meeting to public attention, "I do not want to end up like Roméo Dallaire", which was his reason why Canada needed to intervene in Haiti.[674]

In the House of Commons debate after Haiti's elected president and thousands of local officials were ousted in February 2004, Liberal MP and self-described human rights activist, David Kilgour, repeated the theme. "Canadians have much to learn from the experiences of General Roméo Dallaire in Rwanda. We must intervene when necessary and we must do so expeditiously and multilaterally. This is why I am delighted to hear that 450 Canadian troops are set to join U.S. forces in Haiti."[675]

Dallaire himself linked the overthrow of Haiti's elected government to Rwanda, according to the *Montreal Gazette*. In a story five days after the Canadian-backed coup headlined "Dallaire fears new Rwanda disaster in Haiti: Ex-UN commander urges Canada to act" the former general said, "anywhere people are being abused, the world should be involved."[676]

In justifying the disastrous NATO war on Libya, Dallaire again compared the situation in that country to Rwanda. "When Gaddafi said 'I am going to crush these cockroaches and stay in power,' those were exactly the words that the genociders in Rwanda used."[677] Comparing Darfur in the mid-2000s, Iran in 2011, Syria in 2016 and Myanmar (Rohingya) in 2017 to Rwanda, Dallaire also called for interventions in those countries.[678]

The general is an aggressive proponent of the Responsibility to Protect (R2P) doctrine, which provides an ideological cover to justify Western interventions. Dallaire publicly promoted the Paul Martin government's push to have the UN adopt R2P in 2005 and cited the doctrine (along with many others) to justify the 2011 NATO war on Libya.

Dallaire is co-director of the Will to Intervene Project, which seeks to build "domestic political will in Canada and the United States to prevent future mass atrocities."[679] But the architects of W2I don't mean the "political will" to stop Washington from spurring "mass atrocities" à la Iraq, Vietnam, Somalia, Haiti, Korea, Chile, etc. Human rights rhetoric aside, W2I is an outgrowth of the R2P doctrine, which was used to justify the NATO war in Libya and overthrow of Haiti's elected government. While the less sophisticated neoconservatives simply call for a more aggressive military posture, the more liberal supporters of imperialism prefer a high-minded ideological mask to accomplish the same end. W2I is one such tool.

The Dallaire saviour story is also tied to Ottawa's support for the Uganda/RPF invasion of Rwanda, which destabilized that country and the Congo. The Kagame-inspired genocide story legitimizes his dictatorship and its efforts to physically eliminate opponents. While Kagame's RPF has as much responsibility for the genocidal killings in 1994 as anyone, they've justified repeated invasions of the Congo by the need to disperse *génocidaires*. Kigali justified his 1996 intervention into the Congo as an effort to protect the Banyamulenge (Congolese Tutsi) living in Eastern Congo from the Hutu who fled the country when the RPF took power.[680]

At the time Rwandan forces marched 1,500 km to topple the regime in Kinshasa and then re-invaded after the Congolese government it installed expelled Rwandan troops.[681] This led to a deadly eight-country war between 1998 and 2003. Since

2003 Rwanda and its proxies have repeatedly invaded the Eastern Congo, usually citing Hutu *génocidaires* as pretext.

Peer-reviewed studies by the International Rescue Committee found that up to 5.4 million people were killed as a result of the conflict in Congo.[682] An October 2010 UN report by the Office of the High Commissioner for Human Rights on the Congo from 1993 to 2003, charged Rwandan troops with engaging in mass killings "that might be classified as crimes of genocide."[683]

Progressives who have promoted the 'Dallaire as saviour' story need to grapple with their (ideological) contribution to Congolese and Rwandan suffering as well as their alignment with a liberal imperialist doctrine that has been cited to devastating effect in Haiti, Libya and elsewhere. More generally, left nationalists should interrogate an ideological framework that underplays Canadian power and upholds its mythology. While theoretically possible, an internationalist form of nationalism is unlikely, especially under the world's current economic and political system.

CANADIAN NATIONALISM AND INDIGENOUS PEOPLE

The power of foreign policy nationalism is immense, as illustrated by its effects on the primary victims of Canadian colonialism. Even Indigenous leaders and organizations have been drawn into Canadian wars and mythology.

Dispossessed of 99% of their land, Indigenous people have faced efforts to starve and sterilize them.[684] They've also been made wards of the state, had their movement restricted and religious/cultural ceremonies banned.[685] Residential schools and other so-called child welfare initiatives sought to eradicate their ways, or in the infamous formulation of the deputy superintendent of the Department of Indian Affairs from 1913 to 1932, Duncan Campbell Scott: "Our objective is to continue until there is not a single Indian in Canada that has not been absorbed into the body politic and there is no Indian question."[686]

As part of upending the colonial process, Indigenous representatives/organizations are increasingly important voices on the left. On many issues settlers would do well to seek out the opinion of individuals/groups representing First Nations, but that is generally not the case concerning international affairs (at least defined as Canada's policy towards the rest of the world). Despite an antagonistic relationship to the Canadian state, First Nations have rarely challenged Ottawa's international policies. In fact, they've often backed them.

The dominant Indigenous organizations mostly ignore Canadian policy towards the rest of the world. Searching Google for "Assembly of First Nations" and "Afghanistan war", "Iraq war", "Libya bombing" and "coup in Haiti" failed to elicit any response. Scanning hundreds of AFN resolutions uncovered little about international affairs. While "International Advocacy and Activity" is one of 28 "Policy Areas" listed on the AFN's website, the page is narrowly focused. It's mainly about UN discussions of Indigenous issues and, to a lesser extent, international climate negotiations. The Stephen Harper government's policy of refusing to sign the UN Declaration on the Rights of Indigenous Peoples seems to be the only international issue the AFN forcefully opposed.

While they have rarely challenged foreign policy decisions, Indigenous representatives have occasionally echoed nationalist myth. Alongside Minister of International Development Marie-Claude Bibeau, AFN National Chief

Perry Bellegarde was a keynote speaker at the Canadian Council for International Co-operation's "COME CELEBRATE CANADA'S INTERNATIONAL CONTRIBUTIONS!" event in 2017.[687] Part of Canada's 150th anniversary, the *Global Impact Soirée* included a Global Affairs Canada exhibit titled "25 Years of Excellence in International Development Photography" and "Recognize Canada's 15 international contributions".[688]

At the 2001 World Conference against Racism, Racial Discrimination, Xenophobia and Related Intolerance, AFN leader Matthew Coon Come denounced Canada's "marginalization and dispossession of Indigenous peoples."[689] In what was widely described as a forceful speech, Coon Come labeled Canada "an international advocate of respect for human rights" and said: "Canadians, and the government of Canada, present themselves around the world as upholders and protectors of human rights. In many ways, this reputation is well-deserved. In South Africa, the government of Canada played a prominent role in isolating the apartheid regime. In many other countries, Canada provides impressive international development assistance."[690] (While repeated regularly, Coon Come's characterization of Canada's role in opposing apartheid is incorrect — see above — and aid was largely conceived as a geopolitical tool to blunt radical decolonization.[691])

Indigenous leaders sometimes have ties to the foreign policy establishment. AFN National Chief Shawn A-in-chut Atleo was part of the official Canadian delegation to Nelson Mandela's funeral in South Africa while band council chiefs have been part of government organized "trade, business and investment promotion visits and activities in

Latin America."[692] Global Affairs Canada's website says it "has developed online resources specifically designed to help Aboriginal entrepreneurs who wish to do business abroad" and the international aid agency runs an Aboriginal Procurement Strategy "to promote Aboriginal business development through the federal government procurement process."[693]

Indigenous representatives provide input to arms of the foreign policy apparatus. The AFN, Métis National Council, Inuit Tapiriit Kanatomi and National Association of Friendship Centres provide input on who should be selected for the Aboriginal Leadership Opportunity Year offered by DND's Royal Military College.[694] After consulting the AFN, Native Women's Association of Canada and Métis National Council, CIDA set up the International Aboriginal Youth Internships, which offers 140 Indigenous youth "the opportunity to work in developing countries on Canadian-supported development projects."[695]

Established in 2001, CIDA's Indigenous Peoples Partnership Program (IPPP) "seeks to increase the involvement of Canadian Aboriginal organizations in the delivery of development assistance."[696] The IPPP included "Mining Sector-Indigenous Capacity Building" to spur "two-way learning between Canadian Indigenous peoples and Indigenous partners in Latin America and the Caribbean regarding interactions with mining companies and governments."[697] Presented as a way to empower Indigenous communities living near Canadian mining projects, a consultant who frequently works for the Canadian mining industry developed the project's initial documents.[698]

Mining companies also sought Indigenous support for their international operations. A 1995 Apikan Indigenous

Network, an Ottawa-based consultancy firm, discussion paper titled "Aboriginal Business and International Trade – Canada's Strategic Advantage" claimed: "Canada's Indigenous businesses give us unique advantage in some key international sectors" since "Latin American Indigenous groups ... prefer to work with Canadian Indigenous groups wherever possible."[699] In 2004 the Canadian Embassy in Guatemala paid for a B.C. First Nation leader to address a Mining Forum it organized. Leader of the Tahltan Indian Act band council, Jerry Asp told the Guatemalan audience his community initially opposed industrial mining but ultimately benefited from it (a position contested by many in his community).[700]

Former Assembly of Manitoba Chiefs employee Don Clarke worked with the government and industry to woo Indigenous communities opposed to Canadian mining projects in a number of Latin American countries.[701] In 2007 the embassy in Ecuador brought the member of the Black River First Nation to promote Canadian companies to Indigenous communities. Clarke said, "the Canadian mining industry is committed to responsible mining" and "our people ... are being used by the environmental groups" who are "the modern missionary".[702] In an article titled "Marketing Consent: A journey into the public relations underside of Canada's mining sector" Sandra Cuffe describes Clarke's effort to convince Chile's Diaguita Huascoaltino Indigenous and Agricultural Community to allow the Assembly of Manitoba Chiefs to negotiate with Barrick Gold on its behalf. Clarke was apparently working for Barrick.[703] In describing his work with Indigenous communities internationally Clarke told CBC, "we see a real business opportunity for our First Nations people to capitalize on the knowledge that we have and the experiences."[704] Clarke later took up a position with the mining committee of the Canadian Chamber of Commerce.[705] For its part, the Prospectors and Developers Association of Canada has an Indigenous representative/department, an Aboriginal Program at its annual convention and gives out an Award for Aboriginal Achievement in the mineral industry, which Jerry Asp received in 2011.[706]

As a way to thwart Canadians who associate the plight of First Nations and Palestinians, pro-Israel groups have reached out to Indigenous leaders. In 2006 the Canadian Jewish Congress (CJC) took AFN leaders, including Grand Chief Phil Fontaine, to Israel.[707] Two years later the CJC sponsored a delegation of First Nations women to the Golda Meir Mount Carmel International Training Centre.[708] Other Jewish and Christian Zionist groups have organized a number of missions to Israel for First Nations clergy, educators and leaders. In probably the most appalling case, former grand chief of the AFN and head of the Misipawistik Cree, Ovide Mercredi, participated in at least two Jewish National Fund of Canada tours.[709] This despite the JNF being an explicitly racist and colonial institution.[710]

***

Canadian militarism has been a particularly influential force in shaping First Nations' international outlook. As many as 12,000 Indigenous people fought in World War I, World War II and Korea.[711]

Before those wars British General Garnet Wolseley recruited 60 Mohawk and two-dozen Métis boatmen to navigate the raging cataracts of the Nile River in 1884.[712] With Sudanese forces laying siege to British controlled Khartoum, nearly four hundred Canadian boatmen were recruited to transport soldiers and supplies to defend London's position on the upper Nile.

The Ojibwa, Potawatomi and Odawa of the Saugeen reserve offered to send men to the Boer war in 1899 to "show their loyalty" to the Crown.[713] Their offer was ultimately rejected and it's unknown how many Indigenous men fought in a brutal conflict driven by mining interests, which strengthened British colonial authority in southern Africa and ultimately led to racial apartheid.

Hundreds of Iroquois from Six Nations were members of the part-time militia during this period.[714] In 1908 over 200 "chiefs and warriors" from Six Nations were in the 37th Haldimand Rifles at Niagara, including one of the company's commanders Captain J.S. Johnson.[715] In a 1909 speech Six Nations member and future founder of the League of Indians of Canada, Frederick Onondeyoh Loft told the arch militarist Royal Canadian Military Institute his people were "instinctively soldiers" and should be encouraged to join the militia.[716]

At the outbreak of World War I the Six Nations band council sent $1,500 ($30,000 today) directly to Britain and also offered warriors.[717] A higher proportion of the reserve's population fought than the Canadian public.[718] Additionally, the Six Nations Women's Patriotic League produced materials for the front and published a "Descriptive Booklet of the Part Played by the Six Nations Indians in the Great War."[719]

Women also formed patriotic leagues on many prairie reserves.[720] The Patriotic Fund Board used Indigenous contributions "for propaganda purposes to shame non-Indians into giving more."[721] During WWI Indigenous enlistment rates were twice the national average.[722] On a number of reserves all eligible males volunteered.[723]

As an expression of autonomy the Iroquois Confederacy, which includes Six Nations, declared war on Germany in April 1917.[724] In *For King and Kanata: Canadian Indians and the First World War* Timothy Winegard explains, "for many Indian leaders seeking full and equal sovereignty, support offered directly to the Crown was viewed as a means to lobby the Imperial government to pressure Canada to alter oppressive laws."[725] At an individual level Indigenous men enlisted to escape impoverishment, leave the reserve, be a warrior or demonstrate they were "as capable as Euro-Canadians in so-called European civilized pursuits."[726]

Despite more than 4,000 enlisting, First Nations continued to face extreme racism after the war. An April 1919 Order in Council authorized the expropriation of reserve land for returning white soldiers. Under the law almost 86,000 acres of reserve territory was confiscated and given to European veterans.[727] To protest the theft of their land, an Indigenous community on Vancouver Island cited official war propaganda. The giveaway to white veterans was labeled "unfair to those of our race who are sleeping in France and Flanders. This is what the [German] Kaiser would have done to us all, whites and Indians, if he had won the war."[728] But, the Kaiser wasn't a credible threat to the West Coast.

Over 3,000 Indigenous men enlisted to fight in World War II.[729] Several hundred more volunteered for service in the US-led destruction of Korea.[730] At least 2,300 Indigenous people are part of today's professional military.[731]

Receiving input from its Defence Aboriginal Advisory Group, the Canadian Forces operate various programs focused on Indigenous youth. CF recruiters participate in National Aboriginal Day events and oversee the Aboriginal Entry

Plan, a three-week training.[732] In 1971 the CF introduced the Northern Native Entry Program and the Cadet Corps has long worked with band councils and schools on reserves.[733] Partnering with the Federation of Saskatchewan Indian Nations and the Saskatchewan Indian Veteran's Association, the CF launched Bold Eagle in 1990. It's a "five day Culture Camp" conducted by First Nations elders "followed by a military recruit training course."[734]

(Alongside these outreach efforts, the CF monitors First Nations protesters and has suppressed land struggles.[735] It has also expropriated a great deal of Indigenous land for its bases.[736])

The CF has organized international Indigenous exchanges. In 2015 the military sent twelve members of the Northern Canadian Indigenous Sovereignty Patrol and Surveillance Unit to Australia for a series of trainings and events with the largely aboriginal NORFORCE.[737] Canadian Defence Advisor to Australia Colonel Acton Kilby, Canadian Aboriginal Veterans Association President Richard Blackwolf and former Indigenous NHL player Reggie Leach were part of the delegation.[738]

Fighting with the Canadian military has certainly influenced First Nations' international outlook. Cenotaphs in many Indigenous communities and reserves commemorate those who fought in Canadian/British wars.[739] In 1927 the First Nation of Alderville erected a War Monument to honour 35 sons who volunteered, nine of whom died, during WWI.[740] According to a 2016 *Saugeen Times* story about Remembrance Day, the Saugeen First Nation cenotaph is "to honour the Indigenous soldiers who had served in WWI and WWII, the Korean War, Gulf War and Afghanistan."[741]

In 2017 the Milbrook band council placed 27 Millbrook Remembers Banners to "honour and remember our veterans who served in the First World War, Second World War, Korean War, Vietnam War, NATO conflicts; Bosnia, Kosovo, Afghanistan, Iraq and also those who served during peacetime operations."

The Assembly of First Nations waged a multiyear battle to participate in a Remembrance Day ritual organized by the reactionary, militarist, Royal Canadian Legion. Since winning the right to lay a wreath at the National War Memorial in 1995 the AFN has participated in the yearly Remembrance Day ceremony in Ottawa.[742] In 2015 National Chief Perry Bellegarde described the AFN's effort to "honour the courage of those who gave so much and made such a tremendous contribution in standing strong for this land, our homeland."[743]

"On Remembrance Day we honour our warriors who have come to the defence of Canada in world wars and conflicts around the globe and those who serve in the defence of Canada's interests at home and abroad", said Alvin Fiddler, Grand Chief of the Nishnawbe Aski Nation (NAN), on Remembrance Day in 2016.[744] A Veterans Flag flown in all 49 NAN communities "honours the service and sacrifice of NAN veterans in the defence of Canada's freedom and democracy."[745]

Winnipeg's city council inaugurated National Aboriginal Veterans Day in 1994. The Canadian Aboriginal Veterans and Serving Members Association (alongside other Indigenous veterans groups) pressed the federal government to proclaim November 8 National Aboriginal Veterans Day. In 2016 Veterans Affairs Minister Kent Hehr attended an Ottawa celebration while Indigenous Affairs Minister Carolyn Bennett participated in a Fredericton ceremony. In a statement Hehr noted, "we thank the thousands of Indigenous Canadians in uniform who answered the call of duty and made the ultimate sacrifice. Their contributions and efforts have helped our country in its efforts to make this world a safer place."[746]

A number of monuments, often supported by Veteran Affairs, honour First Nations veterans. In Batoche, Saskatchewan, the Métis Veterans Memorial Monument is dedicated to those who "served alongside other Canadian servicemen and servicewomen in the South African War, World War I, World War II, the Korean War, and in each of the efforts since then to defend our country and contribute to international peace and security."[747] For its part, the National Aboriginal Veterans Monument in Ottawa says it was "raised in sacred and everlasting honour of the contributions of all Aboriginal Canadians in war and peacekeeping operations."[748] Apparently, it's the only official monument in Ottawa commemorating Indigenous peoples or history.[749]

A growing number of landmarks bear the names of Indigenous soldiers. The third Canadian Ranger patrol group headquarters, a monument at CFB Borden and a Parry Sound statue are dedicated to top World War I sniper Francis Pegahmagabow.[750] WWII and Korea veteran Tommy Prince has a statue, school, street, drill hall, CF base, two educational scholarships and a cadet corps named in his honour.[751]

A dozen books and theses, as well as hundreds of articles, detailing First Nations' contribution to Canadian/British wars mostly echo the military's perspective of those conflicts. "Some Métis men were part of the Nile Voyageurs who went to Africa to help the British liberate Khartoum", notes Cathy Littlejohn in *Métis Soldiers of Saskatchewan: 1914 – 1953*, a book published by the Gabrielle Dumont Institute of native studies and applied research.[752] I doubt many Sudanese would employ the term "liberate" to describe London's objective there.

In "The Awakening Has Come": Canadian First Nations in the Great War Era, 1914-1932, Eric Story depicts WWI as a noble affair. "The Great War had put First Nations shoulder to shoulder with Euro-Canadians in a fight for human rights and dignity", writes Story in the *Canadian Military History Journal*.[753]

The editor of *We Were There* says the aim of the Saskatchewan Indian Veterans Association book is to convince kids they fought for "freedom". "I wanted to publish ... to let Indian children know that their fathers and grandfathers fought for the freedom we now cherish."[754]

In a burst of Orwellian doublespeak, a Veterans Affairs book on Indigenous soldiers claims they fought for "world peace". "On each occasion", it notes, "Canada's Indigenous soldiers overcame cultural challenges and made impressive sacrifices and contributions to help the nation in its efforts to restore world peace."[755]

The CF, government commissions and Indigenous veterans' associations, often backed by Veteran Affairs, have produced much of the laudatory literature on aboriginal veterans.[756] But, others without any obvious connection to the CF or veterans' groups also celebrate Canadian militarism by citing Indigenous war deaths. Sometimes they draw on foreign-policy nationalism to justify Canadian colonialism.

In a 2013 Huffington Post blog titled "Whitewashing Remembrance: I Wear A Poppy For Native Veterans" Elizabeth Hawksworth made an antiracist argument for wearing the red poppy. "I choose to wear it because as a woman with Native ancestry, I want to remember those whose faces we never see in the Heritage moments or on the Remembrance Day TV spots. ... I wear the poppy not just as a way to remember, but as a statement: freedom doesn't just belong to white folks."[757] But, the red poppy is the property of, and raises funds for, the jingoist Royal Canadian Legion.[758] Additionally, red poppies were inspired by the 1915 poem "In Flanders Fields" by Canadian army officer John McCrae. The pro-war poem calls on Canadians to "take up our quarrel with the foe" and was used to promote war bonds and recruit soldiers during WWI.[759]

In a 2015 *Newfoundland Independent* column Amelia Reimer, a Métis woman and Support Worker at the St. John's Native Friendship Centre, echoed Hawksworth. In "Lest We Forget Aboriginal Peoples' Sacrifices for Canada" she wrote, "we thank all veterans who fought for our freedom. Please wear your poppy (plain, beaded, or sealskin)", but Reimer ignores antiwar white poppies.[760]

In a TVO interview marking the hundredth anniversary of the outbreak of World War I Joseph Boyden (subsequently criticized over misleading claims of Indigenous ancestry) said Indigenous men enlisted to "do what's right".[761] As he denounced the mistreatment of Indigenous peoples after WWI, the author of *Three Day Road*, a novel dedicated to "the native soldiers who fought in the Great War", called their fighting a "beautiful corner" of Canadian history.[762]

Canadian military experience has shaped Indigenous politics. *Aboriginal Peoples and the Canadian Military: Historical Perspectives* notes: "By the 1960s veterans were in positions of significant influence. This is highlighted by the fact that all leaders of the Union of Saskatchewan Indians during the 1960s ... were Second World War veterans."[763] The influence of former soldiers over Indigenous politics dates to World War I. In a Masters' thesis titled "The Return of the Native (Veteran): Six Nations Troops and Political Change at the Grand River Reserve, 1917-1924" John Moses argues that veterans upended the traditional governance structure. A letter to Indian Affairs signed by 32 Six Nations veterans explained: "After fighting in France, in the World War for three and four years for democracy and freedom, we return to our own country, and to our own home, and right here confronting us we find one of the most flagrant and shining examples of incompetent autocracy imaginable — our hereditary council — which is, and always will be, an insurmountable obstacle to the progress and advancement of the Six Nations. Not only is it a great handicap but a black stain, in that it had during the Great War, not only proven itself disloyal to Canada and the British Empire, but, an actual hindrance, and block to many who but for it, would also have been with us 'Over there.'"[764] Citing support from veterans and some others on the reserve, Indian Affairs abolished the authority of the hereditary council in 1924.[765]

After returning from the Western Front Frederick Ogilvie Loft formed the League of Indians of Canada in 1919, the first pan-Canadian Indigenous political organization. A Mohawk from the Six Nations of the Grand River Reserve, Loft justified the organization to a number of Chiefs in this way: "We have the right to claim and demand more justice and fair play as a recompense for we, too, have fought for the sacred rights of justice, freedom and liberty so dear to mankind."[766] Backed by a number of other veterans, including famed WWI sniper Francis Pegahmagabow, the founding constitution of the League explained: "Not in vain did our young men die in a strange land; not in vain are our Indian bones mingled with the soil of a foreign land … we will take our place side by side with the white people, doing our share of productive work and gladly shouldering the responsibility of citizens in this, our country."[767] The League led directly to today's Indian Association of Alberta and Saskatchewan's Federation of Sovereign Indigenous Nations.[768] "The League was also the forerunner of the National Indian Brotherhood, now known as the Assembly of First Nations", explains an online history of The League of Indians of Canada.[769]

So, ironically, while First Nations have more reason than most to reject the Canadian state's use of force and diplomacy to enforce a neo-colonial world order, ties to the military and other elements of the foreign policy establishment have shaped the outlook of many of their organizations. Of course various other factors have also influenced these institutions' international views. Similar to everyone living in this country, the ideological institutions documented in *A Propaganda System* have shaped Indigenous perspectives. More specifically, First Nations politics are influenced by their financial dependence on the Canadian state (the loss of land has decimated communities' economic base). The AFN, for instance, receives most of its money from Indigenous and Northern Affairs Canada. When former Grand Chief Matthew Coon Come ran afoul of Ottawa in the early 2000s the federal government slashed the AFN's funding. It went from $19.8 million to $12 million in 2001 and was cut another $6 million a year later.[770] According to an Indigenous news outlet, the AFN was "punished" for attempting "to steer a more radical course."[771]

***

Indigenous opinion is, of course, not homogenous. Some leaders and activists have presented an internationalist vision and challenged Canadian foreign policy. Activists have drawn links between Indigenous and Palestinian dispossession at Israeli Apartheid Week and other Palestinian solidarity events. Some chiefs have actively supported Indigenous communities resisting Canadian mining projects in Latin America. Former chief of Manitoba's Roseau River First Nation, Terrance Nelson called on First Nations to forge their own international ties.[772] Nelson even sought out relations with Iran after the Stephen Harper government cut off diplomatic relations with Tehran and listed that country as a state sponsor of terrorism in 2012.

Author of *500 Years of Indigenous Resistance*, Gord Hill criticized First Nations collaboration with the CF. From Kwakwaka'wakw nation, Hill denounces Indigenous leaders supporting recruitment for a force "who continue to loot & plunder not only Indigenous lands here, but also those of tribal peoples in Afghanistan & Haiti."[773]

In the late 1960s and early 1970s the Native Alliance of Red Power opposed "efforts to co-opt native leadership into Canadian imperialism."[774] The Coast Salish (Vancouver) based group protested local residential schools, police brutality, racism, sexism, as well as the war in Vietnam and colonialism in southern Africa.

Further back, many Indigenous people opposed WWI.[775] In *For King and Kanata* Timothy Winegard notes, "the outward support for the war given by most Indian leaders did not in all cases reflect the opinions of those whom they purportedly represented. Many Indians did not endorse the recruitment of their men for a European war."[776] Mohawk leader Thunderwater, for instance, campaigned against indigenous enlistment in what he described as a war "for gold".[777]

Indigenous people's experiences and knowledge should be part of a movement for a just foreign policy. Their experiences with Canadian colonialism, including so-called aid, missionary initiatives and financing of Indigenous organizations, holds lessons for formulating a foreign policy that does no harm. And a foreign policy truth and reconciliation process might be a place to start.

QUÉBEC NATIONALISM

Events in Haiti made me question Québec sovereigntist support for imperialism. Canada helped overthrow the democratically elected government of Jean-Bertrand Aristide in February 2004 and then supported an interim "illegal" government that killed thousands.[778] Québec-based politicians, businesses and NGOs led Canada's violent, undemocratic, policies in Haiti. And the Québec left largely backed them.

The politicians who shaped Ottawa's decision to help overthrow Aristide were all Québec-based Liberals (Pierre Pettigrew, Dennis Coderre and Denis Paradis). But these federalist politicians acted with firm support from the Bloc Québecois. As the International Republican Institute and CIA backed destabilization of the country gained steam, Bloc foreign critic Francine Lalonde released a statement a month before the coup, quoted in an AlterPresse article calling for Aristide's removal. It said the "Canadian government must raise the tone to force respect for human rights in Haiti."[779] The day of the coup Lalonde celebrated Aristide's fall, only complaining "the international community including Canada did not intervene more quickly in Haiti."[780]

Four weeks later the former labour leader suggested Aristide's claim he was forced out of the country by US marines was responsible for "insecurity" in the impoverished nation. In a House of Commons Standing Committee on Foreign Affairs and International Trade debate Lalonde said: "Aristide's departure is the subject of controversy. The United Nations resolution is clear, but newspapers close to Aristide, and Aristide himself, are promoting the idea that he was kidnapped and that what occurred, consequently, was a coup d'état. Are these statements by Aristide helping to maintain the sense of insecurity there?"[781]

During the June 2004 federal election debate Liberal leader Paul Martin and Bloc leader Gilles Duceppe agreed that Canada's involvement in Haiti was a success.[782] Eighteen months later Bloc MP Pierre Paquette criticized the NDP for using the word "removal" to describe the coup against Aristide. At a Standing Committee on Foreign Affairs and International Trade meeting, Paquette insisted the NDP's Alexa McDonough use the word "departure" instead.[783]

In 2009 Bloc MP Thierry St. Cyr called on the Conservative government to rescind its appointment of Pharès Pierre to the Immigration and Refugee Board.[784] The reason was that in 2002 Pierre was chief of staff to Aristide after spending four decades working with a half dozen civil society organizations in Québec (L'Association des Enseignants Haïtiens du Québec, l'Association Mathématique du Québec, etc.).[785]

English Canadian anti-war groups, radical media and even some unions were generally sympathetic to the notion that Canada participated in a brutal coup in Haiti. When progressive media such as *The Dominion*, *New Socialist Magazine* or *Canadian Dimension* published issues focusing on Canadian imperialism in the year after the coup, they all ran at least one article detailing Canadian crimes in Haiti. In contrast, at the height of Canadian-backed repression in Haiti, 'radical' Québec publication À *Babord!* published an issue devoted to Canadian imperialism that failed to even mention Canada's role in Haiti.

In my experience, during three years of campaigning with Haiti Action Montréal a (broad) racial or linguistic pattern emerged: the more "*pure laine*" Québecois a person or institution, the more likely they were to be antagonistic to Haiti's impoverished majority. Left nationalist *Le Devoir*'s coverage of the coup was by far the worst of the city's four dailies. Within *La Presse*, Mauritius-born Jooneed Khan was a singularly sympathetic voice while the *Montreal Gazette* employed a few sympathetic reporters. The *Mirror* and *Hour* were also far better than their francophone alt-weekly counterpart *Voir*. (*L'aut'journal* was an exception to this pattern.)

The story was similar amongst anti-war groups and unions. Canadian Peace Alliance affiliates generally denounced and organized against Canada's role in Haiti. Yet, when members of Montréal's Échec à la guerre, tried to pass a (mild) condemnation of Canada's involvement in Haiti, they were blocked by two of their members, the Canadian Catholic Organization for Development and Peace and AQOCI (an umbrella group representing two dozen Québec NGOs).

In the months after the removal of Haiti's elected government, progressive elements within the Canadian Labour Congress tried to pass a resolution critical of Canada's role in overthrowing Aristide and supporting a murderous dictatorship. The Fédération des travailleurs et travailleuses du Québec (FTQ), which claims responsibility for relations with "French" speaking countries at the CLC, worked to dilute opposition within the CLC. More generally, the FTQ advanced hard line anti-Aristide propaganda and participated in the destabilization of the elected government as discussed in the labour chapter.

Maybe the most disturbing example of a left group siding with imperialism in Haiti was provincial political party Québec Solidaire. Québec Solidaire's spokesperson, Francoise David, traveled to Haiti in the midst of the coup government's crimes and upon returning she publicly (on Radio Canada and elsewhere) parroted the elite's perspective, blaming supporters of the ousted government for violence in Haiti. On March 9, 2006, David spoke at a Concertation pour Haïti, a group of Québec NGOs and unions, event along with Danielle Magloire, a member of the unconstitutional "Council of the Wise" that appointed the brutal coup prime minister Gérard Latortue.[786] In mid-July 2005, Magloire issued a statement on behalf of the seven-member "Council of the Wise" saying that any media that gives voice to "bandits" (code for Aristide supporters) should be shut down.[787] She also asserted that Aristide's Lavalas Family Party should be banned from upcoming elections.

The only example of Québec Solidaire publicly expressing opposition towards the intervention in Haiti I came across was a single line by a candidate running in a heavily Haitian diaspora riding in Montréal. The party even remained quiet when in March 2006 Québec Premier Jean Charest wined and dined bloodstained coup dictator Gerard Latortue.[788]

In fact, the 2004 coup in Haiti was a striking example of left support for Québec imperialism. It also reflects the province/nation's wider relationship to Haiti and the Global South.

Haiti has long been at the centre of Québec's focus on the Global South. Québec missionaries have been on the island for over a century while major cultural exchanges date to the 1930s. But, Catholicism and French represent the colonizers' traditions, reinforcing the tiny, regressive, Haitian elite's dominance of a country with its own language and religion.

Within progressive nationalist intellectual circles Haiti has important cultural cachet. This is partly based on the Haitian diaspora living in Québec, but it predates their arrival and there are three times as many Quebeckers of Italian descent without the same mystique.[789] In *A Place in the Sun: Haiti, Haitians, and the Remaking of Quebec* Sean Mills summarizes the relationship in this way: "Constructed as the only French-speaking country in the Americas (although the vast majority of its population actually spoke Haitian Creole, not French) Haiti was said to be tied to Québec by a special bond, one that French-Canadian intellectuals conceptualized in familial terms."[790]

Beginning in 1903 "Haiti became one of the central sites of French-Canadian missionary activity."[791] About 28% of the country's Catholic clergy were Francophone Canadians by the time François Duvalier rose to power in 1956.[792]

Québec missionaries have received some official support. The initial disbursement of Canadian aid to Haiti went to missionary work and in 1964 Prime Minister Lester Pearson justified sending a Canadian naval vessel to Haiti by noting, "if Canadian nuns or priests should be wounded or killed, it would be difficult to explain why the Canadian government had not ... taken some form of action."[793]

Québec missionaries retain influence in Haiti. In 2007 I stayed at a Québec-run convent in Cap Haitien, which was the largest institution in the neighbourhood. The nun in charge provided a window into Québec missionary thinking. She told me Aristide was the country's biggest drug runner. When pressed on the matter, she said she wasn't there for politics, but to help people.

Much to the dismay of the Catholic Church, the Aristide government supported the voodoo religion, legalizing voodoo marriages, baptisms and funerals in May 2003.[794] Some of Québec's most rabidly anti-Aristide NGOs, most notably Entraide Missionaire and the Catholic Organization for Development and Peace, have religious ties. In March 2006, a Development and Peace Background paper explained: "The international media has shrouded the departure of Aristide on 29 February 2004 with conspiracy theories, going so far in some cases as to claim that the CIA deposed the president in a coup d'état ... In fact, Aristide himself was largely responsible for the circumstances that led to his forced departure."[795]

While now surpassed by NGOs and international media sources, missionaries were Quebeckers' main source of information on Haiti for many decades. Through letters home, articles, books and speaking engagements missionaries played, notes Mills, "a major role in creating and circulating narratives about Haiti and Haitians throughout French-Canadian society."[796]

Purported linguistic ties are central to Québec's interest in Haiti. A 1984 report titled "Canadian Development Assistance to Haiti" explains that country's importance to Quebec: "As the only independent French-speaking country in Latin America and the Caribbean, Haiti is of special importance for the preservation of the French language and culture."[797] But, most Haitians don't speak French. French is the language of Haiti's elite and language has served as a mechanism through which they maintain their privilege (less than 10 per cent of

Haitians speak French fluently while basically everyone speaks Haitian Creole).[798] Whether conscious or not, a French-focused foreigner in Haiti has taken (at least linguistically speaking) a side in the country's brutal class war. The Aristide government promoted Creole at the expense of French, which contributed to many "progressive" Quebecers' antagonism. Québec groups' francophile partners in Haiti transmitted their anti-Aristide bias and hostility to his generally less educated, poor, supporters. While inside Canada the promotion of the French language can be seen as a progressive measure, this is certainly not true in Haiti.

***

Unlike its role supporting the Haiti coup, opposition to Canada participating in a number of wars largely came from Québec. The sovereignty movement has also expressed greater sympathy with national liberation struggles in Palestine, Cuba and elsewhere.

While the movement has included a significant anti-imperialist streak, official Québec nationalism acquiesced to Western imperialism prior to the 1980 independence referendum. Not wanting "to be perceived by the United States as the Cuba of the North", the Parti Québecois' 1979 White Paper (Québec-Canada: A New Deal. The Québec Government Proposal for a New Partnership Between Equals: Sovereignty-Association) said an independent Québec would continue its membership in NATO, NORAD and even the Commonwealth.[799] More recently, the PQ's 2012 election platform pledged to remain in NATO and NORAD.[800]

PQ leaders have participated in tours of Israel organized by the Centre for Israel and Jewish Affairs (or Québec-Israel Committee). So have Bloc Québecois MPs. In 2008

Bloc leader Gilles Duceppe went with his wife on a $17,577 Canada-Israel Committee sponsored trip.[801]

The Bloc also participated in Ottawa's diplomatic circuit, government delegations abroad, Canadian Forces Parliamentary Program, among other initiatives that tie the nationalist party to the Canadian foreign policy establishment.

The Bloc backed Canadian bombing of the former Yugoslavia and Libya.[802] They also supported the war in Afghanistan between 2001 and April 2007 — at which point they supported a Liberal Party motion to withdraw the troops in 2009.[803] During the 2015 federal election Bloc leader Gilles Duceppe embraced bombing Iraq/Syria, which the Liberals and NDP opposed. He said, "an independent Québec would be part of the coalition that is fighting this group (ISIS)" and called for a "discussion with our allies" about deploying ground troops to the region.[804]

Alongside support for Canadian expansionism, Québecois nationalism has directly contributed to international inequities. For example, during the first half of the 20th century Québec was among the leading producers of missionaries in the world per capita.[805] At its height in the 1930s La Ligue missionnaires des écoles in Québec had 150,000 members while a major missionary exhibit at Montréal's St. Joseph's Oratory attracted 225,000 people in 1942.[806] Between 1920 and 1948 French Canadian Catholics gave $10 million ($110 million today) to international missionary endeavours.[807]

Québec missionaries played a sizable role in efforts to 'civilize' Africa. Prominent historian Lionel Groulx found that 1,500 French Canadian Catholics from 48 different religious societies worked on the continent at the end of the colonial period in 1959.[808] In 1862 Francois Allard, a French missionary who laid roots in Québec, brought Catholicism to Basutoland (present-day Lesotho) while Québec priest Arthur Bouchard arrived in Khartoum in 1879 where he spent two years.[809] In 1884 Bouchard was the chaplain who accompanied nearly 400 Canadian Voyageurs sent to defend British control of Khartoum in Sudan.[810]

John Forbes, a Francophone priest from Vaudreuil, Québec, was the first Canadian "White Father" as well as the North American founder of the Catholic missionary group. In 1885 he traveled to the Society of Missionaries of Africa training centre in Algiers, which had been under French control since 1830. After a decade of training and fieldwork, Forbes returned to build support in North America for the White Fathers whose popular nickname came from their Arab-style dress. In 1895 and 1896 he toured Québec, Ontario and parts of the US to recruit missionaries and solicit donations for the Society of Missionaries of Africa. He returned to North Africa for four years and in 1900 began establishing a Canadian chapter of the White Fathers, which included a recruitment and training house in Québec City. At the ceremony where Forbes was ordained bishop in 1918 one White Father described the Québec City school as a place a "where he trained a magnificent cohort of good soldiers to combat against the demons in Africa."[811] In a letter to his brother detailing plans for the recruitment house, Forbes linked the school to British conquest. He wrote that his superior, Bishop Livinhac, asked if it would "not be a good idea for Canadians to join our efforts to convert the countries that have submitted to Great Britain."[812]

Often working with colonial authorities abroad, missionaries encouraged imperialist sentiment at home. Notwithstanding some notable exceptions, their speeches and publications denigrated African traditions and authorities, while ignoring European abuses and the greed and self-interest driving colonial policy. During the 1900s missionaries were a leading source of information on Africa, Asia and Latin America. In *A Place in the Sun: Haiti, Haitians, and the Remaking of Quebec* Sean Mills writes, "missionary accounts, published in journals and crafted in letters home, delivered during speaking tours and articulated in stand-alone books, were the central ways that French-Canadians developed ideas of the Global South."[813]

As religion has declined, French has become more central to Québecois identity and a larger part of the province/nation's international efforts. The 1965 Doctrine Gérin-Lajoie, the basis of Québec's international relations, made projecting the province's linguistic heritage an important objective.[814] To placate growing Québec nationalism during this period Ottawa massively expanded its aid to "Francophone" nations.

Initially Canadian aid was largely focused on former British colonies in Asia and Africa, but to weaken the sovereignty movement Ottawa began an aid program to French Africa. In a January 1962 memo, long time External Affairs official Marcel Cadieux wrote: "[Quebeckers] are going through a period of intense nationalism. In their present mood they are critical of the degree of influence that they have in national affairs and in particular in the field of external affairs. If a scheme of aid for African states should be developed in such a fashion as to provide an outlet to the French-Canadian interests in French-language states, the results in terms of national unity might be quite substantial ... due to the fact that there is little prospect that French-Canadian aspirations are likely to be satisfied as quickly and as easily in other fields of interest to them; e.g. a national flag, repatriation of the constitution, bilingual checks, the status of French in other provinces, etc."[815]

Cadieux's argument that channelling foreign aid to "French" Africa was a politically expedient means of demonstrating concern for Quebecker's aspirations convinced Ottawa decision-makers. Between 1964 and 1971 Canadian aid to Francophone African countries increased more than 200-fold from $300,000 to $64 million annually.[816]

Ottawa ploughed hundreds of millions of dollars into its various French language cultural and educational institutions. Between 1970 and 1983 Canada provided as much as a third of the budget for the institutions of L'Organisation internationale de la Francophonie (OIF), including the Council of African higher education, the agency of cultural and technical cooperation and the Association of Francophone Universities.[817] While OIF is largely designed to strengthen the French language, is there any place aside from Québec where French is the language of the oppressed?

Even more than the English, the French used language as a tool of colonial control. Schooling in French African colonies, for instance, was almost entirely in French, which stunted the written development of local languages as well as the rise of a common national or regional language. It also oriented the intellectual milieu towards the colonial metropole. *In Decolonizing the Mind* Kenyan writer Ngugi wa Thiong'o argues "the domination of a people's language by the languages of the colonizing nations was crucial to the domination of the mental universe of the colonized."[818]

After independence, the place of French in society was politically fraught. According to Patrick Manning in *Francophone sub-Saharan Africa 1880–1995*, "French was written in the city on street signs, posters, newspapers and government documents. French was the language of the national anthem. French was used in vertical relationships among people of uneven rank; people of equal rank tend to speak African languages among themselves."[819]

At the same time as some newly independent countries attempted to promote Indigenous languages, Ottawa spent heavily to link Québec with "French" Africa. After Algeria won its independence, for instance, the government moved to Arabize the nation. Simultaneously, however, Canadian aid to Algeria was channelled through French-speaking Canadians. Efforts to strengthen the 'common' linguistic heritage between Québec and Algeria stunted its moves towards strengthening Arabic. Though less stark, the same dynamic played out in the Congo with the local language of Lingala, in the Central African Republic with Sango and in Senegal with Wolof.

Canada is the second biggest contributor to the Paris-based OIF. It gives $40 million annually to OIF and the other institutions of la Francophonie.[820] A member in its own right, Québec says its provides "over 10 million dollars per year ... to international solidarity activities in developing countries that are members of La Francophonie."[821] Québec's international affairs ministry is named Le Ministère des Relations internationales et de la Francophonie.

Largely ignored by progressive Québec nationalists, OIF reinforces cultural inequities in former French and Belgian colonies. It can also stir linguistic chauvinism within Québec nationalist circles. During the 2016 OIF Summit in Madagascar *Le Devoir* bemoaned the decline of la langue de Molière in the former French colony. Titled "Quel avenir pour le français?: À Madagascar, la langue de Molière s'étiole", the front page story cited an individual calling the post-independence focus on the country's majoritarian, Indigenous language "nothing less than a 'cultural genocide.'"[822] According to the head of OIF's Observatoire de la langue française, Alexandre Wolff, it was "urgent to show French can be useful" in the island nation.[823] The progressive nationalist paper's hostility to Malagasy wasn't even presented as a battle with the dominant colonial language. The story noted that "English is practically absent" there.

Benefiting from strong Canadian lobbying, former Governor General Michaëlle Jean took charge of OIF in 2015. She was the first non-African to hold the position (Québéc diplomat Clément Duhaime was No. 2 at the organization between 2006-15).[824] Founder of *La Lettre du Continent* (*Africa Intelligence* in English) Antoine Glaser pointed out in a 2016 *Afrique Magazine* interview that Ottawa took advantage of OIF to expand its influence on the continent and promote corporate Canada.[825]

Ottawa's interest in former French colonies usually included a corporate aspect. Québec-based businesses benefited from Ottawa's focus on French-speaking Africa in the late 1960s. One of Québec's leading proponents of the French language and former head of CIDA, Paul Gérin-Lajoie (namesake of Québec's international doctrine), used the aid agency to build Québec-based companies. In a history of Canadian development assistance David Morrison writes, "PGL [Paul Gérin-Lajoie] expanded CIDA's commercial base in French-speaking Canada through active use of the contract approval process to build up Québec-based suppliers and consultancy firms, especially SNC and Lavalin."[826] Gérin-Lajoie's underling, Maurice Strong, continued this pattern when he took charge of CIDA. Much to the dismay of External Affairs "Strong hired SNC ... to manage offices on behalf of CIDA in Francophone African countries where there was no Canadian diplomatic representation."[827]

Six years after Algeria won its independence from France, SNC's vice president of development Jack Hahn described their plan to enter Algeria: "They might be interested in North American technology offered in French."[828]

As someone from a family with roots in Québec dating to the 1600s and who grew up attending French-language schools in a predominantly English-speaking city it pains me to admit it, but nationalism is almost as big a barrier in Québec as it is in Canada to creating a just foreign policy.

***

While not an exhaustive discussion, the above examples help explain why the left has backed policies that harm ordinary people around the world. To build a more internationalist left we must examine flaws in our thinking and the ways in which an inequitable economic and political system inspires individual and institutional backing of pro-imperial policies. My point is not to criticize individuals or organizations, but rather to learn from past mistakes.

The concluding chapter will suggest ways to build an alternative to Canada's foreign policy mess.

Conclusion

THIS BOOK PARTLY REFLECTS my personal experience of trying to make sense of Canadian foreign policy and the lack of "left" criticism of this country's role in the world. It echoes the experiences and hopes of someone who has spent a great deal of time researching, writing and acting on these issues. While the first two activities are essential, the point is not simply to describe the world, but to improve it. In that spirit this book will conclude with suggestions for people who feel motivated to act and then a concrete plan to build an organization to challenge Canada's foreign policy zeitgeist.

While the discussion that follows is primarily focussed on moving the "left" to the left on foreign policy issues, this is an important part of improving Canada's role in the world. After all, if the "left" does not fight for a just foreign policy, who will?

***

As discussed above an essential element of a left foreign policy analysis should be "first do no harm". One might think infusing left wing thought with such a sensible approach would be easy, but it is not. For good and bad reasons a "do more" mantra spans the political divide. Ardent militarists want more troops to join the next NATO war. Liberal militarists call for greater contribution to peacekeeping while NGOs demand more "aid". For their part, arms companies seek increased export support and mining companies lobby for more investor rights agreements.

Notwithstanding the dominance of the "do more" ethos, a "first do no harm" policy is rooted in international law. The concept of self-determination is a core principle of the UN Charter and International Covenant on Civil and Political Rights.[829] Peoples' inalienable right to shape their own destiny is based on the truism that they are best situated to run their own affairs.

Alongside the right to self-determination, the UN and Organization of American States prohibit interfering in the internal affairs of another state without consent. Article 2 (7) of the UN Charter states that "nothing should authorize intervention in matters essentially within the domestic jurisdiction of any state."[830]

A military intervention without UN approval is the "supreme international crime". Created by the UN's International Law Commission after World War II, the Nuremberg Principles describe aggression as the "supreme international crime, differing only from other war crimes in that it contains within itself the accumulated evil of the whole."[831] In other words, by committing an act of aggression against Libya in 2011, Ottawa is responsible not only for rights violations it caused directly, but also those that flowed from its role in destabilizing that country and large swaths of Africa's Sahel region. (Ottawa defied the UN Security Council resolution authorizing a no-fly zone to protect Libyan civilians by dispatching ground forces, delivering weaponry to the opposition and bombing in service of regime change.)

Alongside a "first do no harm" perspective, policies should be evaluated on whether the left would want them pursued here. It is often obvious what policies we wouldn't want turned on us. Few want another country to invade Canada or organize a coup against our elected government. The left generally opposes foreign investment agreements that empower multinationals to sue Canada and should oppose Foreign Investment Protection Agreements (FIPA) that Ottawa signs with countries where Canadian companies dominate. Similarly, progressives who think privatized health and education services are a right-wing plot in Canada, should think twice about promoting foreign-funded NGOs that have undermined governmental capacity in Haiti and other highly impoverished nations. How would we like it if our schools and social services were largely run by private foreign charities? This means supporting public social services, just as we do here.

Alongside "first do no harm" and "would we want that for ourselves" perspectives, we should question a policy or doctrine's roots and ask how does/will it function in the real, inequitable, world in which we live. It is important for the left to look beyond high-minded sounding rhetoric. For example, in the abstract, international aid sounds appealing. In a just world, wealthier regions would assist poorer ones. Federal government transfer payments smooth out regional inequities in Canada and there's no reason this type of policy couldn't be internationalized. When looked at narrowly, most aid projects are beneficial (though there are many examples that are not). Schools financed by Canada elsewhere usually benefit some kids and the same can be said regarding money put into a farmers' cooperative or a micro loan program for impoverished women. But as you broaden the lens of analysis the picture changes. Aid takes on a different meaning in the hands of governments run by and for the economic elite.

Initially conceived as a way to blunt radical decolonization in India, Canadian aid is primarily about advancing Ottawa's geopolitical objectives and, to a lesser degree, specific corporate interests. In the 1970s, for instance, Ottawa increased aid to

African states as a way to mitigate their criticism of Canada's economic and political relations with apartheid South Africa.[832] More substantially, the 'intervention equals aid principle' has long seen money channelled into countries where US and Canadian troops are killing people. The $2 billion in aid Canada spent in Afghanistan was at least partially a public relations exercise to justify — to the Canadian public and elite Afghans — its military occupation.[833] Similarly, the huge influx of Canadian aid to Haiti after the 2004 coup was tied to undermining democracy.

While wealthier regions should assist poorer ones, that doesn't mean that the left should uncritically promote Canadian aid. Challenging unambiguous injustices ought to take priority over promoting policy partly designed to put a humanitarian gloss on a broadly self-serving policy.

The Canadian promoted Responsibility to Protect (R2P) doctrine provides another example of a foreign policy tool that sounds appealing on paper, but masks imperial interventions. R2P asserts that where gross human rights abuses occur it is the duty of the international community to intervene, over and above considerations of state sovereignty. "The principle of non-intervention yields to the international responsibility to protect." On paper this Canadian-promoted doctrine is a good idea, unless one considers national borders, usually created through colonial violence, sacrosanct. But who decides when gross human rights abuses are occurring? Was the US responsible for gross human rights abuses in Iraq? Even though credible reports found that the 2003 US invasion and subsequent occupation led to hundreds of thousands of Iraqi deaths, leading R2P proponents never called on the international community to intervene in Washington.

Rather than a tool to improve international human rights standards, R2P has been used by the powerful against the weak. Many liberal commentators invoked R2P to justify NATO's 2011 bombing of Libya, which turned into a humanitarian disaster. In the early 2000s Liberal government officials cited R2P to cut off assistance to Haiti's elected government and to invade that country. Thousands were killed after the US/France/Canada intervention and a highly impoverished society became even poorer. R2P further undermines state sovereignty, which provides the weakest states with some protection from the most powerful. This is the main reason why Latin American, Asian and African countries have largely opposed attempts to incorporate R2P into international law. The author of *Humanitarian Imperialism: Using Human Rights to Sell War* Jean Bricmont notes, "humanitarian intervention goes only one way, from the powerful to the weak. … Nobody expects Bangladesh to interfere in the internal affairs of the United States."[834]

Leftists should err on the side of caution when aligning with official/mainstream media policy, particularly when NATO's war drums are beating. Just because the politicians and dominant media say we have to "do something" doesn't make it so. Libya and the Sahel region of Africa would almost certainly be better off had a "first do no harm" policy won over the interventionists in 2011.

But, that's not to say the enemy of my enemy is my friend. Just because a regime is in the US/Canada crosshairs doesn't make it worth defending. Ruthless regimes do not deserve leftist support, which is not to say one should back an illegal war to oust them. In other words, there are no simple formulas or slogans that can tell us what position to take or political battle to fight. Rather, we must examine every policy, each suggestion by an analyst and every government allocation through a "first do no harm" and "would we want this for ourselves" lens before deciding to support or oppose it. But, this requires knowing about what is being done in our name around the world. A lack of information is a critical problem inhibiting the construction of a democratic and just foreign policy. The military, diplomats and corporations rely on secrecy and disinterest about what's happening elsewhere to ensure that what most Canadians hear about foreign policy is shaped by their PR departments. This process must be disrupted to create a better world.

...

So, where to start in building a movement for a just foreign policy? In part it is simply a matter of amplifying the work of antiwar, mining justice and international solidarity groups that are already active. We need to significantly ramp up their efforts to force issues of peace and international justice into the public sphere through talks, stickers, posters, petitions, rallies, press conferences, legal challenges, disruptions, etc. Their existing activism can give us hope and direction.

While this activism can be the gravel that goes into the foundation for a wider movement, we also need some cement to hold it together and make it stronger. An organization that could make connections and help coordinate activities amongst the various solidarity groups could improve the effectiveness of everyone's campaigns. As well as fostering linkages such an organization could help articulate the bigger picture.

Indigenous people should be part of a movement for a just foreign policy. First Nation experiences with Canadian colonialism, including so-called aid, missionaries and government financing of their organizations, can offer insight into current foreign policy. Some Christian missionaries who worked to undermine Indigenous cultures at the turn of the 20th century pursued similar efforts in colonial Africa. Additionally, a number of the men who helped suppress the 1869-70 Red River Rebellion and 1885 North-West Rebellion fought to expand British influence over Sudan and southern Africa. In a 1951 speech to the Canadian Club, leading post-World War II foreign-policy planner Lester Pearson linked the Korean War and Cold War to the subjugation of First Nations: "We are faced now with a situation similar in some respects to that which confronted our fore-fathers in early colonial days when they plowed the land with a rifle slung on the shoulder. If they stuck to the plow and left the rifle at home, they would have been easy victims for any savages lurking in the woods."[835]

Studying Canadian colonialism helps us learn lessons for developing a just foreign policy. Today the Palestine solidarity movement benefits from growing recognition of the destruction wrought by settler colonialism on Turtle Island. Similarly, the mining injustice movement has benefited from those groups (often Indigenous) challenging capitalist extractivism.

There is also a strategic value in building ties to Indigenous communities and activists promoting an internationalist vision. First Nations impacted by a mining company would tend to be more sceptical of Canadian resource firms' international abuses and interested in building solidarity with Indigenous communities resisting them abroad. Similarly, Indigenous people would generally have less difficulty believing that Ottawa sought to subjugate people elsewhere. Over the longer term an expansion of First Nations autonomy could redefine the Canadian state in a way that helps reset this country's place in the world.

While it has taken a rightward, Islamophobic, turn, the Québec sovereigntist movement also remains an important potential ally that an umbrella foreign policy organization could help link to specific solidarity campaigns. Opposition to Canada participating in a number of wars largely came from Québec. Moreover, the average white Quebecker probably feels less affinity for empire (whether British or American) than someone in Victoria. A resurgent sovereigntist movement led by Québec Solidaire would put a number of important international issues, including Québec's withdrawal from NATO, into the mainstream discussion.

Left nationalism is another political current that can offer a basis on which to build opposition to Canadian foreign policy. While soft on corporate Canada, it includes a critique of US power that can lead individuals towards an anti-imperialist perspective. It's not inconceivable that expanded immigration, Indigenous empowerment and population growth, combined with a socialistic tinged nationalism, could spur the "world's first post-ethnic, democratic, internationalist nationalism", as Gary Engler details in *Great Multicultural North*.[836]

Many of the institutions discussed above could be pushed into taking better foreign policy positions by an organization that coordinated with solidarity groups. With some sympathetic individuals inside, lobbying by a small number of CCPA, Broadbent Institute and Rideau Institute members/donors would likely bear fruit. Maybe the Rideau Institute could sponsor a debate on the tactical/moral rationale of calling for more peacekeeping rather than demilitarization or the CCPA could initiate a public dialogue about Lester Pearson's legacy and the value in citing it today. A coordinating organization could inspire union members and staffers to engage with their international solidarity funds. Members should push for an internal discussion about the political philosophy driving these funds. A question to be asked is why do we seek solidarity for ourselves yet promote charity internationally? Employing a "first do no harm" outlook, solidarity funds should expand their focus on educating members about Canada's role internationally. Reorienting some of the $10-20 million raised by solidarity funds each year towards challenging Canadian foreign policy would have a substantial impact. Beyond the solidarity funds, unions should feel pressure to campaign against obviously anti-working class foreign policy decisions. They should stoke opposition to the investment rights agreements Canada has signed with African countries and the coups Ottawa supported against governments that increased the minimum wage (in Haiti and Honduras most recently).

Just as wealthy patrons of right wing causes have long recognized, a multiplicity of voices is self-reinforcing. When a union releases a statement or commissions a report criticizing an international policy it often finds its way into the media or influences the think tank world. The same can be said for think tanks and when a left commentator with a platform challenges an international policy, it emboldens others in the media to do so. Of course, the most influential left foreign policy voice is the NDP. As an established political entity with a direct foreign policy mandate, when the federal NDP articulates a position it gives sympathetic reporters and commentators political cover to express that perspective. Numerous individuals and institutions operate in politically partisan ways so the NDP backing an issue often stimulates support from party-associated unions, think tanks and commentators. A forceful NDP position on a number of leading issues would substantially expand the parameters of debate on foreign policy.

A foreign policy organization could prod and help the federal NDP pursue an internal assessment of the pros and cons of an electoral strategy that tapped into activism on issues ranging from demilitarization to Palestine, mining justice to Latin America solidarity. Alongside galvanizing some of its historic activist base, a forceful posture on a series of international issues might help NDP leader Jagmeet Singh's bid to increase the party's appeal among immigrants and people of colour (over 20% of Canadians were born outside the country and half of Torontonians and Vancouverites identify as "visible minorities").[837] A more critical foreign policy posture might enable this effort since individuals with a strong connection to another country would tend to be less supportive of Western domination. The Haitian diaspora in Montréal, Arab community in London, Ontario, Somalis in Ottawa and Vancouver's Iranians might be receptive to elements of a counter-hegemonic foreign policy narrative.

But party strategists fear that the dominant media will lambaste the NDP for expressing forthright criticism on many international issues. And this fear is well founded. But the growth of online news and global television stations makes it easier than ever — if the party cared to try — to defend critical positions on international issues. Here are four positions the party could and should take:

> • The NDP should return to its "Canada out of NATO" position. Withdrawing from NATO would dampen pressure to spend on the military and to commit acts of aggression in service of the US-led world order.

• The party should call on the Canada Revenue Agency to stop subsidizing charities supporting illegal Israeli settlements, the Israeli military and racist organizations in that country. The international campaign to defend Palestinian rights is growing and the NDP ought to contribute by demanding that Ottawa stop subsidizing their dispossession.

• The party should denounce the "ugly Canadian" image mining companies have created for this country abroad. It needs to push aggressively for legislation to empower victims to hold companies accountable in Canadian courts and to restrict public support for companies found responsible for significant abuses abroad.

• The NDP should articulate an internationalist perspective on Canada's huge per capita carbon emissions. The party should highlight how the primary victims of climate disturbances reside in parts of Africa and Asia least responsible for global carbon emissions.

While the party could take a few principled foreign policy positions, it's almost certainly too much to expect the NDP to pursue a "first do no harm" or "would we want it here" perspective in the short or medium term. A political party with electoral ambition must bend to the prevailing political culture, which is dominated by corporations and a US-Empire-aligned foreign policy establishment that promotes an interventionist international posture.

Researching the *Black Book of Canadian Foreign Policy* in the mid-2000s I realized a justice-centered foreign policy would take decades to realize. Deeply ingrained structural and ideological biases favouring Canadian corporations and Western geostrategic interests won't be overcome by electing a new government, even one of good will unlike any Canada has ever seen. Here's a sobering way to look at the situation: The 1800s ended with thousands of Canadians fighting in a brutal conflict on behalf of British mining and geostrategic interests in South Africa. While less monstrous, the 1900s concluded with Canada bombing the former Yugoslavia. The struggle is to ensure this century ends differently.

While "victory" may require decades of struggle, major improvements can, and have, been achieved. Over the past half century, there's been a growth of internationalist sentiment and a reduction in racism. Substantial technological changes have also broadened interest and knowledge of international affairs.

Those who campaigned against wars in Korea, Iraq, Afghanistan, etc., as well as nuclear arms and the weapons industry, have civilized the Canadian military. Ditto for those who have built an internationalist culture by standing in solidarity with Cuba, Vietnam, South Africa, Palestine, Central America, Haiti, etc. Unfortunately, however, little of this activism has been institutionalized. While a number of left media outlets reflect this activism, few alternative foreign policy institutions exist and the ones that do reflect specific concerns. Thus the need for a coordinating organization that can link up the various struggles and highlight the bigger foreign policy picture.

CANADIAN FOREIGN POLICY INSTITUTE

While writing this book, I have been engaged in setting up an organization that could help link existing and future solidarity campaigns, coordinate activities amongst the various groups, serve as an information-sharing house and eventually become a powerful voice for a just Canadian foreign policy. Hosted at Foreignpolicy.ca, the Canadian Foreign Policy Institute (CFPI) is an effort to institutionalize critical foreign policy activism. It will monitor diplomatic, aid, intelligence and military policies as well as corporate Canada's international activities. A central objective will be to bridge the gap between public perception and government/corporate propaganda, to inform the public about what is being done in their name around the world.

The CFPI site will offer various educational tools. A Wiki will offer the general reader an introduction to important themes in Canadian foreign policy. For the more seasoned, CFPI will publish or re-post a wide swath of news content and become a repository of critical articles catalogued by theme. It will also produce lists of the best books and documentaries on Canadian foreign policy.

Through social media accounts and a newsletter CFPI will amplify the work of antiwar, mining justice and international solidarity organizations. Its website will offer contacts for activist groups working on these issues and publish their statements and action alerts.

CFPI will offer media and interested organizations a foreign policy speakers bureau, a list of Canadian-based experts on a wide number of regions and topics. It will publish their articles and in time may seek to issue more in-depth reports from these and other individuals.

CFPI will seek to develop ties to international movements, intellectuals and governments challenging unjust Canadian policies. It will publish their work and connect them to interested Canadian media and groups. As a way to highlight their struggles and to spur Canadians to action, CFPI may create an interactive map of groups or individuals confronting Canadian diplomacy, military or corporations. Ideally the individuals would be international officials or activists that have a title that will mean something to those with little knowledge of those countries (i.e. "Canada helped oust my elected government" – Jean-Bertrand Aristide, former president of Haiti).

CFPI will seek to partner with established left media outlets to support internationally focused investigative stories. It will work with progressive radio and TV outlets to do regular video interviews and podcasts.

CFPI will build and mobilize an email list to engage in periodic action requests such as emailing members of a parliamentary committee or attending antiwar protests. The institute may seek to establish a media flak organization — similar to British-based Media Lens — that mobilizes members to respond to particularly egregious examples of bias.

If there is interest CFPI may seek to develop chapters in cities across the country. CFPI Vancouver, for example, might hold public forums and organize local actions concerning specific issues.

While freewheeling in its criticism, CFPI will be non-sectarian. It will work with the NDP, Green, Communist or other political parties' foreign critics. It will try to co-publish reports with the Rideau Institute or CCPA and will seek to work with unions and their solidarity funds. But, CFPI won't shy away from challenging left institutions or commentators for their concessions to the foreign policy establishment. Left self-improvement is not possible without critical discussion.

CFPI will be able to maintain an unyielding but fraternal criticism because it will be a largely volunteer-run online hub. The low-budget initiative will depend on individual contributors and the rare union donation. CFPI will not seek government or corporate funding and doesn't expect a wealthy patron.

CFPI can succeed if it finds funds to pay a modest salary to a coordinator with the bulk of the initiatives hived off to volunteers. An individual or small group will be responsible for producing action alerts. Ditto for media flak campaigns and updating the organization's Twitter, Facebook and website. The regional groups would be autonomous initiatives linked to CFPI through a broad ideological affinity. In sum, CFPI will thrive as a network of foreign policy focused individuals largely linked through the website.

Finding funds for a coordinator won't be easy. CFPI won't be offered a regular platform on the CBC or *Toronto Star* so reaching a mass audience, which can help generate smaller scale donors, will be a constant struggle.

Unshackled by standard institutional constraints, CFPI won't shy away from controversial, even marginalizing, subjects. It will not be deterred from challenging Canada's role in Ukraine/Syria/Rwanda or other regions where the politics are messy and propaganda thick. What's critical is for CFPI to keep its eyes on the prize: Canada's role in the world. To the largest extent possible it will avoid getting drawn into the internal politics of Haiti, Syria, Libya, etc.

While not lacking in ambition, CFPI will also strive to be realistic. Sustaining a regularly updated site, newsletter and social media presence for years would have some effect on the foreign policy debate. If the organization could develop regular action alerts, some corporate media profile and a handful of local chapters the impact would be even greater.

As this book has demonstrated, the obstacles to critical foreign policy discussion in Canada are substantial. Conversely, the needs are enormous. A wealthy country of 35 million people should be able to sustain an unabashedly critical foreign policy institute. This book is one small step in creating such an organization.

The key will be to think small — do what we can — while understanding the big picture. We must see the forest and the trees. Anthropogenic global warming and technological change have made it more important than ever to see ourselves as part of a collective humanity. We are one world now more than ever before and must act accordingly. Fortunately the technology to disrupt human survival and for a small elite to dominate the planet, also enable ordinary people across the globe to coordinate our struggles to build a better world. This book is offered in the spirit of building an internationalism that supports real democracy for people everywhere.

Bibliography

Abella, Irving and John Sigler. The Domestic Battleground: Canada and the Arab-Israeli Conflict, McGill-Queen's University Press, 1989

Abelson, Donald E. Do Think Tanks Matter?, McGill-Queen's University Press, 2014

Auclair, J. Vie de Mgr John Forbes: le premier Père Blanc Canadien, publisher not identified, 1929

Avakumovic, Ivan. The Communist Party in Canada: a History, McClelland and Stewart, 1975

Azzi, Stephen. Walter Gordon and the Rise of Canadian Nationalism, McGill-Queen's University Press, 1999

Babcock, Robert H. Gompers in Canada: a study in American Continentalism before the first world war, University of Toronto Press, 1974

Baum, Daniel J. The Banks of Canada in the Commonwealth Caribbean: Economic Nationalism and Multinational Enterprises of a Medium Power, Praeger, 1974

Beal, John Robinson. Pearson of Canada, Duell, Sloan and Pearce, 1964

Benn, Carl. Mohawks on the Nile: Natives Among the Canadian Voyageurs in Egypt, 1884-1885, Natural Heritage Books, 2009

Bercuson, David. Blood on the Hills: The Canadian Army in the Korean War, University of Toronto Press, 1999

Bercuson, David. Canada and the Birth of Israel: A Study in Canadian Foreign Policy, University of Toronto Press, 1985

Bercuson, David J and JL Granatstein. Dictionary of Canadian Military History, Oxford University Press, 1 1992

Best, Antony and Jussi M Hanhimäki. International History of the Twentieth Century, Routledge, 2015

Black, David R. Canada and Africa in the new millennium: The Politics of Consistent Inconsistency, Wilfrid Laurier University Press, 2015

Blaikie, Bill. The Blaikie Report, United Church Pub. House, 2011

Blum, William Killing Hope: US Military and CIA Interventions Since World War II, Common Courage Press, 2005

Booh Booh, Jacques-Roger. Le patron de Dallaire parle: Révélations sur les dérives d'un général de l'ONU au Rwanda, Duboiris, 2005

Boyden, Joseph. Three-Day Road, Penguin Canada, 2005

Buxton, William and Charles R. Acland. Harold Innis in the New Century: Reflections and Refractions, McGill-Queen's University Press, 2014

Dyers, Michael. Intent for a Nation: What is Canada For?, Douglas & McIntyre, 2007

Campbell, Bruce and Ed Finn. Living with Uncle: Canada-US relations in an age of Empire, J. Lorimer, 2006

Chapnick, Adam. Canada's Voice: The Public Life of John Wendell Holmes, UBC Press, 2009

Charbonneau, Bruno and Wayne S. Cox. Locating Global Order: American Power and Canadian Security after 9/11, UBC Press, 2010

Chomsky, Noam. Deterring Democracy, Hill and Wang, 1992

Daschuk, James. Clearing the Plains: Disease, Politics of Starvation and the Loss of Aboriginal Life, U of R Press, 2013

Dempsey, James. Warriors of the King: Prairie Indians in World War I, Canadian Plains Research Center, University of Regina, 1999

Deneault, Alain. Canada: A New Tax Haven: How the Country That Shaped Caribbean Tax Havens is Becoming One Itself, Talonbooks, 2015

Eayrs, James George. In Defence of Canada: Growing up allied, University of Toronto Press, 1965

Eayrs, James George. In Defence of Canada: Studies in the Structure of Power: Decision-Making in Canada, Vol 1, University of Toronto Press, 1965

Elkins, Caroline. Imperial Reckoning: The Untold Story of Britain's Gulag in Kenya, Henry Holt and Co., 2005

Engler, Gary. Great Multicultural North, Fernwood, 2010

Engler, Yves. A Propaganda System: How Canada's government, corporations, media and academia sell war and exploitation, Fernwood, 2016

Engler, Yves. Black Book of Canadian Foreign Policy, Fernwood, 2009

Engler, Yves. Canada in Africa: 300 years of aid and exploitation, Fernwood, 2015

Engler, Yves. Lester Pearson's Peacekeeping: the truth may hurt, Fernwood, 2012

English, John. Just Watch Me: The Life of Pierre Elliott Trudeau, 1968-2000, Knopf Canada, 2009

English, John. The Worldly Years: Life of Lester Pearson 1949-1972, Vintage Canada, 1993

Evans, Brian L. The Remarkable Chester Ronning: Proud Son of China, The University of Alberta Press, 2013

Fatah, Tarek. The Jew Is Not My Enemy: Unveiling the Myths That Fuel Muslim Anti-Semitism, McClelland & Stewart, 2010

Finkelstein, Norman. Image and Reality of the Israel-Palestine Conflict, Verso, 2003

Finn, Ed. A Journalist's Life on the Left, Boulder Publications, 2013

Freeman, Linda. The Ambiguous Champion: Canada and South Africa in the Trudeau and Mulroney Years, University of Toronto Press, 1997

Gendron, Robin S. Towards a Francophone Community: Canada's Relations with France and French Africa, 1945-1968, McGill-Queen's University Press, 2006

German, Tony. The Sea Is at Our Gates: the History of the Canadian Navy, McClelland & Stewart, 1990

Gonick, Cy. Inflation or Depression: The Continuing Crisis of the Canadian Economy, J. Lorimer, 1975

Gordon, Todd and Jeffery R Webber, Blood of Extraction: Canadian Imperialism in Latin America, Fernwood, 2016

Gough, Barry. Britain, Canada and the North Pacific: Maritime Enterprise and Dominion, 1778–1914, Ashgate, 2004

Granatstein, Jack and Desmond Morton. A nation forged in fire: Canadians and the Second World War, 1939-1945, Lester and Orpen Dennys, 1989

Griffiths, Ann, Richard Gimblett and Peter Haydon, Canadian Gunboat Diplomacy: The Canadian Navy and Foreign Policy, The Centre, 2000

Groulx, Chanoine Lionel. Le Canada Francais Missionnaire: Une Autre Grande Aventure, Fides, 1962

Gupta, Partha. Imperialism and the British Labour Movement, 1914–1964, Holmes and Meier Publishers, 1975

Hall, James L. Radio Canada International: Voice of a Middle Power, Michigan State University Press, 1997

Hart-Landsberg, Martin. Korea: Division, Reunification, and U.S. Foreign Policy, Monthly Review Press, 1998

Herman, Edward and David Peterson. Enduring Lies: The Rwandan Genocide in the Propaganda System, 20 Year Later, Independent Publishing Platform, 2014

Ismael, Tareq Y. Canadian Arab relations: policy and perspectives, Jerusalem International Pub. House, 1984

Isitt, Benjamin. Militant Minority: British Columbia Workers and the Rise of a New Left, 1948-1972, University of Toronto Press, 2011

Kay, Zachariah. Canada and Palestine: the politics of noncommitment, Israel Universities Press, 1978

Kay, Zachary. Diplomacy of Prudence: Canada and Israel, 1948-1958, McGill-Queen's University Press, 1996

Kay, Zachary. The Diplomacy of Impartiality: Canada and Israel, 1958-1968, Wilfrid Laurier University Press, 2010

Kellogg, Paul. Escape from the Staple Trap: Canadian Political Economy after Left Nationalism, University of Toronto Press, 2015

Keshen, Jeffrey A. Propaganda and Censorship during Canada's great war, University of Alberta Press, 1996

Kumar, Pradeep and Chris Schenk. Paths to Union Renewal: Canadian Experiences, University of Toronto Press, 2005

Kurlansky, Mark. Cod: Biography Of The Fish That Changed The World, Vintage Canada, 2011

Lackenbauer, Whitney. Battle Grounds: The Canadian Military and Aboriginal Lands, University of British Columbia Press, 2007

Lackenbauer, Whitney and Craig Leslie Mantle, Aboriginal Peoples and the Canadian Military: historical perspectives, Canadian Defence Academy Press, 2007

Laxer, James. Mission of Folly: Canada and Afghanistan, Between the Lines, 2008

Laxer, Robert M. Canada LTD: The Political Economy of Dependency, McClelland and Stewart, 1973

Leopold, Les. The Man Who Hated Work and Loved Labor: The Life and Times of Tony Mazzocchi, Chelsea Green Publishing, 2007

Lelande, Suzane. SNC: Engineering Beyond Frontiers, Libre Expression, 1992

Levant, Victor. Quiet complicity: Canadian involvement in the Vietnam War, Between the Lines, 1986

Lewis, David. The Good Fight: Political memoirs 1909-1958, Macmillan of Canada, 1981

Lewis, Stephen. Race Against Time: Searching for Hope in AIDS-ravaged Africa, House of Anansi Press, 2006

Leys, Colin and Marguerite Mendell, Culture and Social Change: social movements in Québec and Ontario, Black Rose Books, 1992

Maloney, Sean. Canada and UN Peacekeeping: Cold War by Other Means – 1945-1970, Vanwell Pub, 2002

McCullough, Colin. Creating Canada's Peacekeeping Past, UBC Press, 2016

McFarlane, Peter. Northern Shadows: Canadians and Central America, Between the Lines, 1989

McKay, Ian and Jamie Swift. Warrior Nation: Rebranding Canada in an Age of Anxiety, Between the Lines, 2012

McKenzie, David. Canada and the First World War: Essays in Honor of Robert Craig Brown, University of Toronto Press, 2005

McQuaig, Linda. Holding the Bully's Coat: Canada and the U.S. Empire, Doubleday Canada, 2007

Millman, Brock. Polarity, Patriotism and Dissent in Great War Canada, 1914 – 1919, University of Toronto Press, 2016

Mills, Sean. A Place in the Sun: Haiti, Haitians, and the Remaking of Quebec, McGill-Queen's University Press, 2016

Morgan, Ted. A Covert Life: Jay Lovestone, communist, anti-Communist, and spymaster, Random House, 1999

Morley, J.T. Secular Socialists: The CCF/NDP in Ontario, A Biography, McGill-Queen's University Press, 1984

Morris, George. CIA and American Labor: The Subversion of the AFL-CIO's Foreign Policy, International Publishers, 1967

Morrison, David R. Aid and Ebb Tide: A History of CIDA and Canadian Development Assistance, Wilfrid Laurier University Press, 1998

Morton, Desmond. The New Democrats 1961 – 1986: the Politics of Change, Copp Clark Pitman, 1986

Namikas, Lise. Battleground Africa: Cold War in the Congo, 1960–1965, Stanford University Press, 2013

Naylor, R. T. Canada in the European Age, 1453-1919, McGill-Queen's University Press, 2006

Off, Carol. The Lion, the Fox and the Eagle: a story of generals and justice in Yugoslavia and Rwanda, Random House Canada, 2000

Onana, Charles. Les secrets de la justice internationale: enquêtes truquées sur le génocide rwandais, Duboiris, 2005

Pappe, Ilan. The Ethnic Cleansing of Palestine, Oneworld, 2006

Pearson, Geoffrey A.H. Seize the Day: Lester B. Pearson and Crisis Diplomacy, Carleton University Press, 1993

Pearson, Lester. Mike: The Memoirs of the Right Honourable Lester B. Pearson Vol 1, University of Toronto Press, 1972

Penlington, Norman. Canada and Imperialism: 1896-1899, University of Toronto Press 1965

Philip, Edward. Canadian Development Assistance to Haiti: An Independent Study, North-South Institute, North-South Institute, 1984

Price, John. Orienting Canada: Race, Empire, and the Transpacific, UBC Press, 2011

Razack, Sherene H. Dark Threats and White Knights, University of Toronto Press, 2004

Reid, Escott. Radical mandarin: the memoirs of Escott Reid, University of Toronto Press, 1989

Robertson, Gordon. Memoirs of a Very Civil Servant: Mackenzie King to Pierre Trudeau, University of Toronto Press, 2000

Romero, Federico. The United States and the European trade union movement, 1944 – 1951, University of North Carolina Press, 1992

Saideman, Stephen M. Adapting in the Dust: Lessons Learned from Canada's War in Afghanistan, University of Toronto Press, 2016

Sarty, Roger. The Maritime Defence of Canada, Canadian Institute of Strategic Studies, 1996

Saul, John Ralston. A Fair Country: Telling Truths About Canada, Viking Canada, 2008

Schraeder, Peter J. United States Foreign Policy toward Africa: Incrementalism, Crisis and Change, Cambridge University Press, 1994

Scott, Jack. Yankee Unions go Home: How the AFL helped the U.S. build an empire in Latin America, New Star Books, 1978

Shipley, Tyler. Ottawa and Empire: Canada and the military coup in Honduras, Between the Lines, 2017

Smith, Keith D. Strange Visitors: Documents in Indigenous-Settler Relations in Canada from 1876, University of Toronto Press, 2014

Spooner, Kevin. Canada, the Congo Crisis, and UN Peacekeeping, 1960-64, UBC Press, 2009

Stairs, Denis. The Diplomacy of Constraint: Canada: The Korean War, and the United States, University of Toronto Press, 1974

Stein,, Janice Gross and Eugene Lang. The Unexpected War: Canada in Kandahar, Viking Canada, 2007

Stone, I. F. The Hidden History of the Korean War, Monthly Review Press, 1969

Thorgrimsson, Thor and E. C. Russell. Canadian Naval Operations in Korean Waters, 1950-1955, Dept. of National Defence, Queen's printer, 1965

Villafana, Frank R. Cold War in the Congo: The Confrontation of Cuban Military Forces, 1960-1967, Transaction Publishers, 2009

Warnock, John. Partner to Behemoth: the military policy of a satellite Canada, New Press, 1970

Webster, David. Fire and the Full Moon: Canada and Indonesia in a Decolonizing World, UBC Press, 2009

Whitaker, Reginald and Gary Marcuse. Cold War Canada: The Making of a National Insecurity State, 1945-1957, University of Toronto Press, 1994

Whitehorn, Alan. Canadian socialism: essays on the CCF-NDP, Oxford University Press, 1992

Wilford, Hugh. The CIA, the British Left and the Cold War: calling the tune?, F. Cass, 2003

Winegard, Timothy C. For King and Kanata: Canadian Indians and the First World War, University of Manitoba Press, 2012

Wiseman, Nelson. Social Democracy in Manitoba: a history of the CCF–NDP, University of Manitoba Press, 2014

Wood, Herbert Fairlie. Strange Battleground: The Operations in Korea and Their Effects on the Defence Policy of Canada, Queen's printer, 1966

Young, Roger. Canadian development assistance to Tanzania: an independent study, North-South Institute, 1983

Young, Walter D. Anatomy of a Party: The National C.C.F. 1932 - 61, University of Toronto Press, 1970

Endnotes

1 Regina manifesto (https://en.wikisource.org/wiki/Regina_manifesto)

2 Alan Whitehorn, Canadian socialism: essays on the CCF-NDP, 38

3 Yves Engler, Black Book of Canadian Foreign Policy, 8-12

4 Yves Engler, Canada in Africa: 300 years of aid and exploitation, 67-75

5 Agnes Jean Groome, C.C.F. Foreign Policy as a factor in Mackenzie King's position on Canada's entry into World War II, 25

6 Ibid

7 Roger Sarty, The Maritime Defence of Canada, 124

8 Agnes Jean Groome, C.C.F. Foreign Policy as a factor in Mackenzie King's position on Canada's entry into World War II, 25

9 James Naylor, Pacifism or anti-imperialism?: The CCF response to the outbreak of World War II, Journal of the Canadian historical Association, Vol 8, No 1, 1997

10 John Price, Canadian Labour, the Cold War and Asia, 1945-1955

11 Ibid

12 Nelson Wiseman, Social Democracy in Manitoba: a history of the CCF–NDP, 54

13 John Warnock, Partner to Behemoth: the military policy of a satellite Canada, 44

14 Benjamin Isitt, Confronting the Cold War: The 1950 Vancouver Convention of the Co-operative Commonwealth Federation, Canadian Historical Review, 91, Aug 2010

15 David Lewis, The Good Fight: Political memoirs 1909-1958, 347

16 Antony Best and Jussi M. Hanhimäki, International History of the Twentieth Century, 222

17 Noam Chomsky, Deterring Democracy, 47

18 Ibid

19 Ibid

20 Security and Prosperity: Two Halves of the Same Walnut Speech by Rt. Hon. Lord Robertson of Port Ellen, Secretary General of NATO, to the British Chamber of Commerce in Belgium, Mar 15, 2001 (http://www.nato.int/docu/speech/2001/s010315a.htm)

21 John Warnock, Partner to Behemoth: the military policy of a satellite Canada, 42

22 David Lewis, The Good Fight: Political memoirs 1909-1958, 349

23 Desmond Morton, The New Democrats 1961 – 1986: The Politics of Change, 24

24 Agnes Jean Groome, M. J. Coldwell and C.C.F. foreign policy, 1932 – 1950, 214

25 Nelson Wiseman, Social Democracy in Manitoba: a history of the CCF–NDP, 56

26 Ibid; Reginald Whitaker and Gary Marcuse, Cold War Canada: The Making of a National Insecurity State, 1945-1957, 271

27 Nils Orvik, Semi-Alignment and Western Security, 178; Should Canada leave NATO and NORAD? (http://archive.rabble.ca/babble/ultimatebb.cgi?ubb=get_topic&f=1&t=005806)

28 Roger Annis, Canadian political leaders' non-debate over Ukraine, Aug 11, 2015 (http://rabble.ca/blogs/bloggers/roger-annis/2015/08/canadian-political-leaders-non-debate-over-ukraine)

29 James George Eayrs, In Defence of Canada: Growing up allied, 85

30 Cy Gonick, Inflation or Depression: The Continuing Crisis of the Canadian Economy, 231

31 Hansard Feb 4, 1949, 237

32 David Bercuson, Blood on the Hills: The Canadian Army in the Korean War, 29

33 Denis Stairs, The Diplomacy of Constraint: Canada, the Korean War, and United States, 59-60; Thor Thorgrimsson

and E. C. RusseII, Canadian Naval Operations in Korean Waters, 1950-1955, 2 (https://www.canada.ca/content/dam/themes/defence/caf/militaryhistory/dhh/official/book-1965-korea-navy-en.pdf)

34 David Lewis, The Good Fight: Political memoirs 1909-1958, 383

35 Walter D Young, Anatomy of a Party: The National C.C.F. 1932 - 61, 233; Benjamin Isitt, Militant Minority: British Columbia Workers and the Rise of a New Left, 1948-1972, 94

36 Benjamin Isitt, Confronting the Cold War: The 1950 Vancouver Convention of the Co-operative Commonwealth Federation Canadian Historical Review, Vol 91, 2010

37 I. F. Stone, The Hidden History of the Korean War, 171

38 Carl A. Posey, How the Korean War Almost Went Nuclear, Air & Space Magazine, July 2015 (https://www.airspacemag.com/military-aviation/how-korean-war-almost-went-nuclear-180955324/)

39 Denis Stairs, The Diplomacy of Constraint: Canada, the Korean War, and United States, 177

40 Stockholm Appeal (https://en.wikipedia.org/wiki/Stockholm_Appeal)

41 Walter D Young, Anatomy of a Party: The National C.C.F. 1932 - 61, 281

42 Ivan Avakumovic, The Communist Party in Canada: a history, 186

43 Reginald Whitaker and Gary Marcuse, Cold War Canada: The Making of a National Insecurity State, 1945-1957, 375

44 J.T. Morley, Secular Socialists: The CCF/NDP in Ontario, A Biography, 85

45 Walter D Young, Anatomy of a Party: The National C.C.F. 1932 - 61, 233

46 David Lewis, The Good Fight: Political memoirs 1909-1958, 345

47 Ibid

48 John Price, Canadian Labour, the Cold War and Asia, 1945-1955

49 Aneurin Bevan (http://www.newworldencyclopedia.org/entry/Aneurin_Bevan)

50 J.T. Morley, Secular Socialists: The CCF/NDP in Ontario, A Biography, 86

51 Hansard 1951, Vol 1, 266

52 Ibid

53 July 22, 1960 (http://www.lipad.ca/full/1960/07/22/2/)

54 Yves Engler, Canada in Africa: 300 years of aid and exploitation, 117-122

55 Jan 26, 1961 (http://www.lipad.ca/full/1961/01/26/2/)

56 Daniel Galvin, A role for Canada in an African crisis: perceptions of the Congo crisis and motivations for Canadian participation, University of Guelph Dissertation, 2004, 83

57 Kevin Spooner, Canada, the Congo Crisis, and UN Peacekeeping, 1960-64, 109

58 Ibid, 116

59 Feb 13, 1961 (http://www.lipad.ca/full/1961/02/13/3/)

60 Kevin Spooner, Canada, the Congo Crisis, and UN Peacekeeping, 1960-64, 136

61 Ibid, 130

62 David J. Bercuson, Canada and the Birth of Israel: A Study in Canadian Foreign Policy, 19

63 Zachariah Kay, Canada in Palestine: the politics of noncommitment, 80

64 Ibid, 93

65 Ibid

66 Ibid, 94

67 Ibid, 69

68 Ibid, 94

69 Ibid

70 David Lewis, The Good Fight: Political memoirs 1909-1958, 341

71 Zachariah Kay, Canada in Palestine: the politics of noncommitment, 146

72 David Lewis, The Good Fight: Political memoirs 1909-1958, 341

73 Ibid

74 Ilan Pappe, The Ethnic Cleansing of

Palestine

75 Zachary Kay, Diplomacy of Prudence: Canada and Israel, 1948-1958, 26

76 Zachary Kay, Diplomacy of Prudence: Canada and Israel, 1948-1958, 67

77 Ibid, 86

78 Zachariah Kay, The Diplomacy of Impartiality: Canada and Israel, 1958-1968, 60; Norman Finkelstein, Image and Reality of the Israel-Palestine Conflict, 143

79 Tarek Fatah, The Jew Is Not My Enemy: Unveiling the Myths That Fuel Muslim Anti-Semitism, 88

80 The Workmen's Circle Call: 1967-1972, 54

81 Tareq Y. Ismael, Canadian Arab relations: policy and perspectives, 30

82 Western trade unionists oppose admission of PLO to UN agency, The Canadian Jewish News, July 25, 1975 (http://newspapers.lib.sfu.ca/cjn2-34122/page-4)

83 International Canada, Vol 9, Canadian Institute of International Affairs [and] Parliamentary Centre for Foreign Affairs and Foreign Trade, 1978 (https://books.google.ca/books?id=tREVAAAAYAAJ&q=On+5+May+Mr+Orlikow+(NDP+Winnipeg+North)+asked+the+prime+minister+if+he+was+aware+that+the+statement+of+a+n on-business+relationship+with+Israel+whi ch+was+included+in+the+contract+would +be+%27completely+prohibited+in+the+U nited+States+under+that+country%27s+an ti-+boycott+laws.%27+On+15+May+Mr+S ymes+(NDP+Sault+Ste+Marie)+said+in+th e+adjournment+debate+that+there+was+%2 7some+evidence%27+that,+in+negotiating+ the+contract,+Bell+Canada+might+have+vi olated+the+Canadian)

84 John English, Just Watch Me: The Life of Pierre Elliott Trudeau, 1968-2000, 266

85 Lewis praises Davis for Stand on Israel, Canadian Jewish News, March 18, 1977 (http://newspapers.lib.sfu.ca/cjn2-32540/page-3)

86 Irving Abella and John Sigler, The Domestic Battleground: Canada and the Arab Israeli Conflict, 236

87 Tony Greenstein, Histadrut: Israel's racist "trade union", Mar 9, 2009 (https://electronicintifada.net/content/histadrut-israels-racist-trade-union/8121)

88 Ben White, Don't believe the hype about Israel's Labour Party being progressive – it's just proven that it's decidedly not, Oct 17, 2017 (https://www.independent.co.uk/voices/israel-palestine-labor-party-gabbay-netanyahu-settlements-two-state-bds-movement-a8005136.html)

89 (https://mobile.twitter.com/findonnelly/status/965015092109570049)

90 Michal Biran, Progressives Should Unite Behind a Two-State Solution, Feb 15, 2018 (https://www.nationalnewswatch.com/2018/02/15/progressives-should-unite-behind-a-two-state-solutio/#.WrEwQjch2Uk)

91 Thomas Mulcair – Israel, Right or Wrong (http://ijvcanada.org/2011/thomas-mulcair-israel-right-or-wrong/)

92 Dreaming a Better World: Canadian Governor General Plants a Tree in Jerusalem's Grove of Nations, Nov 7, 2016 (http://www.kkl-jnf.org/about-kkl-jnf/green-israel-news/november-2016/canada-nation-grove/)

93 Negev Dinner Honourees Event At 24 Sussex Dr. (http://site.jnf.ca/index.php/ott/negev-dinner-honourees-event-at-24-sussex-dr/)

94 Board of Directors (http://cija.ca/about-us/board-of-directors/)

95 Elliot Leven, Why Manitoba Jews should vote NDP, Sept 15, 2011 (http://www.winnipegjewishreview.com/article_detail.cfm?id=1490&sec=7)

96 Myron Love, Manitoba-Israel Shared Values Roundtable Aims to Celebrate Common Bonds, Nov 4, 2009 (http://www.

cfhu.org/news/jewish-post-news-article-manitoba-israel-shared-values-roundtable-aims-celebrate-common-bonds)

97 Avi Gafni, My Favourite Zionist Hero May 25, 2017 (https://www.bnaibrith.ca/avi_gafni_my_favourite_zionist_hero)

98 Dan Leon, The Jewish National Fund: How the Land Was 'Redeemed', Vol 12, No 4 (http://www.pij.org/details.php?id=410)

99 Consideration of reports submitted by States parties under articles 16 and 17 of the Covenant, Concluding observations of the Committee on Economic, Social and Cultural Rights, Dec 4, 1998 (https://unispal.un.org/DPA/DPR/unispal.nsf/0/0BC7883100A95730852569AF00575179)

100 Israel and the occupied territories, Bureau of Democracy, Human Rights, and Labor, 2011 Country Reports on Human Rights Practices, May 24, 2012 (https://www.state.gov/j/drl/rls/hrrpt/2011/nea/186429.htm)

101 JNF Canada (https://mobile.twitter.com/jnfca?lang=en)

102 Jewish People Land (http://www.kkl-jnf.org/about-kkl-jnf/kkl-jnf-id/jewish-people-land/)

103 Graham Beverly, Canada: How the NDP facilitates imperialist war Part one: From Yugoslavia to Haiti, Aug 23, 2011 (https://www.wsws.org/en/articles/2011/08/cana-a23.html); Graeme Truelove, Svend Robinson: a life in politics, 219

104 Noam Chomsky, A Review of NATO's War over Kosovo, Z Magazine, Apr 2001 (https://chomsky.info/200005__/)

105 Jerome Klassen and Greg Albo, Empire's Ally: Canada and the War in Afghanistan, 416

106 Tony Seed, The grim reality unfolding right in front of our eyes, Feb 13, 2003 (https://tonyseed.wordpress.com/2003/02/13/the-grim-reality-unfolding-right-in-front-of-our-eyes/)

107 Daniel Leblanc, General's talk of terrorist 'scumbags' praised, July 16, 2005 (https://www.theglobeandmail.com/news/national/generals-talk-of-terrorist-scumbags-praised/article18241070/)

108 Ibid

109 Bill Curry, Layton suggests talks with Taliban, Globe and Mail, Sept 1, 2006

110 Steven Chase, 'This is the wrong mission for Canada,' Layton says, Sept 4, 2006 (https://www.theglobeandmail.com/news/national/this-is-the-wrong-mission-for-canada-layton-says/article18172324/)

111 Roger Annis and Ian Beeching, Canada/NATO Invasion of Afghanistan Sows Destruction and Misery, Oct 9, 2006 (https://www.globalresearch.ca/canada-nato-invasion-of-afghanistan-sows-destruction-and-misery/3429)

112 Graham Beverly, Canada: How the NDP facilitates Imperialist War Part Two: From Kandahar to Libya, Aug 24, 2011 (https://www.wsws.org/en/articles/2011/08/cndp-a24.html)

113 James Laxer, Afghanistan: The Canadian Mission, Mar 15, 2007 (http://rabble.ca/columnists/afghanistan-canadian-mission)

114 Shocking Lancet Study: 8,000 Murders, 35,000 Rapes and Sexual Assaults in Haiti During U.S.-Backed Coup Regime After Aristide Ouster, Aug 31, 2006 (https://www.democracynow.org/2006/8/31/shocking_lancet_study_8_000_murders)

115 Jerome Klassen and Greg Albo, Empire's Ally: Canada and the War in Afghanistan, 416

116 Matthew Brett, NDP abandonment of anti-war stance an outrage, Dec 12, 2008 (https://canadiandimension.com/blog/view/ndp-abandonment-of-anti-war-stance-an-outrage)

117 Jerome Klassen and Greg Albo, Empire's Ally: Canada and the War in Afghanistan, 415

118 2004 Haitian coup d'état (https://

en.wikipedia.org/wiki/2004_Haitian_
coup_d%27%C3%A9tat#Ottawa_Initiative)
119 Anthony Fenton, Haiti is 'Debated' in
the Canadian House of Commons Mar 11,
2004 (http://archives-2001-2012.cmaq.net/
fr/node/15882.html)
120 Tobi Cohen, Harper deploys jets to
Libyan crisis, Mar 19, 2011 (http://www.
winnipegfreepress.com/canada/harper-
deploys-jets-to-libyan-crisis-118289324.
html)
121 Jameson Berkow, Libyan rebels using
Canadian-made reconnaissance drone, Aug
23, 2011 (http://business.financialpost.com/
technology/libyan-rebels-using-canadian-
made-reconnaissance-drone)
122 Statement by Nycole Turmel on death
of Muammar Gaddafi, Oct 20, 2011 (http://
www.ndp.ca/news/statement-nycole-turmel-
death-muammar-gaddafi)
123 Scott Taylor, Chaos in Libya mounts as
rival factions face off, June 26, 2016 (http://
thechronicleherald.ca/opinion/1375657-
on-target-chaos-in-libya-mounts-as-rival-
factions-face-off)
124 Baird: 'No knowledge' of outside
military action against Iran, Sept 9, 2012
(https://www.ctvnews.ca/politics/baird-
no-knowledge-of-outside-military-action-
against-iran-1.948382)
125 Jessica Hume, NDP backtracks on
Iran comment, Sept 11, 2012 (http://www.
thewhig.com/2012/09/11/ndp-backtracks-
on-iran-comment)
126 Irwin Cotler leads Parliamentary
"Iran Accountability Week", May 22,
2012 (https://irwincotler.liberal.ca/blog/
irwin-cotler-leads-parliamentary-iran-
accountability-week/)
127 Yitzhak Benhorin, The man who fights
Iran, Apr 26, 2011 (http://www.ynetnews.
com/articles/0,7340,L-4060499,00.html)
128 Kenneth Rapoza, One Year After Russia
Annexed Crimea, Locals Prefer Moscow
to Kiev, Mar 20, 2015 (https://www.forbes.
com/sites/kenrapoza/2015/03/20/one-year-
after-russia-annexed-crimea-locals-prefer-
moscow-to-kiev/#6bda6670510d)
129 Maidan in Canada Part I: NGOs,
Ukrainian Revolutionaries, Bulletproof Vests
& Ontario's Top Politicians, Mar 3, 2014
(http://www.genuinewitty.com/2014/03/11/
maidan-in-canada-part-i-ngos-ukrainian-
revolutionaries-bulletproof-vests-queens-
park-politicians/)
130 Murray Brewster, Canadian embassy
used as safe haven during Ukraine uprising,
investigation finds, Jul 12, 2015 (http://
www.cbc.ca/news/politics/canadian-
embassy-used-as-safe-haven-during-ukraine-
uprising-investigation-finds-1.3148719)
131 Mark MacKinnon, Agent Orange: Our
secret role in Ukraine, Globe and Mail, Apr
14, 2007
132 3.1 Summary of Plans and Priorities
for 2006-2009 ARCHIVED - RPP 2006-
2007 Department of Foreign Affairs and
International Trade (https://www.tbs-sct.
gc.ca/rpp/2006-2007/fait-aeci/fait-aeci03-
eng.asp)
133 Counter Russia's impact: MacKay,
Montreal Gazette, July 19, 2007 (https://
www.pressreader.com/canada/montreal-
gazette/20070719/281719790179320)
134 Ibid
135 Roger Annis, Canadian political leaders'
non-debate over Ukraine, Aug 11, 2015
(http://rabble.ca/blogs/bloggers/roger-
annis/2015/08/canadian-political-leaders-
non-debate-over-ukraine)
136 Ibid ; Steven Chase, Canadians can
still do business with Rosneft, despite new
sanctions, Globe and Mail, Feb 18, 2015
137 NDP calls for suspension of military
sales with Russia, Mar 21, 2014 (http://
www.ndp.ca/news/ndp-calls-suspension-
military-sales-russia)
138 Conservatives shield Russian business
elite from sanctions, Aug 6, 2014 (http://
www.ndp.ca/news/conservatives-shield-

russian-business-elite-sanctions)
139 Mike Blanchfield, Canada backs recommendation for Magnitsky Act targeting human rights violators, May 17, 2017 (https://www.thestar.com/news/canada/2017/05/17/canada-backs-recommendation-for-magnitsky-act-targeting-human-rights-violators.html)
140 Lee Berthiaume, Trudeau will face pointed questions on Canada's NATO role at Poland summit, July 7, 2016 (https://www.thestar.com/news/canada/2016/07/07/trudeau-will-face-pointed-questions-on-canadas-nato-role-at-poland-summit.html)
141 Canada's Support to Ukraine in Crisis and Armed Conflict, Report of the Standing Committee on National Defence Stephen Fuhr, Chair (http://www.ourcommons.ca/Content/Committee/421/NDDN/Reports/RP9313861/nddnrp08/nddnrp08-e.pdf)
142 Emmanuel Dreyfus, Ukraine Beyond Politics, Le Monde Diplomatique, Mar 2014 (https://mondediplo.com/2014/03/02ukraine)
143 Michael Laxer, What is far-right organization Right Sector doing marching in Toronto's Ukrainian Festival Parade?, Sept 19, 2016 (http://theleftchapter.blogspot.ca/2016/09/what-is-far-right-organisation-right.html)
144 Susana Mas, Harper to raise Syria crisis on China trip, Feb 5 2012 (http://www.cbc.ca/news/politics/harper-to-raise-syria-crisis-on-china-trip-1.1204508) ; Les Whittington, NDP grill Tories over Suncor's operations in Syria, Nov 21 2011 (https://www.thestar.com/news/canada/2011/11/21/ndp_grill_tories_over_suncors_operations_in_syria.html)
145 Catherine Cullen, NDP pushes for Syrian 'White Helmets' to win Nobel Peace Prize, Sep 15, 2016 (http://www.cbc.ca/m/touch/politics/story/1.3764121)
146 Hélène Laverdière, Mar 29, 2018 (https://twitter.com/HLaverdiereNPD/status/979382336595750919?s=20) ; Jolson Lim, MPs look to support Syrian rescue workers after 'riveting' Ottawa appearance, Apr 11, 2018 (https://www.hilltimes.com/2018/04/11/gripped-harrowing-stories-syrian-rescue-workers-mps-want-federal-support-white-helmets-continue/140138)
147 Max Blumenthal and Ben Norton, Yet another video shows U.S.-funded white helmets assisting public-held executions in rebel-held Syria, May 25, 2017 (https://www.salon.com/2017/05/25/yet-another-video-shows-u-s-funded-white-helmets-assisting-public-held-executions-in-rebel-held-syria_partner/)
148 Ibid
149 Our Partners (http://syriacivildefense.org/our-partners) ; 'We don't hide it': White Helmets openly admit being funded by Western govts, Oct 19, 2016 (https://www.rt.com/news/363363-white-helmets-funded-west/)
150 Nobel Peace Prize nominees White Helmets to visit five Canadian cities, News Release, Dec 6 2016 (https://www.canada.ca/en/global-affairs/news/2016/12/modification-nobel-peace-prize-nominees-white-helmets-visit-five-canadian-cities.html?=undefined&wbdisable=true) ; Statement by Foreign Affairs Minister on Seven Years of Conflict in Syria Statement, Global Affairs Canada, Mar 26, 2018 (https://www.canada.ca/en/global-affairs/news/2018/03/statement-by-foreign-affairs-minister-on-seven-years-of-conflict-in-syria.html)
151 Levon Sevunts, Canada condemns Venezuela's 'undemocratic' vote but is not ready to follow U.S. sanctions yet, Jul 31, 2017 (http://www.cbc.ca/news/politics/venezuela-sanctions-regime-vote-1.4229930)
152 NDP statement on the situation in Venezuela, June 3, 2016 (http://helenelaverdiere.ndp.ca/ndp-statement-on-the-situation-in-venezuela)

153 Uruguay's Mujica: Opposition, OAS Leader Almagro Endangering Venezuela and Region, April 30, 2017 (https://www.telesurtv.net/english/news/Uruguays-Mujica-Opposition-OAS-Leader-Almagro-Endangering-Venezuela-and-Region-20170430-0030.html)

154 Maria Carolina Marcello, Just 5 percent approve of Brazilian leader Temer's gov't: poll, Jul 27, 2017 (https://www.reuters.com/article/us-brazil-politics-poll/just-5-percent-approve-of-brazilian-leader-temers-govt-poll-idUSKBN1AC2A8)

155 Nick Taylor-Vaisey, The House is unanimous about Venezuela, Feb 28, 2014 (http://www.macleans.ca/politics/the-house-is-unanimously-concerned-about-venezuelan-unrest/)

156 Barney Henderson, Donald Trump threatens Venezuela's Nicolas Maduro with military action, Aug 12, 2017 (http://www.telegraph.co.uk/news/2017/08/11/donald-trump-threatens-venezuelas-nicolas-maduro-military-option/)

157 Tillerson Hints at Military Coup in Venezuela, Feb 2, 2018 (https://venezuelanalysis.com/News/13636)

158 David Ljunggren, Canada to impose sanctions on Venezuela's Maduro and top officials, Sept 22 2017 (https://www.reuters.com/article/us-venezuela-canada/canada-to-impose-sanctions-on-venezuelas-maduro-and-top-officials-idUSKCN1BX2PV) ; Noam Chomsky, Danny Glover slam Canadian, U.S. sanctions on Venezuela, Mar 9 2018 (https://www.theglobeandmail.com/news/world/noam-chomsky-danny-glover-slam-canadian-us-sanctions-on-venezuela/article38259253/)

159 Peter Hum, Stepping back from hotspot diplomacy, Ben Rowswell hopes to better the world with tech, Aug 19, 2017 (http://ottawacitizen.com/news/local-news/ben-rowswell)

160 Susanne Gratius, Assessing Democracy Assistance Venezuela, FRIDE, May 2010 (http://fride.org/descarga/IP_WMD_Venezuela_Eng_jul2310.pdf)

161 Anthony Fenton, The Revolution Will Not Be Destabilized: Ottawa's democracy promoters target Venezuela, Apr 3, 2009 (http://www.dominionpaper.ca/articles/2557)

162 Yves Engler, Recognition and little else: Canada's Anti-Venezuela Diplomacy, Oct 20, 2006 (http://www.dominionpaper.ca/foreign_policy/2006/10/20/recognitio.html) ; Carmona Decree (https://en.wikipedia.org/wiki/Carmona_Decree)

163 Lee Berthiaume, Liberals' second budget leaves big questions on vets' pensions, defence spending, Mar 22 2017 (http://atlantic.ctvnews.ca/mobile/liberals-second-budget-leaves-big-questions-on-vets-pensions-defence-spending-1.3336568)

164 David Cochrane, Defence spending increase won't boost deficit, Finance Department says, Jun 8, 2017 (http://www.cbc.ca/news/politics/defence-policy-deficit-spending-1.4151769)

165 Murray Brewster, Liberals planning $600M down payment on defence strategy, June 20, 2017 (http://www.cbc.ca/news/politics/dnd-budget-boost-1.4170340)

166 Althia Raj, Liberals Silence Opposition By Fulfilling Their Defence-Spending Promises, June 10, 2017 (https://www.huffingtonpost.ca/althia-raj/liberals-defence-spending-harjit-sajjan-tories-ndp_b_17032948.html)

167 Canada's top soldier says troops ready and eager for new overseas missions, Canadian Press, July 7, 2012 (https://www.cp24.com/news/canada-s-top-soldier-says-troops-ready-and-eager-for-new-overseas-missions-1.869849)

168 Kevin Libin, Pacifist NDP leans right on foreign policy, May 8, 2011 (http://news.nationalpost.com/full-comment/kevin-libin-pacificist-ndp-leans-right-on-foreign-policy)

169 Matthew Behrens, Canada's massive

military budget is off the table in federal election, Apr 26, 2011 (http://rabble.ca/news/2011/04/canadas-massive-military-budget-table-federal-election)

170 Lee Berthiaume, Radar upgrades raise questions about ultimate cost of Liberal's defence review plan, Aug 30, 2017 (http://www.cbc.ca/news/politics/liberals-cost-defence-review-norad-1.4269488)

171 Marco Vigliotti, Conservatives, NDP call on Liberal government to match rhetoric with action on NORAD, Hill Times, Nov 27, 2017

172 Steven Chase, New warships to cost more than $100-billion, Ottawa estimates, Nov 13, 2013 (https://www.theglobeandmail.com/news/politics/ottawa-estimates-new-warships-to-cost-more-than-100-billion/article15407360/)

173 Carmen Chai, Layton vows to fix 'broken' defence system, Apr 8, 2011 (http://nationalpost.com/news/politics/layton-vows-to-fix-broken-defence-system)

174 NDP slams Conservatives over lack of decision on naval supply ship, May 28, 2015 (https://www.ctvnews.ca/politics/ndp-slams-conservatives-over-lack-of-decision-on-naval-supply-ship-1.2395503)

175 2015 NDP Platform (https://docslide.com.br/documents/2015-ndp-platform.html)

176 Tony German, The Sea Is at Our Gates: the History of the Canadian Navy, 317/ 323

177 Ann Griffiths, Richard Gimblett and Peter Haydon, Canadian Gunboat Diplomacy: The Canadian Navy & Foreign Policy, 30

178 Marc Milner, The Invasion Of El Salvador: Navy, Part 14, Mar 1, 2006 (https://legionmagazine.com/en/2006/03/the-invasion-of-el-salvador/)

179 Ann Griffiths, Richard Gimblett and Peter Haydon, Canadian Gunboat Diplomacy: The Canadian Navy & Foreign Policy, 151

180 Target asks veterans to sell poppies outside stores, Sept 23, 2013 (http://atlantic.ctvnews.ca/target-asks-veterans-to-sell-poppies-outside-stores-1.1467411)

181 Laura Stone, Make Remembrance Day a legal holiday, NDP MP says, Nov 5, 2014 (https://globalnews.ca/news/1653402/make-remembrance-day-a-legal-holiday-ndp-mp-says/)

182 Remembrance Day ceremonies at National War Memorial honour the fallen, Nov 10, 2015 (http://www.cbc.ca/news/politics/remembrance-day-2015-ceremony-ottawa-1.3313522)

183 Nelson Wiseman, Social Democracy in Manitoba: a history of the CCF–NDP, 51

184 Ibid

185 Benjamin Isitt, Militant Minority: British Columbia Workers and the Rise of a New Left, 1948-1972, 89

186 Justin Podur, NDP purge of pro-Palestine candidates plays into Harper's hands, Aug 25, 2015 (https://ricochet.media/en/562/ndp-purge-of-pro-palestine-candidates-plays-into-harpers-hands)

187 Morgan Wheeldon, Kings-Hants NDP candidate, resigns over Israel comments, Aug 10 2015 (http://www.cbc.ca/news/canada/nova-scotia/morgan-wheeldon-kings-hants-ndp-candidate-resigns-over-israel-comments-1.3185485) Lizzie Dearden, Israel-Gaza conflict: 50-day war by numbers, Aug 27 2014 (http://www.independent.co.uk/news/world/middle-east/israel-gaza-conflict-50-day-war-by-numbers-9693310.html)

188 Email to author from Barry Weisleder

189 Yves Engler, Insiders suppress 'Palestine Resolution' at NDP convention, Mar 10, 2018 (http://rabble.ca/blogs/bloggers/yves-englers-blog/2018/03/insiders-suppress-palestine-resolution-ndp-convention)

190 Ibid

191 NDP Rejects Right Turn at Vancouver Convention, NDP Socialist Caucus, Jun 28,

2011 (http://ndpsocialists.ca/ndp-rejects-right-turn-vancouver-convention/)

192 Resolutions 22nd Biennial Convention New Democratic Party of Canada, Quebec City, Sept 8–10 2006 (http://www.stephentaylor.ca/archives/ndp-resolutions1.pdf)

193 Barry Weisleder, NDP Demands "Troops Out Now" (http://www.laborstandard.org/New_Postings/NDP_Canada.htm)

194 NDP ranks reject turn to right, July 8, 2011 (https://socialistaction.ca/2011/07/08/ndp-ranks-reject-turn-to-right/)

195 Patrick Cockburn, Amnesty questions claim that Gaddafi ordered rape as weapon of war, June 23, 2011 (http://www.independent.co.uk/news/world/africa/amnesty-questions-claim-that-gaddafi-ordered-rape-as-weapon-of-war-2302037.html)

196 Peter O'Neil, The legacy of Svend Robinson: book excerpt, Sept 14, 2013 (http://www.vancouversun.com/life/legacy+svend+robinson+book+excerpt/8909774/story.html)

197 Robert H Babcock, Gompers in Canada: a study in American Continentalism before the first world war, 26

198 George Morris, CIA and American Labor: The Subversion of the AFL-CIO's Foreign Policy, 36; The Canadian Forum, Jan 1925, Vol V, no 52

199 Lorne Brown, The Great War: A Crime Against Humanity, Vol 48, Nov 2014 (https://canadiandimension.com/articles/view/the-great-war-a-crime-against-humanity)

200 Jack Scott, Yankee Unions go Home: How the AFL helped the U.S. build an empire in Latin America, 257

201 Robert H Babcock, Gompers in Canada: a study in American Continentalism before the first world war, 107

202 David McKenzie, Canada and the First World War: Essays in Honor of Robert Craig Brown, 233

203 Jeffrey A Keshen, Propaganda and Censorship during Canada's great war, 5

204 Gregory S. Kealey and Andrew Parnaby, A War on Two Fronts, Mar 13, 2017 (http://www.canadahistory.ca/Explore/Politics-Law/A-War-on-Two-Fronts)

205 Margaret Randall and Jack Scott, Canadian Workers, US Unions, 112

206 Ibid

207 Brock Millman, Polarity, Patriotism and Dissent in Great War Canada, 1914 – 1919, 179

208 Ibid

209 James George Eayrs, In Defence of Canada: Studies in the Structure of Power: Decision-Making in Canada, Vol 1, 36

210 Canadian Congress Journal, Vol 7, Oct 1928, 19

211 The Stockholm Conference, Canadian Congress Journal, Aug 1930

212 League of Nations Society in Canada 15th annual national conference, Canadian Congress Journal, June 1937 ; A Journal of Foreign Affairs, Canadian Congress Journal, Vol 7, Aug 1928

213 The West Indies Steamship Service, Canadian Congress Journal, Vol 8, Aug 1929

214 Ibid

215 Development of Trade with the West Indies, Canadian Congress Journal, Vol 7, Dec 1928

216 Mark Kurlansky, Cod: Biography Of The Fish That Changed The World, 83

217 Development of Trade with the West Indies, Canadian Congress Journal, Vol 7, Dec 1928

218 Canadian Congress Journal, Vol 4, Sept 1925, 50

219 Yves Engler, Canada in Africa: 300 Years of Aid and Exploitation, 67-75

220 International Relationships, Canadian Congress Journal, Vol 7, Aug 1928, 32 ;

Canadian Congress Journal, Vol 3, No 4, 33 ; Canadian Congress Journal, Vol 3, No 1, 1924 ; Commonwealth Trade Union Conference, Canadian Congress Journal, Aug 1950

221 Empire Settlement, Canadian Congress Journal, Vol 3, No 6, 1924

222 Canadian Congress Journal, June 1927 Vol 6, 31

223 Canadian Congress Journal, June 1953, 8

224 Wendy Cuthbertson, Labour Goes to War: The CIO and the Construction of a New Social Order, 1939-45, 13

225 Tristin Hopper, The prime minister with a man crush for Hitler, May 15, 2017 (http://nationalpost.com/news/canada/he-loves-flowers-the-insane-true-story-of-the-day-canadas-prime-minister-met-hitler)

226 Jack Granatstein and Desmond Morton, A nation forged in fire: Canadians and the Second World War, 1939-1945, 11

227 Peace!, Canadian Congress Journal, Aug 1945

228 Labour is acclaimed for atomic bomb Aid, Canadian Congress Journal, Aug 1945

229 John Price, Orienting Canada: Race, Empire, and the Transpacific, 146

230 John Price, Canadian Labour, the Cold War and Asia, 1945-1955

231 Ibid

232 Ibid

233 Reginald Whitaker and Gary Marcuse, Cold War Canada: The Making of a National Insecurity State, 1945-1957, 320

234 Federico Romero, The United States and the European trade union movement, 1944 – 1951, 117

235 Ibid, 177

236 Ibid, 163

237 International Confederation of Free Trade Unions, Canadian Congress Journal, Jan 1950

238 Hugh Wilford, the CIA, the British Left and the Cold War: calling the tune?, 93

239 Ibid ; Federico Romero, the United States and the European trade union movement, 1944 – 1951, 95

240 Ibid, 130

241 Ibid

242 Percy Bengough (http://www.thecanadianencyclopedia.ca/en/article/percy-bengough/)

243 The Canadian Labour Congress and Free Trade Unions Throughout the World, The Empire Club of Canada Addresses, Feb 7, 1957 (http://speeches.empireclub.org/59958/data)

244 Caroline Elkins, Imperial Reckoning: The Untold Story of Britain's Gulag in Kenya

245 Katherine Slavka Nastovski, Towards Transformative Solidarities: Wars of Position in the Making of Labour Internationalism in Canada, 228

246 Ibid, 236

247 Partha Gupta, Imperialism and the British Labour Movement, 100

248 Ted Morgan, A Covert Life: Jay Lovestone, communist, anti-Communist, and spymaster, 313

249 Ibid

250 Michael Joseph Murphy, The Canadian International Development Agency and the Canadian Labour Congress: A Developing Partnership, 55

251 Michael Joseph Murphy, The Canadian International Development Agency and the Canadian Labour Congress: A Developing Partnership, 55

252 John Price, Canadian Labour, the Cold War and Asia, 1945-1955

253 David Webster, Fire and the Full Moon: Canada and Indonesia in a Decolonizing World, 50

254 John Price, Canadian Labour, the Cold War and Asia, 1945-1955

255 Hansard May 14, 1951, 3003

256 Report of the Executive Council, Canadian Labour Congress, Fourth

Constitutional Convention, 1962, 70 ; James Hall, Radio Canada International, 113

257 The Canadian Labour Congress First Convention, report of proceedings, 1956, 92

258 Report of the Executive Council, Canadian Labour Congress, Second Constitutional Convention, 1958, 105

259 Ibid

260 Report of the Executive Council, Canadian Labour Congress, Third Constitutional Convention, 1960, 88

261 Report of the Executive Council, Canadian Labour Congress, Fourth Constitutional Convention, 1962, 31

262 Canadian Labour Congress Convention Proceedings 1976, 70

263 John Price, Canadian Labour, the Cold War and Asia, 1945-1955

264 Who is for peace?, Canadian Congress Journal, Aug 1950

265 John Price, Canadian Labour, the Cold War and Asia, 1945-1955

266 Martin Hart-Landsberg, Korea: Division, Reunification, and U.S. Foreign Policy, 121

267 John Price, Orienting Canada: Race, Empire, and the Transpacific, 180

268 65th Convention Liquidates Communism, Canadian Congress Journal, Oct 1950 ; John Price, Canadian Labour, the Cold War and Asia, 1945-1955

269 Benjamin Isitt, Militant Minority: British Columbia Workers and the Rise of a New Left, 1948-1972, 58

270 Reginald Whitaker and Gary Marcuse, Cold War Canada: The Making of a National Insecurity State, 1945-1957, 349

271 Ibid, 345

272 Ibid, 354

273 John Price, Canadian Labour, the Cold War and Asia, 1945-1955

274 The Canadian Labour Congress and Free Trade Unions Throughout the World, The Empire Club of Canada Addresses, Feb 7, 1957 (http://speeches.empireclub.

org/59958/data)

275 Report of the Executive Council, Canadian Labour Congress, Fourth Constitutional Convention, 1962, 71

276 Frank R. Villafana, Cold War in the Congo. The Confrontation of Cuban Military Forces, 1960-1967, 25

277 William Blum, Killing Hope: US Military and CIA Interventions Since World War II, 158

278 Lise Namikas, Battleground Africa: Cold War in the Congo, 1960–1965, 89

279 Peter J. Schraeder, United States Foreign Policy toward Africa: Incrementalism, Crisis and Change, 55

280 Report of the Executive Council, Canadian Labour Congress, Fourth Constitutional Convention, 1962, 52

281 Fall of Peron, Canadian Congress Journal, Oct 1955

282 Jack Scott, Yankee unions, go home: How the AFL helped the U.S. build an empire in Latin America, 222

283 Ed Finn, A Journalist's Life on the Left, 74

284 Ibid

285 Katherine Slavka Nastovski, Towards Transformative Solidarities: Wars of Position in the Making of Labour Internationalism in Canada, 246

286 Ibid, 242

287 Ibid, 242

288 Ibid, 244

289 Les Leopold, The Man Who Hated Work and Loved Labor: The Life and Times of Tony Mazzocchi, 338

290 Reginald Whitaker and Gary Marcuse, Cold War Canada: The Making of a National Insecurity State, 1945-1957, 362

291 Michael Joseph Murphy, The Canadian International Development Agency and the Canadian Labour Congress: A Developing Partnership, 108

292 Ibid, 1115

293 Marv Gandall, Foreign Affairs: The

CLC Abroad, This Magazine, Feb 1986
294 Ibid
295 Michael Joseph Murphy, The Canadian International Development Agency and the Canadian Labour Congress: A Developing Partnership, 16
296 Ibid, 86
297 Marv Gandall, Foreign Affairs: The CLC Abroad, This Magazine Feb 1986
298 Michael Joseph Murphy, The Canadian International Development Agency and the Canadian Labour Congress: A Developing Partnership, 86
299 Marv Gandall, Foreign Affairs: The CLC Abroad, This Magazine Feb 1986
300 Colin Leys and Marguerite Mendell, Culture and Social Change: social movements in Québec and Ontario, 120
301 Marv Gandall, Foreign Affairs: The CLC Abroad, This Magazine Feb 1986
302 Ibid
303 Colin Leys and Marguerite Mendell, Culture and Social Change: social movements in Québec and Ontario, 120
304 Ibid
305 Mordechai Briemberg, Canadian Trade Unions in Palestine, The United Nations Seminar on the Question of Palestine, 1983
306 Zachariah Kay, Canada in Palestine: the politics of noncommitment, 85
307 Mordechai Briemberg, Canadian Trade Unions and Palestine, The United Nations Seminar on the Question of Palestine, 1983
308 Fifth Constitutional Convention of the Canadian Labour Congress, Apr 1964, 89
309 Tony Greenstein, Histadrut: Israel's racist "trade union", Mar 9, 2009 (https://electronicintifada.net/content/histadrut-israels-racist-trade-union/8121)
310 Ibid
311 Ibid
312 The Canadian Labour Congress First Convention, report of proceedings, 1956, 92
313 Barry Bristman, In the Strategic Interests of Canada: Canadian Arms Sales to Israel and Other Middle East States, 1949-1956. MA thesis, University of Calgary (1992)
314 Canada-Israel Friendship: The First Thirty Years, 141 ; International Perspectives, Vol 16, 1988, 38
315 Mordechai Briemberg, Canadian Trade Unions in Palestine, The United Nations Seminar on the Question of Palestine, 1983
316 Canadian Middle East Digest, Vol 1, No 4
317 Senate Mideast report is labelled anti-Israel, Globe and Mail, June 27, 1985
318 Gilbert Levine, Canadian labor loosens historic ties to Israel, Toronto Star May 16, 1990
319 Disposition of Matters Referred to the Executive Council by the 17th Constitutional Convention of the Canadian Labour Congress, 1998, 13
320 Andy Ajzenkopf-Levy, Israel and Canadian Unions: a strained relationship?, Canadian Jewish News Apr 28, 2005
321 Ibid
322 Steve Buist, Labour union's father-son team to be honoured at Negev Dinner, Hamilton Spectator, June 7, 2000
323 CAW's Hargrove Urges Canadian Islamic Congress Leader To Step Down (http://archive.rabble.ca/babble/ultimatebb.cgi?ubb=get_topic&f=12&t=000677)
324 Muslims, Arabs Call on B'nai Brith to Repudiate "Terror" Comments 2004/11/01 (http://www.caf.ca/2004/11/muslims-arabs-call-on-bnai-brith-to-repudiate-terror-comments/)
325 CUPE boycott of Israel won't help cause of peace (http://archive.is/RhnOo)
326 CAW Calls on Prime Minister to Take Leadership Role (http://www.caw.ca/en/3791.htm)
327 Ibid
328 Casualties of the 2006 Lebanon War (https://en.wikipedia.org/wiki/Casualties_of_the_2006_Lebanon_War)

329 Buzz Hargrove, Laying It On The Line: Buzz Hargrove, 306

330 Lisa Green, Shades of Indigo, May 18, 2006 (http://www.jpost.com/Jewish-World/Jewish-Features/Shades-of-Indigo)

331 Yves Engler, What's Left of Quebec Left?, Apr 12, 2008 (https://canadiandimension.com/blog/view/canadian-dimension-special-whats-left-of-quebec-left)

332 Ibid

333 Ibid

334 Roland Oliphant, Ukraine crisis: dozens killed in Odessa fire as violence spreads to country's south, May 2, 2014 (https://www.telegraph.co.uk/news/worldnews/europe/ukraine/10805412/Ukraine-crisis-dozens-killed-in-Odessa-fire-as-violence-spreads-to-countrys-south.html)

335 Unifor: Statement on Ukraine, Mar 6, 2014 (https://www.unifor.org/sites/default/files/brief-statements/statement_on_ukraine.pdf)

336 Report of the Executive Council, Canadian Labour Congress, Sixteenth Constitutional Convention, 1986 (under headline international affairs department)

337 Carleton Mourns Loss of William H. Barton, Nov 12, 2013 (http://newsroom.carleton.ca/2013/11/12/carleton-mourns-loss-william-h-barton/) ; Geoffrey Pearson and Nancy Gordon, Shooting Oneself in the Head: the demise of CIIPS, in Canada Among Nations 1993–94 ; Roy McFarlane, Pearson Discusses Peace and Security Institute, Peace Magazine, May 1985 (http://peacemagazine.org/archive/v01n3p09.htm) ; George Gray Bell (https://en.wikipedia.org/wiki/George_Gray_Bell)

338 Report of the Executive Council, Canadian Labour Congress, Eighth Constitutional Convention, 1970, 72

339 Katherine Slavka Nastovski, Towards Transformative Solidarities: Wars of Position in the Making of Labour Internationalism in Canada, 207

340 Mordechai Briemberg, Canadian Trade Unions and Palestine, The United Nations Seminar on the Question of Palestine, 1983

341 Adam Chapnick, Canada's Voice: The Public Life of John Wendell Holmes, 205 ; Alex I. Inglis, The Institute and the Department, International Journal, Vol 33, No 1, Winter 1977-78 ; Canadian Institute of International Affairs Annual Report, 1988

342 Spotlight Canada: The Canadian Institute of International Affairs (https://anticommunistarchive.wordpress.com/edmund-burke-society/f-paul-fromm/spotlight-canada-the-canadian-institute-of-international-affairs/)

343 Donald E. Abelson, Do Think Tanks Matter?, 43

344 Report of the Executive Council, Canadian Labour Congress, Eighth Constitutional Convention, 1970, 37

345 45 Years of History (http://www.parlcent.org/en/who-we-are/our-story/) ; Thomas M. Franck and Edward Weisband, Secrecy and Foreign policy, 148

346 Report of the Executive Council, 24th Constitutional Convention, 2005, 50

347 David R. Morrison, Aid and Ebb Tide: A History of CIDA and Canadian Development Assistance, 70

348 Ibid

349 Lee Berthiaume, Cutting out the development NGO 'heart', Embassy, June 9, 2010

350 Pradeep Kumar and Chris Schenk, Paths to Union Renewal: Canadian Experiences, 226

351 Canadian Labour: Travailleur Canadien, Vol 30-31

352 Member's Report, Steelworkers Humanity Fund, June 2016 (http://www.usw.ca/act/activism/humanity/resources/document/SHF_annual_report2016_web.pdf)

353 Canadian Labour Congress, Member

Profile, Apr 2012 (http://www.ccic.ca/members/profiles/CLC_2012-04_e.php)

354 Pradeep Kumar and Chris Schenk, Paths to Union Renewal: Canadian Experiences, 227

355 Political activities, Policy statement, Reference number CPS-022, Sept 2, 2003 (http://www.cra-arc.gc.ca/chrts-gvng/chrts/plcy/cps/cps-022-eng.html#4-0)

356 Dean Beeby, Revenue Canada targets Steelworkers charity for political activities, Apr 12, 2015 (http://www.cbc.ca/news/politics/revenue-canada-targets-steelworkers-charity-for-political-activities-1.3026863)

357 Gregory Thomas, Putting Unions on the Same Playing Field as Charities (http://www.taxpayer.com/commentaries/putting-unions-on-the-same-playing-field-as-charities)

358 Colombia Advocating for strong trade unions in the oil sector (http://www.unifor.org/sites/default/files/attachments/sjf-casestudy-oiltradeunions-en-v1.0.pdf)

359 Haiti Rebuilding together (http://www.unifor.org/sites/default/files/attachments/sjf-casestudy-haitiearthquake-en-v1.0.pdf)

360 Report of the Executive Council, Canadian Labour Congress, Third Constitutional Convention, 1960,

361 Michael Joseph Murphy, The Canadian International Development Agency and the Canadian Labour Congress: A Developing Partnership, 10

362 Report of the Executive Council, Canadian Labour Congress, Eighth Constitutional Convention, 1970, 36

363 Katherine Slavka Nastovski, Towards Transformative Solidarities: Wars of Position in the Making of Labour Internationalism in Canada, 256

364 Ibid

365 Michael Joseph Murphy, The Canadian International Development Agency and the Canadian Labour Congress: A Developing Partnership, 16

366 Michael Joseph Murphy, The Canadian International Development Agency and the Canadian Labour Congress: A Developing Partnership, 4

367 Katherine Slavka Nastovski, Towards Transformative Solidarities: Wars of Position in the Making of Labour Internationalism in Canada, 272

368 Why Do Tories Keep Funding Leftists?, Mar 27, 2012 (http://www.henrymakow.com/why_does_right-wing_govt_fund.html#sthash.o6nFkrSD.dpuf)

369 Katherine Slavka Nastovski, Towards Transformative Solidarities: Wars of Position in the Making of Labour Internationalism in Canada, 272

370 Report of the executive Council, 22nd Constitutional Convention, 1999, 110

371 Canadian Labour Congress, Member Profile, Apr 2012 (http://www.ccic.ca/members/profiles/CLC_2012-04_e.php)

372 Resolutions, 16th Constitutional Convention, Canadian Labour Congress, 1986, 70

373 Mordechai Briemberg, Canadian Trade Unions and Palestine, The United Nations Seminar on the Question of Palestine, 1983

374 John Price, Canadian Labour, the Cold War and Asia, 1945-1955

375 Katherine Slavka Nastovski, Towards Transformative Solidarities: Wars of Position in the Making of Labour Internationalism in Canada, 217

376 John Price, Canadian Labour, the Cold War and Asia, 1945-1955

377 Report of the Executive Council, Canadian Labour Congress, Second Constitutional Convention, 1958, 85

378 Mordechai Briemberg, Canadian Trade Unions and Palestine, The United Nations Seminar on the Question of Palestine 1983

379 Report of the Executive Council, Canadian Labour Congress, Ninth Constitutional Convention, 1972, 38 ;

Report of the Executive Council, Canadian Labour Congress, Eighth Constitutional Convention, 1970, 35

380 Michael Joseph Murphy, The Canadian International Development Agency and the Canadian Labour Congress: A Developing Partnership, 88

381 Katherine Slavka Nastovski, Towards Transformative Solidarities: Wars of Position in the Making of Labour Internationalism in Canada, 265

382 Ibid, 266 ; Michael Joseph Murphy, The Canadian International Development Agency and the Canadian Labour Congress: A Developing Partnership, 21

383 Report of the Executive Council, Canadian Labour Congress, 1980, 27

384 Mordechai Briemberg, Canadian Trade Unions and Palestine, The United Nations Seminar on the Question of Palestine 1983

385 Michael Joseph Murphy, The Canadian International Development Agency and the Canadian Labour Congress: A Developing Partnership, 22 ; John Clark, Canadian Labour Congress as an International Actor, International Perspectives, Sep 1980

386 Africa Society Profile of Mr. H. John Harker Canadian Foreign Policy Advisor on Africa (https://sites.ualberta.ca/~afso/documents/harkerProfile.pdf)

387 Michael Joseph Murphy, The Canadian International Development Agency and the Canadian Labour Congress: A Developing Partnership, 20-21

388 Michael Joseph Murphy, The Canadian International Development Agency and the Canadian Labour Congress: A Developing Partnership, 20-21

389 Mordechai Briemberg, Canadian Trade Unions and Palestine, The United Nations Seminar on the Question of Palestine 1983 ; Katherine Slavka Nastovski, Towards Transformative Solidarities: Wars of Position in the Making of Labour Internationalism in Canada, 217

390 Katherine Slavka Nastovski, Towards Transformative Solidarities: Wars of Position in the Making of Labour Internationalism in Canada, 217

391 Building Peace in the 21st Century - reflections over 30 years, Science4Peace, Feb 27, 2014 (https://www.youtube.com/watch?v=Y-u1J1eKGWk)

392 Ibid

393 Former UN Ambassador for Disarmament to Head Rideau Institute, Media Release, June 26, 2014 (http://www.rideauinstitute.ca/2014/06/26/former-un-ambassador-for-disarmament-to-head-rideau-institute/)

394 Advisory board, Peggy Mason (http://www.wfmcanada.org/about/advisory-board/)

395 (http://www.rideauinstitute.ca/category/blog/releases/)

396 J L Granatstein, The new peace movement, National Post, Aug 20, 2008

397 Ibid

398 Ms. Peggy Mason (As an Individual) at the National Defence Committee, Oct 25, 2012 (https://openparliament.ca/committees/national-defence/41-1/53/peggy-mason-1/only/)

399 Peggy Mason, LinkedIn (https://ca.linkedin.com/in/peggy-mason-76325b4b)

400 Standing Committee on National Defence No 053 11st Session 41st Parliament, Oct 25, 2012 (http://www.parl.gc.ca/HousePublications/Publication.aspx?Language=e&Mode=1&Parl=41&Ses=1&DocId=5790033)

401 Ibid

402 Ibid

403 Who is pushing Canada to become a global arms dealer?, Oct 9, 2016 (https://www.ceasefire.ca/who-is-pushing-canada-to-become-a-global-arms-dealer/)

404 Sean Maloney, Canada and UN Peacekeeping: Cold War by Other Means – 1945-1970, xii

405 Steven Staples, Marching Orders. How

Canada Abandoned Peacekeeping and Why the UN Needs Us Now More than Ever, a report commissioned by the Council of Canadians, 2006

406 Gloria Galloway, 800 Canadian soldiers going to Haiti, Jan 15, 2010 (http://www.theglobeandmail.com/news/world/800-canadian-soldiers-going-to-haiti/article4302078/)

407 Canada feared popular uprising in Haiti after quake, The Canadian Press, Mar 31, 2011 (https://www.ctvnews.ca/canada-feared-popular-uprising-in-haiti-after-quake-1.625850)

408 Brendan Kennedy, Earthquake rescue teams remain grounded in Canada, Jan 17, 2010 (https://www.thestar.com/news/world/2010/01/17/earthquake_rescue_teams_remain_grounded_in_canada.html)

409 Murray Dobbin, Mea Culpa on Haiti, Jan 23, 2010 (https://www.globalresearch.ca/mea-culpa-on-haiti/17174)

410 Peggy Mason, Why good peacekeeping training really matters, Mar 1, 2016 (http://rabble.ca/blogs/bloggers/views-expressed/2016/03/why-good-peacekeeping-training-really-matters)

411 Is Remembrance Day too much about war, and not enough about peace?, Nov 10, 2011 (http://www.ceasefire.ca/?p=9128)

412 Ibid

413 Dr Walter Dorn, Department of Defence Studies (http://www.cfc.forces.gc.ca/136/286-eng.html)

414 Walter Dorn, Keeping Watch: monitoring, technology and innovation in US Peace Operations, xxiv (http://walterdorn.net/pdf/KeepingWatch_Dorn_CompleteBook-NoCover_UNUP_2011.pdf)

415 Ibid, xxi

416 LECTURES & PRESENTATIONS (SELECTED) (http://walterdorn.net/pres)

417 Walter Dorn, Intelligence-led Peacekeeping: The United Nations Stabilization Mission in Haiti (MINUSTAH), 2006–07, Intelligence and National Security, Vol 24, No 6, Dec 2009

418 Ibid

419 Jeb Sprague, Invisible Violence: Ignoring murder in post-coup Haiti, Fairness and Accuracy in Reporting, Nov 26, 2006 (https://jebsprague.blogspot.ca/2010/08/invisible-violence-ignoring-murder-in.html)

420 The Cite Soleil Massacre Declassification Project, Keith Yearman, Assistant Professor of Geography, College of DuPage (http://www.cod.edu/people/faculty/yearman/cite_soleil.htm)

421 Eyewitnesses Describe Massacre by UN Troops in Haitian Slum, July 11, 2005 (https://www.democracynow.org/2005/7/11/eyewitnesses_describe_massacre_by_un_troops)

422 US Embassy in Haiti acknowledges excessive force by UN, Jan 24, 2007 (http://haitiaction.net/News/HIP/1_23_7/1_23_7.html)

423 Ibid

424 Haiti: We Must Kill the Bandits (https://www.youtube.com/watch?v=25Mf7Lv5Qo8)

425 LECTURES & PRESENTATIONS (SELECTED) (http://walterdorn.net/presentations)

426 Roger Annis, Canadian military tests its new base in Jamaica, Aug 12 2011 (http://nbmediacoop.org/2011/08/12/canadian-military-tests-its-new-base-in-jamaica/)

427 Paul Weinberg, From Peacekeeping to Partisan Policing?, Jan 18, 2012, IPS (http://www.ipsnews.net/2012/01/from-peacekeeping-to-partisan-policing/)

428 Ibid

429 Canada joining Brazilian-led peacekeeping mission in Haiti, The Canadian Press, June 18, 2013 (http://www.cbc.ca/news/canada/canada-joining-brazilian-led-peacekeeping-mission-in-haiti-1.1326851)

430 Dan Beeton, Soldiers Without a Cause:

Why Are Thousands of UN Troops Still in Haiti?, NACLA Report on the Americas, Spring 2012 (http://cepr.net/publications/op-eds-columns/soldiers-without-a-cause-why-are-thousands-of-un-troops-still-in-haiti)

431 Harriet Agerholm, UN admits playing role in cholera outbreak that killed almost 10,000 people in Haiti, Aug 19, 2016 (http://www.independent.co.uk/news/world/americas/un-cholera-role-haiti-outbreak-deaths-united-nations-peacekeepers-helped-spread-a7198861.html)

432 Yves Engler, Minustah's filthy record in Haiti, Sep 11, 2011 (https:// www.theguardian.com/commentisfree/ cifamerica/2011/sep/11/haiti-unitednations-minustah-cholera)

433 Ibid

434 Daniel Galvin, A role for Canada in an African crisis: perceptions of the Congo crisis and motivations for Canadian participation, University of Guelph Dissertation, 2004, 83

435 Walter Dorn, Canadian Peacekeeping: Proud Tradition, Strong Future? Canadian Foreign Policy Journal, Vol 12, No 2 (Fall 2005) (http://walterdorn.net/32-canadian-peacekeeping-proud-tradition-strong-future)

436 Noam Chomsky, Restoring the Traditional Order, Excerpted from What Uncle Sam Really Wants, 1992 (https:// chomsky.info/unclesam03/)

437 Herbert Fairlie Wood, Strange Battleground: The Operations in Korea and Their Effects on the Defence Policy of Canada, 6

438 John Price, Orienting Canada. Race, Empire, and the Transpacific, 183

439 Denis Stairs, The Diplomacy of Constraint: Canada: The Korean War, and the United States, 15

440 Mitch Potter, Can Canada's army return to peacekeeping?, Mar 29, 2015 (http:// www.thestar.com/news/world/2015/03/29/ can-canadas-army-return-to-peacekeeping. html)

441 Walter Dorn and Joshua Libben, Unprepared for Peace? The Decline of Canadian Peacekeeping Training (and What to Do About It), Feb 2, 2016 (https://www. policyalternatives.ca/publications/reports/ unprepared-peace)

442 Walter Dorn and Andrew Wedgwood, NATO's Libya Campaign 2011: Just or Unjust to What Degree?, Diplomacy & Statecraft, Vol 26, Issue 2, 2015 (http:// walterdorn.net/pub?id=215)

443 Mark Piesing, Why are UN Peacekeepers so badly equipped for modern conflict?, Aug 8 2011 (http://www. independent.co.uk/news/world/politics/why-are-un-peacekeepers-so-badly-equipped-for-modern-conflict-2334052.html)

444 Mitch Potter, Can Canada's army return to peacekeeping?, Mar 29, 2015 (https:// www.thestar.com/news/world/2015/03/29/ can-canadas-army-return-to-peacekeeping. html)

445 David Pugliese, Traditional peace-keeping not enough to maintain a Syrian deal, Feb 9, 2016 (http://nationalpost.com/ news/canada/traditional-peace-keeping-not-enough-to-maintain-a-syrian-deal-un-report-looks-to-satellites-crowdsourcing-for-solutions)

446 Richard Sanders, Canada's Leading Role in the Militarisation of Space (http:// coat.ncf.ca/our_magazine/links/58/blurb-58. htm)

447 COMPLETE LIST OF PRESENTATIONS Walter Dorn, Dec 31, 2011 (http://walterdorn. net/pdf/PresentationsLst_Dorn_ForWeb_31Dec2011.pdf)

448 Steven Staples, Breaking Rank: A citizens' review of Canada's military spending (https://d3n8a8pro7vhmx. cloudfront.net/polarisinstitute/pages/31/ attachments/original/1411065431/breaking_ rank.pdf?1411065431)

449 Ibid

450 Marco Vigliotti, Greater Role in International Crises Could Bolster Domestic Defence Manufacturers, Hill Times, Jun 1, 2016

451 Michelle Zilio, Afghanistan: The mission that changed our military, May 9, 2014 (http://ipolitics.ca/2014/05/09/afghanistan-the-mission-that-changed-our-military/)

452 Michael Valpy, 'This is Stephen Harper's war', Globe and Mail (http://v1.theglobeandmail.com/servlet/story/RTGAM.20070818.wwshuffle18/front/Front/Front/)

453 Michael Byers, Smart Defence: A Plan for Rebuilding Canada's Military, June 2015 (http://www.rideauinstitute.ca/wp-content/uploads/2015/06/Rebuilding-Canadas-Military.pdf)

454 Ibid

455 Michael Byers and Stewart Webb, Stuck in a Rut: Harper Government Overrides Canadian Army, Insists on Buying Outdated Equipment, Sept 2013 (https://www.policyalternatives.ca/sites/default/files/uploads/publications/National%20Office/2013/09/Stuck_in_a_Rut.pdf)

456 Bill Robinson, Canadian military spending 2010-11, CCPA Foreign Policy Series, Mar 2011 (https://www.policyalternatives.ca/sites/default/files/uploads/publications/National%20Office/2011/03/Canadian%20Military%20Spending%202010.pdf)

457 Living with Uncle: Canada – US relations in an age of Empire, 62

458 Ibid

459 Bill Robinson, Canadian military spending 2010-11, CCPA Foreign Policy Series, Mar 2011 (https://www.policyalternatives.ca/sites/default/files/uploads/publications/National%20Office/2011/03/Canadian%20Military%20Spending%202010.pdf)

460 Michael Byers and William Schabas, Trudeau can now get at war crimes truth, June 13, 2016 (https://www.thestar.com/opinion/commentary/2016/06/13/trudeau-can-now-get-at-war-crimes-truth.html)

461 Michael Byers, Saudi arms sale: Still time to reverse a terrible mistake, May 11, 2016 (http://www.theglobeandmail.com/opinion/saudi-arms-sale-still-time-to-reverse-a-terrible-mistake/article29983723/)

462 Yves Engler, Lester Pearson's Peacekeeping: the truth may hurt, 84-89

463 Linda Freeman, Ambiguous Champion: Canada and South Africa in the Trudeau and Mulroney years, 261

464 Yves Engler, Black Book of Canadian Foreign Policy, 135/197/220

465 Murray Dobbin, War Is Peace, Orwell wrote the Harper doctrine, Apr 8, 2008 (https://thetyee.ca/Views/2008/04/08/WarIsPeace/)

466 Stephen M Saideman, Adapting in the Dust: Lessons Learned from Canada's War in Afghanistan, 52

467 Steve Mertl, Take lead in Darfur, Layton urges Canada, May 8, 2006 (http://www.theglobeandmail.com/news/national/take-lead-in-darfur-layton-urges-canada/article965990/)

468 Thomas Walkom, Afghanistan, Libya and the fallacy of the good war, June 22 2011 (https://www.thestar.com/news/canada/2011/06/22/walkom_afghanistan_libya_and_the_fallacy_of_the_good_war.html) ; Murray Dobbin, War is peace, Apr 10 2008 (http://rabble.ca/columnists/war-peace)

469 Ed Finn, Canada after Harper: his ideology-fuelled attack on Canadian society and values, and how we can resist and create the country we want, 362

470 Ed Finn, A Journalist's Life on the Left, 100

471 Ibid, 108

472 Tyler Shipley, Ottawa and Empire: Canada and the military coup in Honduras,

141
473 Bruce Campbell and Ed Finn, Living with Uncle: Canada US relations in an age of Empire, 10

474 Janice Gross Stein and Eugene Lang, The Unexpected War: Canada in Kandahar, 126-27

475 Noam Chomsky interviewed by Vincent Navarro, July 18, 2008 (https://chomsky.info/20080718/)

476 Linda McQuaig, Keep Pearson out of it, Toronto Star, Feb 5, 2008 (https://www.thestar.com/opinion/columnists/2008/02/05/keep_pearson_out_of_it.html)

477 Linda McQuaig, Holding the Bully's Coat: Canada and the US Empire, 149

478 Reginald Whitaker and Gary Marcuse, Cold War Canada: The Making of a National Insecurity State, 1945-1957, 68 ; Lester Pearson, Mike: The Memoirs of the Right Honourable Lester B. Pearson 1, 234

479 James L. Hall, Radio Canada International: Voice of a Middle Power, 57

480 Hansard Mar 28, 1949, 2095

481 John Robinson Beal, Pearson of Canada, 96

482 Linda McQuaig, Holding the Bully's Coat: Canada and the US Empire, 150

483 Escott Reid, Radical mandarin: the memoirs of Escott Reid, 252

484 Linda McQuaig, Holding the Bully's Coat: Canada and the US Empire, 155

485 Tareq Y. Ismael, Canadian Arab relations: policy and perspectives, 17

486 Hansard Feb 12, 1953, 1865 ; Hansard Jan 14, 1957, 179

487 Hansard Jan 14, 1957, 175

488 Robin Gendron, Towards a Francophone Community, 41

489 Ibid, 38

490 Yves Engler, Canada in Africa 300 Years of Aid and Exploitation, 90-92

491 Geoffrey A.H. Pearson, Seize the Day: Lester B. Pearson and Crisis Diplomacy, 157

492 Linda McQuaig, Holding the Bully's

Coat: Canada and the U.S. Empire, 146

493 Ibid, 145

494 Victor Levant, Quiet complicity: Canadian involvement in the Vietnam War, 197

495 John Tirman, Why do we ignore the civilians killed in American wars?, Jan 6, 2012 (https://www.washingtonpost.com/opinions/why-do-we-ignore-the-civilians-killed-in-american-wars/2011/12/05/gIQALCO4eP_story.html?utm_term=.a12ee7d494f5)

496 John English, The Worldly Years: Life of Lester Pearson 1949-1972, 366

497 Yves Engler, Lester Pearson's Peacekeeping: the truth may hurt, 132-134

498 Ibid

499 Bonny Ibhawoh, A Voice for Africa: Stephen Lewis and the Race Against Time, Journal of Canadian Studies, Vol 41, Jan 2008

500 Selina Chignall, Canada not doing enough for world health, says Stephen Lewis, Sept 30, 2015 (https://ipolitics.ca/2015/09/30/canadas-are-not-doing-enough-for-world-health-says-stephen-lewis/)

501 The Discovery of Human Rights, Dec 10, 2015 (http://www.cbc.ca/radio/ideas/the-discovery-of-human-rights-1.3358890?autoplay=true)

502 Mike Cowie (Oredakedo), The Stephen Lewis Rave (http://www.mikesanddislikes.com/politics_africa_the_stephen_lewis_rave)

503 Samuel Getachew, Stephen Lewis Is a Great Supporter of the African Community, May 28, 2015 (http://www.huffingtonpost.ca/samuel-getachew/stephen-lewis-african_b_7453836.html)

504 Brent Jang and Paul Waldie, Canadian firms in Africa fail fight against AIDS, Stephen Lewis says, Dec 12, 2006 (https://www.theglobeandmail.com/news/national/canadian-firms-in-africa-fail-fight-against-

aids-stephen-lewis-says/article972988/)

505 Ibid

506 Stephen Lewis, Race Against Time: Searching for Hope in AIDS-ravaged Africa, 34

507 Robin S. Gendron, Towards a Francophone Community: Canada's Relations with France and French Africa, 1945-1968, 66 ; Yves Engler, Canada in Africa 300 Years of Aid and Exploitation, 112-116

508 Ibid, 123-126

509 Ibid, 127-138

510 Lawrence K. Altman, U.N. Official Assails South Africa on Its Response to AIDS Aug 19, 2006 (http://www.nytimes.com/2006/08/19/world/africa/19aids.html)

511 Remarks by Stephen Lewis at the 10th annual Policy Forum of The Institute for Inclusive Security, Jun 29, 2009 (https://www.stephenlewisfoundation.org/news-resources/speeches?id=4056)

512 Lydia Polgreen, In Zimbabwe Land Takeover, a Golden Lining, July 20, 2012 (http://www.nytimes.com/2012/07/21/world/africa/in-zimbabwe-land-takeover-a-golden-lining.html) ; Blessing-Miles Tendi, Why Robert Mugabe scored a landslide victory in Zimbabwean elections, Aug 5, 2013 (https://www.theguardian.com/world/2013/aug/05/robert-mugabe-zimbabwe-election-zanu-pf)

513 Hillels Remember Kristallnacht, Hillel News, Nov 15, 2004 (http://www.hillel.org/about/news-views/news-views---blog/news-and-views/2004/11/15/hillels-remember-kristallnacht)

514 'An ally that he trusted and loved': Citizens and politicians praise Mandela's attachment to Canada, Dec 6, 2013 (http://nationalpost.com/news/canada/an-ally-that-he-trusted-and-loved-citizens-and-politicians-praise-mandelas-attachment-to-canada) ; Stephen Lewis recalls Mandela's deep respect for Canada, Mulroney, Dec 8, 2013 (https://globalnews.ca/news/1016956/mandelas-deep-respect-for-canada-mulroney/)

515 Linda Freeman, Ambiguous Champion: Canada and South Africa in the Trudeau and Mulroney years, 261

516 Ibid, 194

517 Race Against Time, Stephen Lewis, Race Against Time: Searching for Hope in AIDS-Ravaged Africa, 18

518 National Review of Medicine 2008

519 Yves Engler, Canada in Africa: 300 Years of Aid and Exploitation, 127-138

520 Stephen Lewis, Race Against Time: Searching for Hope in AIDS-Ravaged Africa, 178

521 Stephen Lewis, No funding for peace talks unless women are at the table, 10th annual Policy Forum, The Institute for Inclusive Security (http://www.africafiles.org/printableversion.asp?id=19966)

522 The Rwanda Genocide: How Does Madeleine Albright Live with Herself?, July 11, 2000 (https://www.democracynow.org/2000/7/11/the_rwanda_genocide_how_does_madeleine)

523 Stephen Lewis and Gerald Caplan, Don't blame Africa for its wars, July 12, 2000 (https://www.theglobeandmail.com/opinion/dont-blame-africa-for-its-wars/article768708/)

524 Stephen Lewis, Race Against Time: Searching for Hope in AIDS-Ravaged Africa, 185

525 Fred Mwasa, Pressure mounts to ease delivery of ARVs to Rwanda, April 3, 2009 (http://www.rnancws.com/health/1118-pressure-mounts-to-ease-delivery-of-arvs-to-rwanda)

526 Edward S. Herman and David Peterson, The Kagame-Power Lobby's dishonest attack on BBC documentary on Rwanda, Nov 12, 2014 (http://www.pambazuka.org/governance/kagame-power-lobby%E2%80%99s-dishonest-attack-bbc-documentary-rwanda)

527 Edmund Kagire, Rwanda suspends BBC Kinyarwanda service, Oct 25, 2014 (http://www.theeastafrican.co.ke/news/Rwanda-suspends-BBC-Kinyarwanda-service/2558-2499120-bbvju9z/index.html)

528 Edward S. Herman and David Peterson, The Kagame-Power Lobby's dishonest attack on BBC documentary on Rwanda, Nov 12, 2014 (http://www.pambazuka.org/governance/kagame-power-lobby%E2%80%99s-dishonest-attack-bbc-documentary-rwanda)

529 The Rwanda Genocide: How Does Madeleine Albright Live with Herself?, July 11, 2000 (https://www.democracynow.org/2000/7/11/the_rwanda_genocide_how_does_madeleine) ; Douglas G. Anglin, Rwanda: the preventable genocide. The Report of the International Panel of Eminent Personalities to Investigate the 1994 Genocide in Rwanda & the Surrounding Events, International Journal, 56, 2001

530 Peter Erlinder, Rwanda: No Conspiracy, No Genocide Planning ... No Genocide?, Dec 24, 2008 (https://www.commondreams.org/views/2008/12/24/rwanda-no-conspiracy-no-genocide-planning-no-genocide)

531 Geoffrey York and Judi Rever, Probe revisits mystery of assassination that triggered Rwandan genocide, Oct 11, 2016 (https://www.theglobeandmail.com/news/world/probe-revisits-mystery-of-assassination-that-triggered-rwandan-genocide/article32316139/)

532 The Rwanda Genocide: How Does Madeleine Albright Live with Herself?, July 11, 2000 (https://www.democracynow.org/2000/7/11/the_rwanda_genocide_how_does_madeleine)

533 Chris McGreal, Xan Rice and Lizzy Davies, Leaked UN report accuses Rwanda of possible genocide in Congo, Aug 26, 2010 (https://www.theguardian.com/world/2010/aug/26/un-report-rwanda-congo-hutus)

534 Stephen Lewis, No funding for peace talks unless women are at the table, 10th annual Policy Forum, The Institute for Inclusive Security (http://www.africafiles.org/printableversion.asp?id=19966)

535 Élaine Audet, Fémicide au Congo, Nov 21, 2008 (http://sisyphe.org/spip.php?article2767)

536 Michael Laxer, On the 40th anniversary of the expulsion of the Waffle, June 25, 2012 (http://rabble.ca/blogs/bloggers/michael-laxer/2012/06/40th-anniversary-expulsion-waffle)

537 Tokunbo Ojo, Africa in the Canadian media: The Globe and Mail's coverage of Africa from 2003 to 2012, Ecquid Novi: African Journalism Studies, Vol 35, Issue 1, 2014

538 Ibid

539 David R. Black, Canada and Africa in the new millennium: The Politics of Consistent Inconsistency, 95

540 James Naylor, Pacifism or anti-imperialism?: The CCF response to the outbreak of World War II, Journal of the Canadian historical Association, Vol 8, No 1, 1997

541 Michiel Horn, Frank Underhill's Early Drafts of the Regina Manifesto 1933, Canadian Historical Review, Vol 54, Issue 4, Dec 1973 (http://www.utpjournals.press/doi/abs/10.3138/CHR-054-04-02?journalCode=chr)

542 Hélène Laverdière, Landmine treaty should remind Liberals what multilateralism means, Dec 1, 2017 (http://ottawacitizen.com/opinion/columnists/laverdiere-landmine-treaty-should-remind-liberals-what-multilateralism-means)

543 Ibid

544 Donna Jacobs, John Baird: warm manner, blunt talk, Feb 8, 2012 (http://diplomatonline.com/mag/2012/02/john-baird-warm-manner-blunt-talk/); Laura

Payton, John Baird resigns: 'You need to be defined by your values', Feb 3, 2015 (http://www.cbc.ca/news/politics/john-baird-resigns-you-need-to-be-defined-by-your-values-1.2942832)

545 Joël-Denis Bellavance, Le NPD vise une soixantaine de sièges au Québec, Feb 3, 2015 (http://www.lapresse.ca/actualites/politique/politique-canadienne/201502/03/01-4840803-le-npd-vise-une-soixantaine-de-sieges-au-quebec.php)

546 Chester Ronning (https://en.wikipedia.org/wiki/Chester_Ronning)

547 Brian L. Evans, The Remarkable Chester Ronning: Proud Son of China, 94

548 Bill Blakie, The Blakie Report, 149

549 Desmond Morton (historian) (https://en.wikipedia.org/wiki/Desmond_Morton_(historian))

550 Ibid

551 Bill Blakie, The Blakie Report, 39

552 Ibid, 150

553 Ibid, 48/117

554 Ibid, 156/175

555 Ibid, 117

556 Ibid, 151

557 Ibid, 152

558 Jane Taber, When parliamentarians go to war, Oct 22, 2010 (http://www.theglobeandmail.com/news/politics/ottawa-notebook/when-parliamentarians-go-to-war/article1381081/)

559 Matthew Behrens, Canada's massive military budget is off the table in federal election, Apr 26, 2011 (http://rabble.ca/news/2011/04/canadas-massive-military-budget-table-federal-election)

560 Louise Rousseau, Parliamentarians in Uniform (http://www.revparl.ca/english/issue.asp?param=59&art=23)

561 Tim Naumetz, Mulcair off to Asia on committee trip, Nov 30, 2017 (https://ipolitics.ca/2017/11/30/mulcair-off-asia-committee-trip/)

562 Baird arrives in Iraq to deliver sharp message to new government, Sept 3, 2014 (https://www.thestar.com/news/canada/2014/09/03/baird_arrives_in_iraq_to_deliver_sharp_message_to_new_government.html)

563 Gordon Robertson, Memoirs of a Very Civil Servant: Mackenzie King to Pierre Trudeau, 43

564 Bill Blaikie, The Blakie Report, 154

565 Ibid, 163

566 List of Associations and Interparliamentary Groups (https://www.parl.ca/IIA/Associations.aspx?Language=E&DCId=4&DTId=6&P=list)

567 Patrick Smith, Bon Voyage: Members of Parliament took more than 100 sponsored trips in 2013, Ottawa Citizen, Apr 7, 2014

568 Elizabeth Thompson, Sponsored travel helping Israel win over Canadian MPs, Aug 13, 2014 (https://ipolitics.ca/2014/08/13/sponsored-travel-helping-israel-win-over-canadian-mps/)

569 Steve Rennie, Mining industry lobbied nine of 24 MPs who helped kill ethics bill, Nov 11, 2010 (https://www.theglobeandmail.com/news/politics/mining-industry-lobbied-nine-of-24-mps-who-helped-kill-ethics-bill/article1241708/) ; Bill C-300 a High Water Mark for Mining and Government Accountability, Nov 16, 2010 (https://miningwatch.ca/blog/2010/11/16/bill-c-300-high-water-mark-mining-and-government-accountability)

570 Catherine Solyom, Attempt to enact legislation failed, Dec 19, 2012 (http://www.montrealgazette.com/news/attempt+enact+legislation+failed/7711071/story.html)

571 Union asks NDP to keep Saudi armoured vehicles deal 'under wraps,' fearing 'significant' job losses, Sep 30, 2015 (http://nationalpost.com/news/politics/union-asks-ndp-to-keep-saudi-armoured-vehicles-deal-under-wraps-fearing-significant-job-losses)

572 Carl Bronski, Unifor demands NDP keep silent on Canada-Saudi Arabia arms deal, Oct 13, 2015 (https://www.wsws.org/en/articles/2015/10/13/caun-o13.html)

573 Tom MacGregor, Funding Available For New Cenotaphs, Mar 26, 2011 (https://legionmagazine.com/en/2011/03/funding-available-for-new-cenotaphs/)

574 Benedict Anderson, Imagined Communities: Reflections on the Origin and Spread of Nationalism, 9

575 Deborah Campbell, What is Canada For? (https://www.adbusters.org/article/what-is-canada-for/)

576 Bruce Campion-Smith, Liberals courting risk with upcoming peace mission, Dec 27, 2016 (https://www.thestar.com/news/canada/2016/12/27/liberals-courting-risk-with-upcoming-peace-mission.html) ; Walter Dorn, Canadian Peacekeeping: A Proud Tradition, Jul 2006 (http://peacemagazine.org/archive/v22n3p15.htm)

577 Colin McCullough, Creating Canada's Peacekeeping Past, 5

578 Ian McKay and Jamie Swift, Warrior Nation: Rebranding Canada in an Age of Anxiety, 136

579 Peter C Newman, Canada: Peaceable Kingdom no More, Maclean's, Mar 15, 2006

580 Robert M Laxer, Canada LTD: The Political Economy of Dependency, 10

581 The Waffle Manifesto: For an Independent Socialist Canada (1969) (http://www.socialisthistory.ca/Docs/Waffle/WaffleManifesto.htm)

582 Council of Canadians (http://www.thecanadianencyclopedia.ca/en/article/council-of-canadians/)

583 Ivan Avakumovic, The Communist Party in Canada: a History, 64

584 Ibid, 183

585 Leslie Morris, Look on Canada, now, and see history a new: selected writings of Leslie Morris, 109 ; Paul Kellogg, Escape from the Staple Trap: Canadian Political Economy after Left Nationalism, 173

586 Ibid, 62

587 Ibid, 7

588 Ibid

589 Duncan Cameron@duncancameron

590 Chris Varcoe, Foreign exodus from oilsands has followed investment frenzy, Sep 29, 2017 (http://calgaryherald.com/business/energy/foreign-exodus-has-followed-investment-frenzy)

591 Paul Kellogg, Escape from the Staple Trap: Canadian Political Economy after Left Nationalism, 60

592 Stephen Azzi, Walter Gordon and the Rise of Canadian Nationalism, page 1 of photos

593 Ibid, 4

594 Mel Watkins (https://en.wikipedia.org/wiki/Mel_Watkins)

595 Paul Kellogg, Escape from the Staple Trap: Canadian Political Economy after Left Nationalism, 10

596 Chris Harty, The 10 Nations With The Highest GDPs Per Capita (http://www.therichest.com/business/economy/the-10-nations-with-the-highest-gdp-per-capita/)

597 Daniel Tencer, Canadian Cities Jump In Rankings Of Top Financial Centres, But Calgary Plummets, Sep 14, 2017 (http://www.huffingtonpost.ca/2017/09/14/canadian-cities-jump-in-rankings-of-worlds-top-financial-centres_a_23208966/)

598 Foreign direct investment, 2014, Released: 2015-04-24 (http://www.statcan.gc.ca/daily-quotidien/150424/dq150424a-eng.htm)

599 Bill Burgess, Canada: Imperialist or Imperialized? Paper presented to IX Encuentro International de Economistas, Globalización y Problemas del Desarrollo, La Habana del 5 al 9 de febrero de 2007 (http://www.kpu.ca/sites/default/files/downloads/Burgess_Canada2834.pdf)

600 About Us (https://www.garda.com/about-us)

601 JahanZaib Mehmood Chaudhary, Ranking: The World's 100 Largest Banks, May 17, 2017 (https://marketintelligence. spglobal.com/our-thinking/ideas/ranking-the-world-s-100-largest-banks)

602 Dave Dean, 75% of the World's Mining Companies Are Based in Canada, Jul 9, 2013 (https://www.vice.com/en_ca/article/wdb4j5/75-of-the-worlds-mining-companies-are-based-in-canada)

603 Yves Engler, Black Book of Canadian Foreign Policy, 8-12

604 Alain Deneault, Canada: A New Tax Haven: How the Country That Shaped Caribbean Tax Havens is Becoming One Itself, 264

605 Ibid, 268

606 Last Post, Vol 1, 1969, 46

607 Ann L. Griffiths, Peter T.Haydon, and Richard H. Gimblett, Canadian Gunboat Diplomacy: The Canadian Navy and Foreign Policy, 163

608 Ibid

609 Alain Deneault, Canada: A New Tax Haven: How the Country That Shaped Caribbean Tax Havens is Becoming One Itself, 268

610 James Laxer, Mission of Folly: Canada and Afghanistan, 141

611 Andrew Potter, introduction to the 40th anniversary edition of George Grant's Lament for a Nation, XXVIII

612 Ibid, 70

613 Ibid, 5

614 James Daschuk, Clearing the Plains: Disease, Politics of Starvation and the Loss of Aboriginal Life

615 George Grant, Lament for a Nation, 70-71

616 George Monro Grant (https://en.wikipedia.org/wiki/George_Monro_Grant) ; George Robert Parkin (https://en.wikipedia.org/wiki/George_Robert_Parkin)

617 Andrew Potter, introduction to the 40th anniversary edition Lament for a Nation, XXVIII

618 Andrew Potter, introduction to the 40th anniversary edition Lament for a Nation, LIX

619 Norman Penlington, Canada and Imperialism: 1896-1899, 5

620 David J Bercuson and JL Granatstein, Dictionary of Canadian Military History, 30

621 Barry Gough, Britain, Canada and the North Pacific: Maritime Enterprise and Dominion, 1778–1914, 357

622 House of Commons Debates, Vol 45, June 21, 1897, 4817

623 Yves Engler, Canada in Africa: 300 Years of Aid and Exploitation, 21-48

624 Ibid

625 William Buxton and Charles R. Acland, Harold Innis in the New Century: Reflections and Refractions, 112

626 Robert Fatton Jr, Killing Haitian Democracy, July 22, 2015 (https://www.jacobinmag.com/2015/07/monroe-doctrine-1915-occupation-duvalier)

627 Robert H Babcock, Gompers in Canada: a study in American Continentalism before the first world war, 29

628 Daniel J Baum, The Banks of Canada in the Commonwealth Caribbean: Economic Nationalism and Multinational Enterprises of a Medium Power, 19

629 R. T. Naylor, Canada in the European Age, 1453-1919, 482

630 Peter McFarlane, Northern Shadows: Canadians and Central America, 38

631 Acheson, Dean G. (https://www.encyclopedia.com/history/encyclopedias-almanacs-transcripts-and-maps/acheson-dean-g)

632 Ian Brown, A look inside Palm Beach, where wealthy Canadians are one degree of separation from Donald Trump, Globe and Mail, Dec 30, 2016

633 Lukin Robinson, The Tragedy of Rwanda, Dec 1, 2003 (https://

monthlyreview.org/2003/12/01/the tragedy-of-rwanda/)

634 Judi Rever, Did Rwanda's Paul Kagame trigger the genocide of his own people?, Apr 8, 2018 (https://www.thestar.com/news/insight/2018/04/08/did-rwandas-paul-kagame-trigger-the-genocide-of-his-own-people.html)

635 Edward S. Herman and David Peterson, The Kagame-Power Lobby's dishonest attack on BBC documentary on Rwanda, Nov 12, 2014 (https://www.pambazuka.org/governance/kagame-power-lobby%E2%80%99s-dishonest-attack-bbc-documentary-rwanda)

636 Collins Mwai, Kagame confers National Order of Outstanding Friendship, Nov 19, 2017 (http://www.newtimes.co.rw/section/read/223889/)

637 Lukin Robinson, The Tragedy of Rwanda, Dec 1, 2003 (https://monthlyreview.org/2003/12/01/the-tragedy-of-rwanda/)

638 Carol Off, The Lion, the Fox and the Eagle: a story of generals and justice in Yugoslavia and Rwanda, 66

639 Carol Off, The Lion, the Fox and the Eagle: a story of generals and justice in Yugoslavia and Rwanda, 21

640 Chapter 5: A coup by any other name... (http://www.taylor-report.com/Rwanda_1994/index.php?id=ch5)

641 Jacques-Roger Booh Booh, Le patron de Dallaire parle: Révélations sur les dérives d'un général de l'ONU au Rwanda, 161

642 Ibid, 71/95

643 Charles Onana, Les secrets de la justice internationale: enquêtes truquées sur le génocide rwandais, 127

644 Edward Herman and David Peterson in Enduring Lies: The Rwandan Genocide in the Propaganda System, 20 Year Later, 45

645 Mel Watkins, Peacemakers· How People Around the World Are Building a World Free of War, Peace Magazine Jul

2014 (http://peacemagazine.org/archive/v30n3p28a.htm)

646 Ellie Kirzner, Fall Guide Politics NOW critics' picks, Sept 30, 2004 (https://nowtoronto.com/news/fall-guide-politics/)

647 Michael Byers, Intent for a Nation: What is Canada For?, 25 ; Sherene H Razack, Dark Threats and White Knights, 170

648 Does Canada still stand for something? (http://www.adbusters.org/article/does-canada-still-stand-for-something/) ; Iran Jails Baha'i Educators, Calling Their Canadian Degrees Illegal Feb 24, 2012 (https://news.ca.bahai.org/iran-jails-baha%E2%80%99i-educators-calling-their-canadian-degrees-illegal)

649 Marites N. Sison, Ex-vice regal 'at home' in communion, Dec 1, 2005 (http://www.anglicanjournal.com/articles/ex-vice-regal-at-home-in-communion-6642)

650 What should we say to Sen. Romeo Dallaire?, Feb 21, 2014, Ceasefire Action Alerts (http://www.ceasefire.ca/?p=17757)

651 Michael Lewis and Alex Ballingall, NBA courts controversy with Rwandan president all-star appearance, Feb 13, 2016 (https://www.thestar.com/news/gta/2016/02/13/nba-courts-controversy-with-rwandan-president-all-star-appearance.html) ; Daniel Sabiiti, Rwandans Eager To Watch 'Rwanda -The Royal Tour' Documentary, Apr 24, 2018 (http://ktpress.rw/2018/04/rwandans-eager-to-watch-rwanda-the-royal-tour-documentary/)

652 Ann Garrison, Rwanda, the Clinton Dynasty, and the Case of Dr. Léopold Munyakazi, July 27, 2016 (https://www.counterpunch.org/2016/07/27/rwanda-the-clinton-dynasty-and-the-case-of-dr-leopold-munyakazi/)

653 John Ralston Saul, A Fair Country: Telling Truths About Canada

654 Chris Black, View from Rwanda: The Dallaire Genocide Fax: A Fabrication, Inside

Track, Dec 1, 2005 (http://www.scoop.co.nz/stories/HL0512/S00081.htm)

655 Edward Herman and David Peterson, Enduring Lies: The Rwandan Genocide in the Propaganda System, 20 Year Later, 60

656 Ibid, 59

657 Ibid, 62

658 Ibid, 64

659 Ibid, 63

660 Ibid, 56

661 Ibid, 63

662 Gerald Caplan, The Genocide Problem: "Never Again" All Over Again, Oct 12, 2004 ; Gerald Caplan, For Roméo Dallaire, the war ends, but the battle doesn't, Jan 9, 2017 (https://www.theglobeandmail.com/news/politics/for-romeo-dallaire-the-war-ends-but-the-battle-doesnt/article33556235/)

663 The Rwanda Genocide: How Does Madeleine Albright Live with Herself?, July 11, 2000 (https://www.democracynow.org/2000/7/11/the_rwanda_genocide_how_does_madelein) ; Douglas G. Anglin, Rwanda: the preventable genocide. The Report of the International Panel of Eminent Personalities to Investigate the 1994 Genocide in Rwanda & the Surrounding Events, International Journal 56, 1 (2001)

664 Gerald Caplan, For Roméo Dallaire, the war ends, but the battle doesn't, Jan 9, 2017 (https://www.theglobeandmail.com/news/politics/for-romeo-dallaire-the-war-ends-but-the-battle-doesnt/article33556235/)

665 Gerry Caplan, Rwanda's tragic legacy should warn Canada not to repeat past in Burundi, Jan 5, 2016 (http://rabble.ca/blogs/bloggers/gerry-caplan/2016/01/rwandas-tragic-legacy-should-warn-canada-not-to-repeat-past-buru)

666 Gerry Caplan, Why does the University of Toronto's radio station promote genocide denial? Apr 30, 2013 (http://rabble.ca/blogs/bloggers/gerry-caplan/2013/04/why-does-university-torontos-radio-station-promote-genocide-deni)

667 Gerry Caplan, Inflammatory falsehood poor homage to twentieth anniversary of Rwanda genocide, Feb 24, 2014 (http://rabble.ca/blogs/bloggers/gerry-caplan/2014/02/inflammatory-falsehood-poor-homage-to-twentieth-anniversary-rwan)

668 Ibid

669 Yves Engler, A Propaganda System: How Canada's government, corporations, media and academia sell war and exploitation, 109

670 Mission and Highlights (http://onf-nfb.gc.ca/en/about-the-nfb/organization/mandate/)

671 Yves Engler, A Propaganda System: How Canada's government, corporations, media and academia sell war and exploitation, 110

672 Ibid

673 2004 Haitian coup d'état (https://en.wikipedia.org/wiki/2004_Haitian_coup_d%27%C3%A9tat#Ottawa_Initiative)

674 Michel Vastel, Haïti mise en tutelle par l'ONU?, Mar 15, 2003 (http://lactualite.com/monde/2003/03/15/haiti-mise-en-tutelle-par-lonu/)

675 David Kilgour, Mar 11, 2004 (https://openparliament.ca/politicians/2993/?page=5)

676 Allison Lampert, Dallaire fears new Rwanda disaster in Haiti: Ex-UN commander urges Canada to act, Montreal Gazette, Mar 5, 2004

677 Joshua Ostroff, Romeo Dallaire: Senator Warns Of Dangerous Parallels Between Violence In Iran and Syria and Rwandan Genocide, Dec 6, 2011 (http://www.huffingtonpost.ca/2011/12/06/romeo-dallaire-syria-iran-rwanda_n_1132469.html)

678 Ibid ; Nick Logan, World should have intervened in Syria a year ago: Dallaire, Aug 28, 2013 (https://globalnews.ca/news/807685/world-should-have-intervened-in-syria-a-year-ago-dallaire/)

Dominic Waghorn, Rohingya crisis is 'very deliberate genocide', former UN general Romeo Dallaire says, Dec 14, 2017 (https://news.sky.com/story/rohingya-crisis-is-very-deliberate-genocide-former-un-general-romeo-dallaire-says-11169354)

679 Will to Intervene (W2I) (https://www.concordia.ca/research/migs/projects/will-to-intervene.html)

680 William Macpherson, Rwanda in Congo: Sixteen Years of Intervention, July 9, 2012 (http://africanarguments.org/2012/07/09/rwanda-in-congo-sixteen-years-of-intervention-by-william-macpherson/)

681 John Pomfret, Rwandans Led Revolt In Congo, Washington Post, July 9, 1997 (http://www.washingtonpost.com/wp-srv/inatl/longterm/congo/stories/070997.htm)

682 Lydia Polgreen, Congo's Death Rate Unchanged Since War Ended, Jan 23, 2008 (http://www.nytimes.com/2008/01/23/world/africa/23congo.html)

683 DR Congo: UN Report Exposes Grave Crimes, Oct 1, 2010 (https://www.hrw.org/news/2010/10/01/dr-congo-un-report-exposes-grave-crimes)

684 Arthur Manuel, Until Canada gives Indigenous people their land back, there can never be reconciliation, Jan 18, 2017 (http://rabble.ca/blogs/bloggers/views-expressed/2017/01/until-canada-gives-Indigenous-people-their-land-back-there-ca)

685 Potlatch (http://www.thecanadianencyclopedia.ca/en/article/potlatch/)

686 Until There Is Not a Single Indian in Canada (https://www.facinghistory.org/stolen-lives-Indigenous-peoples-canada-and-indian-residential-schools/historical-background/until-there-not-single-indian-canada)

687 Global Impact Soirée CCIC Conference (https://www.globaldev150.ca/global-impact-soiree/)

688 Ibid

689 Matthew Coon Come, Remarks of National Chief Matthew Coon Come, World Conference against Racism, Durban, South Africa, Aug 30 2001 (https://beta.groups.yahoo.com/neo/groups/Racism_Against_Indigenous_Peoples/conversations/messages/596)

690 Ibid

691 Linda Freeman, The Ambiguous Champion: Canada and South Africa in the Trudeau and Mulroney Years

692 Sandra Cuffe, Marketing Consent: A journey into the public relations underside of Canada's mining sector, Aug 22, 2012 (http://www.dominionpaper.ca/articles/4569)

693 9.40. Procurement Strategy for Aboriginal Business (https://buyandsell.gc.ca/policy-and-guidelines/supply-manual/section/9/40)

694 Aboriginal Leadership Opportunity Year (ALOY) Joining Instructions 2017 (https://www.rmc-cmr.ca/en/training-wing/aboriginal-leadership-opportunity-year-aloy-joining-instructions)

695 Minister Oda Announces International Aboriginal Youth Internship Initiative, Feb 9, 2011 (http://www.marketwired.com/press-release/minister-oda-announces-international-aboriginal-youth-internship-initiative-1393033.htm)

696 Indigenous Peoples and the Right to Participate in Decision-Making A Submission by the Government of Canada to the United Nations Expert Mechanism on the Rights of Indigenous Peoples, July 2010 (http://www.marketwired.com/press-release/canada-announces-changes-to-program-for-Indigenous-peoples-in-the-americas-535038.htm)

697 Sandra Cuffe, Marketing Consent: A journey into the public relations underside of Canada's mining sector, Aug 22, 2012 (http://www.dominionpaper.ca/articles/4569)

698 Ibid

Left, Right

699 Aboriginal Business and International Trade – Canada's Strategic Advantage (Discussion Paper), Apr 5, 2012 (http://www.slideshare.net/waynedunn/aboriginal-business-and-international-trade-canadas-strategic-advantage)

700 Todd Gordon and Jeffery R Webber, Blood of Extraction: Canadian Imperialism in Latin America, 85

701 Sandra Cuffe, Marketing Consent: A journey into the public relations underside of Canada's mining sector, Aug 22, 2012 (http://www.dominionpaper.ca/articles/4569)

702 Todd Gordon and Jeffery R Webber, Blood of Extraction: Canadian Imperialism in Latin America, 225

703 Sandra Cuffe, Marketing Consent: A journey into the public relations underside of Canada's mining sector, Aug 22, 2012 (http://www.dominionpaper.ca/articles/4569)

704 Native groups encouraged to capitalize on past conflicts, Mar 19, 2007 (http://www.cbc.ca/news/canada/manitoba/native-groups-encouraged-to-capitalize-on-past-conflicts-1.636664)

705 Ibid

706 PDAC 2011 Skookum Jim Award winner - Jerry Asp, Prospectors and Developers Association of Canada (PDAC) (https://www.facebook.com/thePDAC/videos/vb.190183217710201/10150803993995487/?type=3&permPage=1)

707 Grand Chief of Canada's First Nations Visits Israeli Knesset (http://rabble.ca/babble/national-news/grand-chief-canadas-first-nations-visits-israeli-knesset)

708 Reuven Bulka, Phil Fontaine and Sylvain Abitbol, Two solitudes break their isolation together, Globe and Mail, July 31, 2008 (https://www.theglobeandmail.com/opinion/two-solitudes-break-their-isolation-together/article715223/)

709 http://www.jpost.com/Green-Israel/Innovative-Research/Unique-merger-formed-with-Misipawistik-Cree-community

710 Yves Engler, Canada must stop subsidizing this racist, colonial, institution, Oct 24, 2017 (https://yvesengler.com/2017/10/24/canada-must-stop-subsidizing-this-racist-colonial-institution/)

711 Lee Berthiaume, Indigenous Canadians remember ancestors who fought, died in war, Nov 8, 2016 (https://www.theglobeandmail.com/news/national/Indigenous-canadians-remember-ancestors-who-fought-died-in-war/article32725644/)

712 Lawrence Barkwell, The Nile Voyageurs 1884-1885: Manitoba Metis and Indians of the Nile Expedition (http://www.metismuseum.ca/media/db/07194) ; Carl Benn, Mohawks on the Nile: Natives Among the Canadian Voyageurs in Egypt, 1884-1885, 33

713 Timothy C Winegard, For King and Kanata: Canadian Indians and the First World War, 36 ; Militarism, Sovereignty, and Nationalism: Six Nations and the First World War, 37

714 Mike O'Brien. Manhood and the Militia Myth: Masculinity, Class and Militarism in Ontario, 1902-1914, Labour/Le Travail, Vol 42, Fall 1998

715 Ibid

716 Ibid

717 Six Nations Support of WWI, Great War Centenary Association (http://www.doingourbit.ca/six-nations-support-war)

718 First Nations in the Great War (http://vimyridge.valourcanada.ca/the-road-to-vimy-ridge/battling-on/first-nations/)

719 Timothy C Winegard, For King and Kanata: Canadian Indians and the First World War, 141

720 James Dempsey, Warriors of the King: Prairie Indians in World War I, 35

721 Ibid, 34

722 Jonathan F Vance, Death so Noble: Memory, Meaning, and the First World War, 246

723 Amelia Reimer, Lest We Forget

Aboriginal Peoples' sacrifices for Canada, Nov 11, 2015 (http://theindependent.ca/2015/11/11/lest-we-forget-aboriginal-peoples-sacrifices-for-canada/)

724 Timothy C Winegard, For King and Kanata: Canadian Indians and the First World War, 130

725 Ibid, 53

726 Ibid, 8

727 Ibid, 155

728 Ibid

729 Indigenous People in the Second World War (http://www.veterans.gc.ca/eng/remembrance/history/historical-sheets/aborigin)

730 Aboriginal Veterans (http://www.veterans.gc.ca/public/pages/publications/system-pdfs/Aboriginal-pi-e.pdf)

731 ARCHIVED - Aboriginal Peoples in the Canadian Armed Forces, Project number: BG - 13.016, May 19, 2016 (http://www.forces.gc.ca/en/news/article.page?doc=aboriginal-peoples-in-the-canadian-armed-forces/hie8w98n)

732 Gord Hill, Canadian Forces Target Aboriginal Youth, Feb 11, 2011 (https://warriorpublications.wordpress.com/2011/02/11/canadian-forces-target-aboriginal-youth/)

733 Ibid ; Fred Gaffen, Forgotten Soldiers, 30

734 Canadian Armed Forces Aboriginal Entry Plans, Aug 23, 2017 (http://www.nndfn.com/wp-content/uploads/2017/09/CF-Aboriginal-Enrolment-Plans-2017.pdf)

735 Steven Chase, Military intelligence unit keeps watch on native groups, Oct 12, 2011 (https://www.theglobeandmail.com/news/politics/military-intelligence-unit-keeps-watch-on-native-groups/article557423/)

736 Whitney Lackenbauer, Battle Grounds: The Canadian Military and Aboriginal Lands

737 Canadian Rangers Make Indigenous Connections in Australia's Top End, Dec 22, 2015 (http://www.canadainternational.gc.ca/australia-australie/eyes_abroad-coupdoeil/EA-CanRangers.aspx?lang=eng)

738 Ibid

739 Timothy C Winegard, For King and Kanata: Canadian Indians and the First World War, 170

740 Peterborough, Ontario during the First World War 1914 - 1918, Oct 29, 2012 (http://ptbowwi.blogspot.ca/2012/10/the-native-alderville-cenotaph-and-war.html)

741 Sandy Lindsay, Saugeen First Nation observes Remembrance Day, Nov 12, 2016 (http://www.saugeentimes.com/113%20x/Feature%20Saugeen%20First%20Nations%20Remembrance%20Nov%2012%202016/Template.htm)

742 AFN National Chief Bellegarde Reinvigorates Longstanding Commitment to First Nations Veterans, Nov 10, 2016 (http://www.afn.ca/2016/11/14/10-11-16-afn-national-chief-bellegarde-reinvigorates-longstanding-comm/)

743 Assembly of First Nations National Chief Honours First Nations Veterans on Remembrance Day, will Participate in Ceremony at National War Memorial, CNW, Nov 10, 2015 (https://www.newswire.ca/fr/news-releases/assembly-of-first-nations-national-chief-honours-first-nations-veterans-on-remembrance-day-will-participate-in-ceremony-at-national-war-memorial-545214332.html?$G1Ref)

744 NAN Honours Veterans, Nov 12, 2016 (http://www.wawataynews.ca/breaking-news/nan-honours-veterans)

745 News Release, Nov10 2016 NAN Honours Veterans (http://www.nan.on.ca/upload/documents/nr-remembranceday-nov-10-2016-final.pdf)

746 Lee Berthiaume, National Aboriginal Veterans Day Honours Soldiers Who Fought, Died For Canada, Nov 8, 2016 (http://www.huffingtonpost.ca/2016/11/08/growing-debate-around-remembrance-of-canada-s-aboriginal-veterans_n_12858204.

html)

747 Métis Veterans Memorial Monument Unveiled in Batoche, July 19, 2014 (http://www.metisnation.ca/index.php/news/metis-veterans-memorial-monument-unveiled-in-batoche)

748 National Aboriginal Veterans Monument (http://www.veterans.gc.ca/eng/remembrance/memorials/canada/national-aboriginal-veterans-monument)

749 Amira Hass, Redundant Monuments and the Contest of Victimhood, Oct 31, 2017 (https://www.haaretz.com/opinion/.premium-redundant-monuments-and-the-contest-of-victimhood-1.5461315)

750 John Boileau, Voyageurs On The Nile, Jan 1, 2004 (https://legionmagazine.com/en/2004/01/voyageurs-on-the-nile/)

751 Timothy C Winegard, For King and Kanata: Canadian Indians and the First World War, 171

752 Cathy Littlejohn, Métis Soldiers of Saskatchewan: 1914 – 1953, 3

753 Eric Story, "The Awakening Has Come": Canadian First Nations in the Great War Era, 1914-1932, Canadian Military History Vol 24, Nov 23, 2015 (http://scholars.wlu.ca/cgi/viewcontent.cgi?article=1777&context=cmh)

754 Conclusion (http://www.veterans.gc.ca/eng/remembrance/those-who-served/aboriginal-veterans/native-soldiers/conclusion)

755 Ibid

756 Whitney Lackenbauer and Craig Leslie Mantle, Aboriginal Peoples and the Canadian Military: historical perspectives, 210-212

757 Elizabeth Hawksworth, Whitewashing Remembrance: I Wear A Poppy For Native Veterans Nov 10, 2013 (http://www.huffingtonpost.ca/elizabeth-hawksworth/native-veterans-remembrance-day_b_4246946.html)

758 Yves Engler, Royal Canadian Legion Has A Dark History We Must Also Remember, Nov 11, 2016 (http://www.huffingtonpost.ca/yves-engler/royal-canadian-legion_b_12903124.html)

759 In Flanders Fields (https://en.wikipedia.org/wiki/In_Flanders_Fields)

760 Amelia Reimer, Lest We Forget Aboriginal Peoples' sacrifices for Canada, Nov 11, 2015 (http://theindependent.ca/2015/11/11/lest-we-forget-aboriginal-peoples-sacrifices-for-canada/)

761 The Agenda with Steve Paikin Joseph Boyden: First Nations and the First World War (https://tvo.org/video/programs/the-agenda-with-steve-paikin/joseph-boyden-first-nations-and-the-first-world-war)

762 Joseph Boyden, Three-Day Road, acknowledgments

763 Whitney Lackenbauer and Craig Leslie Mantle, Aboriginal Peoples and the Canadian Military: historical perspectives, 223

764 John Moses, The Return of the Native (Veteran): Six Nations Troops and Political Change at the Grand River Reserve, 1917-1924, M.A. Carleton University, 2008, 88

765 Ibid, 107

766 Keith D. Smith, Strange Visitors: Documents in Indigenous-Settler Relations in Canada from 1876, 130

767 Aboriginal People in the Canadian Military: Chapter Five: The World Wars (http://www.cmp-cpm.forces.gc.ca/dhh-dhp/pub/boo-bro/abo-aut/chapter-chapitre-05-eng.asp)

768 Introduction: The League of Indians of Canada (http://www.collectionscanada.gc.ca/008/001/008001-5000-e.php?&e=1&brws=1&st=Aboriginal%20Documentary%20Heritage:%20Historical%20Collections%20of%20the%20Canadian%20Government&ts_nbr=4&)

769 Ibid

770 Lloyd Dolha, AFN Leader Seeks to Reorganize National Body by First Nations

Drum, Aug 9, 2003

771 Rick Harp, Why a truly independent First Nations political voice could be just $1 or $2 away, July 19 2012 (https://www.mediaindigena.com/why-a-truly-independent-first-nations-voice-could-be-just-1-or-2-away/)

772 Kathryn Blaze Carlson, Concern that First Nations will be 'used as pawns' as former chief to meet Iranian leaders, Oct 4, 2012 (http://nationalpost.com/news/canada/concern-that-first-nations-will-be-used-as-pawns-as-former-chief-to-meet-iranian-leaders)

773 Gord Hill, Canadian Forces Target Aboriginal Youth, Feb 11, 2011 (https://warriorpublications.wordpress.com/2011/02/11/canadian-forces-target-aboriginal-youth/)

774 Ray Bobb, Overview of Red Power Movement in Vancouver – 1967-1975 (https://revolutionary-initiative.com/2012/04/26/overview-of-red-power-movement-in-vancouver-1967-1975/)

775 James Dempsey, Warriors of the King: Prairie Indians in World War I, 39

776 Timothy C Winegard, For King and Kanata: Canadian Indians and the First World War, 53

777 P Whitney Lackenbauer, Battle Grounds: the Canadian military and aboriginal lands, 69

778 A Very Canadian Coup d'état in Haiti: The Top 10 Ways that Canada's Government Helped the 2004 Coup and its Reign of Terror, Press for Conversion!, Mar 2007 (http://coat.ncf.ca/our_magazine/links/60/60.htm)

779 Pourquoi Aristide doit-il partir ? Feb 17, 2004 (http://www.alterpresse.org/spip.php?article1166#.WrCCXDch2Uk)

780 Le Canada participera à la mission internationale, La Presse, Mar 1, 2004

781 37th PARLIAMENT, 3rd SESSION Standing Committee on Foreign Affairs and International Trade, Mar 25, 2004 (http://www.ourcommons.ca/DocumentViewer/en/37-3/FAIT/meeting-8/evidence)

782 Yves Engler, The Canadian Left is Failing to Stand Up for Haiti (http://www.dominionpaper.ca/pdf/dominion-issue20.pdf)

783 38th PARLIAMENT, 1st SESSION Standing Committee on Foreign Affairs and International Trade, Oct 4, 2005 (http://www.ourcommons.ca/DocumentViewer/en/38-1/FAAE/meeting-54/evidence)

784 Alec Castonguay, Commission de l'immigration et du statut de réfugié - Le gouvernement conservateur nomme quatre militants du parti, Mar 27, 2009 (http://www.ledevoir.com/politique/canada/242025/commission-de-l-immigration-et-du-statut-de-refugie-le-gouvernement-conservateur-nomme-quatre-militants-du-parti)

785 Forum Haiti : Des Idées et des Débats sur l'Avenir d'Haiti (http://www.forumhaiti.com/t5981-pour-mettre-l-affaire-phares-pierre-en-contexte)

786 Yves Engler, What's Left of Quebec Left?, Canadian Dimension, Apr 12, 2008 (https://canadiandimension.com/blog/view/canadian-dimension-special-whats-left-of-quebec-left)

787 Ibid

788 Ibid

789 Demographics of Quebec (https://en.wikipedia.org/wiki/Demographics_of_Quebec)

790 Sean Mills, A Place in the Sun: Haiti, Haitians, and the Remaking of Quebec, 5

791 Ibid, 55

792 Ibid, 69

793 Ann Griffiths, Richard Gimblett and Peter Haydon, Canadian Gunboat Diplomacy: The Canadian Navy and Foreign Policy, 150

794 Carol J. Williams, Haitians Hail the 'President of Voodoo', Aug 3, 2003 (http://articles.latimes.com/2003/aug/03/world/

fg-voodoo3)

795 Roger Annis, Haitian Masses Move Forward Against Foreign Occupation (http://www.socialistvoice.ca/?p=120)

796 Sean Mills, A Place in the Sun: Haiti, Haitians, and the Remaking of Quebec, 41

797 Edward Philip, Canadian Development Assistance to Haiti: An Independent Study, North-South Institute, 23

798 Arika Okrent, Haiti is teaching kids in the wrong language, Feb 8, 2013 (http://theweek.com/articles/467846/haiti-teaching-kids-wrong-language)

799 Québec-Canada: A New Deal. The Québec Government Proposal for a New Partnership Between Equals: Sovereignty-Association Government of Québec, Nov 1, 1979 (https://english.republiquelibre.org/Qu%C3%A9bec-Canada:_A_New_Deal._The_Qu%C3%A9bec_Government_Proposal_for_a_New_Partnership_Between_Equals:_Sovereignty-Association)

800 Jack Granatstein, How a separate Quebec would transform our defence policy, Sept 7, 2012 (http://news.nationalpost.com/full-comment/j-l-granatstein-how-a-separate-quebec-would-transform-our-defence-policy)

801 Elizabeth Thompson, Trips to Israel a hit with MPs, including ours, Feb 4, 2009 (http://www.intelligencer.ca/2009/02/04/trips-to-israel-a-hit-with-mps-including-ours)

802 Keith Jones, From "peacekeeper" to war hawk—Canada and NATO's war on Serbia, April 30, 1999 (https://www.wsws.org/en/articles/1999/04/can-a30.html)

803 Bruno Charbonneau and Wayne S. Cox, Locating Global Order: American Power and Canadian Security after 9/11, 119 ; Daniel Leblanc, Bloc firm on support for Afghan mission, Sept 13 2006 (http://www.theglobeandmail.com/news/national/bloc-firm-on-support-for-afghan-mission/article18172859/) ; Government will fall if Afghan mission doesn't end in 2009, Bloc warns, Aug 23 2007 (http://www.cbc.ca/news/canada/government-will-fall-if-afghan-mission-doesn-t-end-in-2009-bloc-warns-1.633316?ref=rss)

804 Gilles Duceppe says 'no choice but to intervene' against ISIS, Sep 16, 2015 (http://www.cbc.ca/news/politics/canada-election-2015-duceppe-bloc-military-isis-iraq-1.3230912)

805 Sean Mills, A Place in the Sun: Haiti, Haitians, and the Remaking of Quebec, 55

806 Ibid

807 Ibid

808 Chanoine Lionel Groulx, Le Canada Francais Missionnaire: Une Autre Grande Aventure, 263

809 Yves Engler, Canada in Africa: 300 years of aid and exploitation, 50

810 Ibid

811 J. Auclair, Vie de Mgr John Forbes: le premier Père Blanc Canadien, 225

812 Ibid

813 Sean Mills, A Place in the Sun: Haiti, Haitians, and the Remaking of Quebec, 58

814 Paul Gérin-Lajoie (http://www.encyclopediecanadienne.ca/fr/article/gerin-lajoie-paul/)

815 Robin S. Gendron, Educational Aid for French Africa: And the Canada-Quebec Dispute over Foreign Policy in the 1960s, International Journal Vol 56, No 1, Winter 2000/2001

816 David R. Morrison, Aid and Ebb Tide: A History of CIDA and Canadian Development Assistance, 78

817 Africa Research Bulletin Sept 1965 ; Africa Research Bulletin Mar 1970; Michel Houndjahoué, A propos de la cooperation dominante et marginale: la France et le Canada en Afrique francophone, Revue canadienne d'études Vol 4, no 1, 1983

818 Yukio Tsuda, The Hegemony of English and Strategies for Linguistic Pluralism: Proposing the Ecology of Language

Paradigm (http://miresperanto.com/en/english_as_intern/hegemony_of_english.htm)

819 Patrick Manning, Francophone sub-Saharan Africa: 1880 – 1995, 189

820 Canada and La Francophonie (http://international.gc.ca/world-monde/international_relations-relations_internationales/francophonie/index.aspx?lang=eng)

821 Québec and solidarity (http://www.mrif.gouv.qc.ca/en/solidarite-internationale/quebec-et-la-solidarite/portrait)

822 Christian Rioux, Quel avenir pour le français?: À Madagascar, la langue de Molière s'étiole, Le Devoir, Nov 25, 2016

823 Ibid

824 Clément Duhaime (https://www.francophonie.org/Clement-Duhaime.html)

825 Antoine Glaser, La France est comme ce vieil oncle que l'on recoit encore par politesse, Afrique Magazine, June 2016

826 David R. Morrison, Aid and Ebb Tide: A History of CIDA and Canadian Development Assistance, 131

827 Ibid, 67

828 Suzane Lelande, SNC: Engineering Beyond Frontiers, 152

829 Purposes and Principles of the United Nations (http://www.un.org/en/sc/repertoire/principles.shtml#rel1) ; International Covenant on Civil and Political Rights Adopted and opened for signature, ratification and accession by General Assembly resolution 2200A (XXI) of 16

December 1966 entry into force 23 March 1976, in accordance with Article 49 (http://www.ohchr.org/EN/ProfessionalInterest/Pages/CCPR.aspx)

830 Charter of the United Nations, Chapter I — Purposes and Principles (http://legal.un.org/repertory/art2_7.shtml)

831 The Nuremberg Judgment, Oct 5, 1946 (https://www.economist.com/node/14205505)

832 Roger Young, Canadian development assistance to Tanzania: an independent study, 41

833 Kim Mackrael, Canada's role in Iraq could mirror Afghanistan, foreign minister says, Mar 5, 2015 (http://www.theglobeandmail.com/news/politics/foreign-affairs-minister-nicholson-to-speak-about-secret-trip-to-iraq/article23305564/)

834 Jean Bricmont, The Case for a Non-Interventionist Foreign Policy, Feb 20, 2012 (https://www.counterpunch.org/2012/02/20/the-case-for-a-non-interventionist-foreign-policy/)

835 John Price, Orienting Canada: Race, Empire, and the Transpacific, 229

836 Gary Engler, Great Multicultural North

837 Alex Ballingall, A majority of Torontonians now identify themselves as visible minorities, Oct 25, 2017 (https://www.thestar.com/news/gta/2017/10/25/a-majority-of-torontonians-now-identify-themselves-as-visible-minorities-census-shows.html)